Risk Analysis for
Islamic Banks

Risk Analysis for
Islamic Banks

Hennie van Greuning and Zamir Iqbal

THE WORLD BANK
Washington, D.C.

ISBN-13: 978-0-8213-7141-1
eISBN-13: 978-0-8213-7142-8
DOI: 10.1596/978-0-8213-7141-1

Library of Congress Cataloging-in-Publication data has been applied for.

CONTENTS

FIGURES

TABLES

FOREWORD

Islamic finance is a rapidly growing part of the financial sector in the world. Indeed, it is not restricted to Islamic countries and is spreading wherever there is a sizable Muslim community. More recently, it has caught the attention of conventional financial markets as well. According to some estimates, more than 250 financial institutions in over 45 countries practice some form of Islamic finance, and the industry has been growing at a rate of more than 15 percent annually for the past five years. The market's current annual turnover is estimated to be $350 billion, compared with a mere $5 billion in 1985.

An institutional infrastructure to support development of the Islamic financial sector has been evolving since 1975, with the establishment of the Islamic Development Bank (IsDB) as a regional development institution to promote economic development in Muslim countries and the Islamic Financial Services Board (IFSB) in 2002, with a mandate to promote regulatory standards, corporate governance, and capital markets. In addition, other bodies such as AAOIFI have made significant contributions to developing accounting standards for Islamic financial institutions.

Major, globally-active financial services firms with foundations in conventional finance now offer Shariah compatible financial services through a dedicated subsidiary or through Islamic "windows."

Islamic finance is not new to the World Bank Group. It has been involved in diverse activities including financial transactions, research, publications, and presentations regarding the regulation of risk in Islamic financial institutions. Both IFC and IBRD have met a portion of their financing requirements via *Sukuk* issues.

This publication expands on the work of previous researchers who have already explained the fundamental principles and functions of an economic, banking, and financial system operating under Shariah. With its focus on corporate governance and risk analysis, the present volume complements earlier publications in this area by World Bank Treasury colleagues.

We trust that the ideas proposed will contribute to the debate on the application of risk analysis for Islamic banks themselves and for their regulators and supervisors.

Kenneth G. Lay, CFA
Vice President and Treasurer
The World Bank

FOREWORD

Globally, there has been significant interest and explosion in literature on risk analysis and management in the past decade or so. This has emerged largely because of a combination of developments. First, there has been greater reflection on risk mitigation and management in the wake of frequent episodes of financial crises. Second, financial diversification and product innovation have brought new dimensions and types of risks to the forefront. Third, the endeavours of the financial community to develop and innovate financial architecture, which, among other things, have resulted in agreements on Basel II that have evolved after a rich debate and understanding of how to measure, monitor, and cushion for different types of risks facing financial institutions and markets.

However, all these developments have thus far revolved around the conventional finance system, benefiting incrementally from the financial engineering and innovation of esoteric products and structures. While Islamic finance has grown substantively in the last few years, appreciation of its risk architecture and profile is still evolving. *Risk Analysis for Islamic Banks* not only aims to fill the gap in knowledge, but it also enriches the debate on risk management. While offering perspective on the size and dimensions of Islamic finance, this book's value lies in its success in bringing to the forefront some new presentations and a perspective that offers new insights into the risk structure and dimensions of Islamic finance.

The book recognizes up front that Islamic finance, governed by *Shariah* principles, offers its own unique approach to risk sharing and management. To illustrate this, it brings out effectively and simply the dynamics of specific risks inherent in Islamic banks and products by analyzing each of the products and their risks. It also examines a typical structure of financial statement for Islamic banks in order to get some aggregate perspective on risk at the institutional level. This helps in understanding the underpinnings of the theoretical framework of risk on both the asset and liability sides of the Islamic financial institution. The risk profile of assets depends on the structure of Islamic financial instruments and contracts and their functionality and maturity profile. In addition, on the liability side, equity risks are recognized to differ for depositors and investment account holders. It is therefore inevitable that there will be important differences in the size and types of risks in Islamic banks versus conventional banks, depending on the nature of transactions, products, and partnership arrangements that carry profit and the risk-sharing elements relative to credit risk that are more relevant in loan products. Credit risk for Islamic products is specialized. Islamic banks also face additional externalities on account of counterparty risks. Finally, Islamic banks tend to be more concentrated in trade and commodity financing, which tend to be less risky and of shorter maturity.

This book illustrates well through balance sheet analysis what Islamic banks need to watch out for in the changing dynamics in business and commodity markets, given the important differentiation in their asset and liability book relative to conventional banks. The book makes the important observation that—while in theory Islamic banking should be exposed to less risk given that Islamic finance offers a "pass through" of risk to investors and depositors—in practice this is not being pursued.

The book further makes a potent argument that while Islamic finance offers its own ideological framework and ethical standards, as well as some new perspectives on risk framework, Islamic banks are eventually prone to some of the same risks as conventional banks. As such, it is critical that it be reinforced that Islamic institutions need to adapt similar frameworks and principles for analyzing their risks and exposures and for effectively managing fiduciary responsibility interlinked with issues of conflict of interest and asymmetric information, and so on.

In line with this, the book articulates well the internationally well-accepted risk management and corporate governance framework in a simple and lucid manner. Consistent with the best practices of the corporate governance framework, the book elaborates well that Islamic banks need to conform to the well-accepted and time-tested principles of corporate governance, while recognizing that *Shariah* offers a stakeholder-oriented model of corporate governance implicit in Islamic property and contract provisions. Also, the model of governance is affected by the role of investors as depositors, in addition to the oversight of Islamic banks by Shariah Advisory Boards considered to be critical for ensuring credibility and sanctity. The authors argue well the fiduciary responsibility of the shareholders and squarely place the ultimate responsibility for oversight of the banks on boards of directors and the responsibility for operations on management. The significance of audit committees and the role of auditors in the assessment of risk management and implementation is well placed. Other stakeholders, such as Multilateral Development Banks and newly created standard setters for Islamic banking industry and accounting, also share the responsibility for encouraging proper risk management practices in this emerging area of finance.

Drawing from the specific features of Islamic finance and its inherent features of risk sharing, the book argues that materiality of financing transactions under Islamic banking—which may alter the risk profile of the balance sheet—would also involve changes in capital requirements. On one hand, the materiality of investments changes risks. On the other hand, quasi liability products such as investment account holders and other forms of risk sharing deposits, may reduce the need for a safety cushion. Islamic banks, while maintaining capital, have booked the shareholders' portion of the profit equalization reserve, while it excludes hybrid or subordinated interest-based debt products. It is these matters that have driven Islamic Financial Services Board to set some standards and norms for how to assess the risk associated and assign proper risk weights for the specific transaction and features of Islamic banking.

With its particular focus on Islamic banks, representing an important mode of Islamic financial intermediation, this book makes a timely and valuable contribution to the above objective. The value of this book lies in its comprehensiveness. It balances well Islamic financing strengths with the need to recognize the value of conventional approaches and systems that have a proven track record of corporate governance, which is central to risk management. The authors have aptly emphasized the macro and micro aspects of risk management and moved beyond the discussion on the overall risk management framework to deal with the institutional challenges of asset-liability management and the measurement of different risk types. The importance of a high level of transparency and improvement in governance has also been accentuated.

Finally, *Risk Analysis for Islamic Banks* is an important contribution to the existing literature on risk management of Islamic banks and will be useful for all stakeholders, including practitioners and academics.

Dr. Shamshad Akhtar
Governor, The State Bank of Pakistan
Former Director-General, Asian Development Bank

ACKNOWLEDGMENTS

The authors are grateful to Mr. Kenneth Lay, Vice President and Treasurer of the World Bank, who has always emphasized the importance of financial analysis and interpretation of risk-based information. He has supported this publication as a means to further the risk management debate in our client countries and facilitate a greater understanding of Islamic banking with its distinct risk management challenges. Without his support, this project would not have been completed.

Wafik Grais, senior advisor in the World Bank financial sector practice, has been the champion for greater investigation of the potential for expanding Islamic banking among World Bank colleagues. He has written and lectured extensively on the topic and we have been fortunate to have had access to the many outputs he has produced over the years. This publication is a tribute to the groundbreaking work he has performed.

John Gandolfo approved participation in conferences and workshops that might have appeared peripheral to the major outputs demanded of his quantitative strategies, risk, and analytics department—assisting us in refining our thought processes in order to identify where the next round of research into this topic might lie.

Other colleagues in the World Bank Treasury shared their insights into the complexities of developing Islamic capital markets. We benefited greatly from hours of conversation with those colleagues. In the early stages of this project, Osman Ul Haq assisted us in organizing our material during his internship with the World Bank Treasury.

John Wiley & Sons (Asia) Pte Ltd allowed the adaptation of material that we have previously prepared for them. For this we are grateful as it saved us time in the preparation of this manuscript.

Through the years, the Islamic Financial Services Board and related organizations have invited us to workshops and conferences, allowing us to learn from the many scholars presenting at those gatherings.

Despite the extent and quality of the inputs received, we are solely responsible for the contents of this publication.

Zamir Iqbal   Hennie van Greuning

ABOUT THE AUTHORS

Hennie van Greuning is a senior advisor in the World Bank Treasury and has previously worked as a sector manager for financial sector operations in the Bank. He has had a career as a partner in a major international accounting firm and as chief financial officer in a central bank, in addition to heading bank supervision in his home country. He is a CFA Charterholder and qualified as a Chartered Accountant. He holds doctorate degrees in both accounting and economics. His publications include *Analyzing Banking Risk*, as co-author, and *International Financial Reporting Standards: A Practical Guide.*

Zamir Iqbal is a principal financial officer with the Quantitative Strategies, Risk and Analytics (QRA) Department of the World Bank Treasury. He earned his Ph.D. in international finance from the George Washington University, where he also serves as adjunct faculty of international finance. He has written extensively in the area of Islamic finance in leading academic journals and has presented at several international forums. His research interests include financial engineering, structured finance, risk management, and corporate governance. He co-authored *An Introduction to Islamic Finance: Theory and Practice.*

ACRONYMS AND ABBREVIATIONS

AAOIFI	Accounting and Auditing Organization for Islamic Financial Institutions
ALM	Asset-liability management
ARCIFI	Arbitration and Reconciliation Centre for Islamic Financial Institutions
CAMEL	Capital adequacy, asset quality, management, earnings, and liquidity
CAR	Capital adequacy ratio
CIBAFI	General Council of Islamic Banks and Financial Institutions
DJIM	Dow Jones Islamic Market Index
EBIT	Earnings before interest and taxes
EBITDA	Earnings before interest, taxes, depreciation, and amortization
EBT	Earnings before taxes
ECO	Extended co-financing operation
FIFO	First in, first out
GAAP	Generally Accepted Accounting Principles
GCC	Gulf Cooperation Council
HSBC	Hong Kong and Shanghai Banking Corporation
IAS	International Accounting Standards
ICD	Islamic Corporation for the Development of the Private Sector
IDB	Islamic Development Bank
IFC	International Finance Corporation
IFRS	International Financial Reporting Standards
IFSB	Islamic Financial Services Board
IICCS	Islamic inter-bank check clearing system
IIFM	International Islamic Financial Market
IIRA	International Islamic Rating Agency

IMF	International Monetary Fund
IRB	Internal ratings-based approach
IRR	Investment risk reserve
IRTI	Islamic Research and Training Institute
ITFC	Islamic Trade Finance Corporation
LIFO	Last in, first out
LIBOR	London Interbank Offered Rate
OIC	Organization of Islamic Countries
PAR	Profit at risk
PER	Profit equalization reserve

One

Principles and Key Stakeholders

1

Principles and Development of Islamic Finance

slamic finance is a rapidly growing part of the financial sector in the world. Indeed, it is not restricted to Islamic countries and is spreading wherever there is a sizable Muslim community. More recently, it has caught the attention of conventional financial markets as well. According to some estimates, more than 250 financial institutions in over 45 countries practice some form of Islamic finance, and the industry has been growing at a rate of more than 15 percent annually for the past five years. The market's current annual turnover is estimated to be $350 billion, compared with a mere $5 billion in 1985.[1] Since the emergence of Islamic banks in the early 1970s, considerable research has been conducted, focusing mainly on the viability, design, and operation of "deposit-accepting" financial institutions, which function primarily on the basis of profit- and loss-sharing partnerships rather than the payment or receipt of interest, a prohibited element in Islam.

Whereas the emergence of Islamic banks in global markets is a significant development, it is dwarfed by the enormous changes taking place in the conventional banking industry. Rapid innovations in financial markets and the internationalization of financial flows have changed the face of conventional banking almost beyond recognition. Technological progress and deregulation have provided new opportunities, increasing competitive pressures among banks and non-banks alike. The growth in international financial markets and the proliferation of diverse financial instruments have provided large banks with wider access to funds. In the late 1980s, margins attained from the traditional business of banking diminished. Banks have

---

Key Messages

- Institutions offering financial instruments and services compatible with the principles of Islam are emerging rapidly in domestic and international financial markets.
- The basic framework for an Islamic financial system is a set of rules and laws, collectively referred to as *Shariah*, governing economic, social, political, and cultural aspects of Islamic societies.
- Prohibition of *riba* —a term literally meaning "an excess" and interpreted as "any unjustifiable increase of capital whether in loans or sales"—is the central tenet of the system. Such prohibition is applicable to all forms of "interest" and therefore eliminates "debt" from the economy.
- Efforts to develop financial intermediation without interest started in the 1960s. Several Islamic banks were established in the 1970s, and their number has been growing since then.
- The last decade has witnessed rapid developments in the areas of financial innovation, risk management, regulation, and supervision.

---

responded to these new challenges with vigor and imagination by forging ahead into new arenas. At the same time, markets have expanded, and opportunities to design new products and provide more services have arisen. While these changes have occurred more quickly in some countries than in others, banks everywhere are developing new instruments, products, services, and techniques. Traditional banking practice—based on the receipt of deposits and the granting of loans—is only one part of a typical bank's business today and often the least profitable.

New information-based activities, such as trading in financial markets and generating income through fees, are now a major source of a bank's profitability. Financial innovation has also led to the increased market orientation and marketability of bank assets, which entail the use of assets such as mortgages, automobile loans, and export credits as backing for marketable securities, a process known as securitization. A prime motivation for innovation has been the introduction of prudential capital requirements, which has led to a variety of new financial instruments. Some instruments are technically very complicated and poorly understood except by market experts, while many others pose complex problems for the measurement, management, and control of risk. Moreover, profits associated with some of these instruments are high and, like the financial markets from which they are derived, are highly volatile and expose banks to new or higher degrees of risk.

These developments have increased the need for and complicated the function of risk measurement, management, and mitigation (control assessment). The quality of corporate governance of banks has become a hot topic, and the approach to regulation and supervision has changed dramatically. Within an individual bank, the new banking environment and increased market volatility have necessitated an integrated approach to asset-liability and risk management.

Rapid developments in conventional banking have also influenced the reshaping of Islamic banks and financial institutions. There is a growing realization among Islamic financial institutions that sustainable growth requires the development of a comprehensive risk management framework geared to their particular situation and requirements. At the same time, policy makers and regulators are taking serious steps to design an efficient corporate governance structure as well as a sound regulatory and supervisory framework to support development of a financial system conducive to Islamic principles.

This publication provides a comprehensive overview of topics related to the assessment, analysis, and management of various types of risks in the field of Islamic banking. It is an attempt to provide a high-level framework (aimed at non-specialist executives) attuned to the current realities of changing economies and Islamic financial markets. This approach emphasizes the accountability of key players in the corporate governance process in relation to the management of Islamic financial risk.

PRINCIPLES OF ISLAMIC FINANCIAL SYSTEMS

The Islamic financial system is not limited to banking; it also covers capital formation, capital markets, and all types of financial intermediation and risk transfer. The term "Islamic financial system" is relatively new, appearing only in the mid-1980s. In fact, earlier references to commercial or mercantile activities conforming to Islamic principles were made under the umbrella of either "interest-free" or "Islamic" banking. However, interpreting the Islamic financial system simply as free of interest does not capture a true picture of the system as a whole. Undoubtedly, prohibiting the receipt and payment of interest is the nucleus of the system, but it is supported by other principles of Islamic doctrine advocating social justice, risk sharing, the rights and duties of individuals and society, property rights, and the sanctity of contracts.

An Islamic economic system is a rule-based system formulated by Islamic law, known as *Shariah*. The *Shariah* consists of constitutive and regulative rules according to which individual Muslims, and their collectivity, must conduct their affairs. The basic source of the law, in Islam, is the Qur'an, whose centrality in Islam and influence on the life of Muslims cannot be overemphasized. Its chapters constitute the tissues out of which the life of a Muslim is tailored, and its verses are the threads from which the essence of his or her soul is woven. It includes all the necessary constitutive rules of the law as "guidance for mankind." However, it contains many universal statements that need further explanation before they can become specific guides for human action. Hence, after the *Qur'an*, the Prophet Muhammad's sayings and actions are the most important sources of the law and a fountainhead of Islamic life and thought.

The philosophical foundation of an Islamic financial system goes beyond the interaction of factors of production and economic behavior. Whereas the conventional financial system focuses primarily on the economic and financial aspects of transactions, the Islamic system places equal emphasis on the ethical, moral, social, and religious dimensions, which seek to enhance equality and fairness for the good of society as a whole. The system can be fully appreciated only in the context of Islam's teachings on the work ethic, distribution of wealth, social and economic justice, and role of the state. The Islamic financial system is founded on the absolute prohibition of the payment or receipt of any predetermined, guaranteed rate of return. This closes the door to the concept of interest and precludes the use of debt-based instruments.

Given an understanding of the role of institutions, rules, the law, and ideology of Islam, one can make the following propositions regarding the economic system:[2]

- The foremost priority of Islam and its teaching on economics is *justice and equity*. The notion of justice and equity, from production to distribution, is deeply embedded in the system. As an aspect of justice, social justice in Islam consists of the creation and provision of equal opportunities and the removal of obstacles equally for every member of society. Legal justice, too, can be interpreted as meaning that all members of society have equal status before the law, equal protection of the law, and equal opportunity under the law. The notion of economic justice, and its attendant concept of distributive justice, is characteristic of the Islamic economic system: rules governing permissible and forbidden economic behavior on the part of consumers, producers, and government, as well as questions of property rights and the production and distribution of wealth, are all based on the Islamic concept of justice.
- The Islamic paradigm incorporates a spiritual and moral framework that values human relations above material possessions. In this way, it not only is concerned about material needs but also establishes a balance between the material and spiritual fulfillment of human beings.

■ Whereas conventional thinking focuses on the individual, society, or community and appears as a mere aggregate having no independent significance, the Islamic system creates a balanced relationship between the individual and society. Self-interest and private gains of the individual are not denied, but they are regulated for betterment of the collectivity. Maximizing an individual's pursuit of profit in enterprise or satisfaction in consumption is not the sole objective of society, and any wasteful consumption is discouraged.

■ The recognition and protection of the property rights of all members of society are the foundation of a stakeholder-oriented society, preserving the rights of all and reminding them of their responsibilities.

To assure justice, the *Shariah* provides a network of ethical and moral rules of behavior for all participates in the market and requires that these norms and rules be internalized and adhered to by all (see box 1.1). This concept of market is based on the basic principle forbidding any form of behavior leading to the creation of instantaneous property rights without commensurate equity created by work. In this context, market imperfection refers to the existence of any factor considered not to be permissible by the *Shariah*, such as fraud, cheating, monopoly practices, coalitions and all types of combinations among buyers and sellers, underselling, speculative hoarding, and bidding up of prices without the intention to purchase. The freedom of contract and obligation to fulfill it, consent of the parties to a transaction, full access to the market for all buyers and sellers, honesty in transactions, and provision of full information regarding the quantity, quality, and prices of factors and products to buyers and sellers before the start of negotiation and bargaining are prescribed.

Beginning with the notion of property as a sacred trust, as well as prohibitions also present in other monotheistic religions, *Shariah* protects property from any exploitation through unjust and unfair dealings. Prohibition of *riba* (interest), elimination of *gharar* (contractual ambiguity), and restrictions on other forms of exploitation are some of the implications of this core principle. (See appendix A for a glossary of Islamic terms.) The significance of contracts and the related obligations cannot be overstated. In this context, financial transactions are no different from any other set of contracts subject to compliance with *Shariah* principles. Primarily, a financial transaction is considered valid if it meets the basic requirements of a valid legal contract and does not contain certain elements, such as *riba, gharar, qimar* (gambling), and *maysur* (games of chance involving deception). While the prohibition of *riba* is the most

BOX 1.1   Principles of an Islamic Financial System

The basic framework for an Islamic financial system is a set of rules and laws, collectively referred to as *Shariah*, governing economic, social, political, and cultural aspects of Islamic societies. *Shariah* originates from the rules dictated by the *Qur'an* and its practices and explanations rendered (more commonly known as *Sunnah*) by the Prophet Muhammad. Further elaboration of the rules is provided by scholars in Islamic jurisprudence within the framework of the *Qur'an* and Sunnah. The basic principles of an Islamic financial system can be summarized as follows.

Prohibition of interest. Prohibition of *riba*—a term literally meaning "an excess" and interpreted as "any unjustifiable increase of capital whether in loans or sales"—is the central tenet of the system. More precisely, any positive, fixed, predetermined rate tied to the maturity and the amount of principal (that is, guaranteed regardless of the performance of the investment) is considered *riba* and is prohibited. The general consensus among Islamic scholars is that *riba* covers not only usury but also the charging of "interest" as widely practiced. This prohibition is based on arguments of social justice, equality, and property rights. Islamic law encourages the earning of profits but forbids the charging of interest because profits, determined ex post, symbolize successful entrepreneurship and creation of additional wealth, whereas interest, determined ex ante, is a cost that is accrued irrespective of the outcome of business operations and may not create wealth. Social justice demands that borrowers and lenders share rewards as well as losses in an equitable fashion and that the process of accumulating and distributing wealth in the economy be fair and representative of true productivity.

Money as "potential" capital. Money is treated as "potential" capital—that is, it becomes actual capital only when it joins hands with other resources to undertake a productive activity. Islam recognizes the time value of money, but only when it acts as capital, not when it is "potential" capital.

Risk sharing. Because interest is prohibited, suppliers of funds become investors instead of creditors. The provider of financial capital and the entrepreneur share business risks in return for a share of the profits. The terms of financial transactions need to reflect a symmetrical risk-return distribution that each party to the transaction may face. The relationship between the investors and the financial intermediary is based on profit- and loss-sharing principles, and the financial intermediary shares the risks with the investors.

Prohibition of speculative behavior. An Islamic financial system discourages hoarding and prohibits transactions featuring extreme uncertainties, gambling, and risks.

Sanctity of contracts. Islam upholds contractual obligations and the disclosure of information as a sacred duty. This feature is intended to reduce the risk of asymmetric information and moral hazard.

Shariah-approved activities. Only those business activities that do not violate the rules of *Shariah* qualify for investment. For example, any investment in business dealing with alcohol, gambling, or casinos is prohibited.

Social justice. In principle, any transaction leading to injustice and exploitation is prohibited. A financial transaction should not lead to the exploitation of any party to the transaction. Exploitation entails the absence of information symmetry between parties to a contract.

critical and gets the most attention, one cannot dispute the criticality of *gharar* and other elements. Historically, jurists or *Shariah* scholars did not interfere unnecessarily in economic activities and gave economic agents full freedom to contract as long as certain basic requirements—that is, the prohibition of *riba*—were met.

Prohibition of interest is not due to any formal economic theory as such but is directly prohibited by the divine order in the *Qur'an*. Verses of the *Qur'an* clearly prohibit dealing with *riba* but do not define it precisely. Such omission is often attributed to the fact that the concept was not vague at the time of prohibition, so there was no need to provide a formal definition. Defining the term in any language other than Arabic adds further complexity. For example, no single English word captures the essence of *riba*. This has caused much of the confusion in explaining the concept both to the lay person and to scholars.

Literally, the Arabic term *riba* refers to excess, addition, and surplus, while the associated verb implies "to increase, to multiply, to exceed, to exact more than was due, or to practice usury." E. W. Lane's Arabic-English Lexicon presents a comprehensive meaning that covers most of the earlier definitions of *riba*:[3]

> To increase, to augment, swellings, forbidden "addition," to make more than what is given, the practicing or taking of usury or the like, an excess or an addition, or an addition over and above the principal sum that is lent or expended.

While the original basis for the prohibition of interest was divine authority, Muslim scholars recently have emphasized the lack of a theory to justify the use of interest. Muslim scholars have rebutted the arguments that interest is a reward for savings—a productivity of capital—and constitutes the difference between the value of capital goods today and their value tomorrow. Regarding interest being a reward for savings, they argue that interest could be justified only if it resulted in reinvestment and subsequent growth in capital and was not a reward solely for forgoing consumption. Regarding interest as productive capital, modern Muslim scholars argue that the interest is paid on the money and is required regardless of whether or not capital is used productively and thus is not justified. Finally, regarding interest as an adjustment between the value of capital goods today and their value tomorrow, they argue that this only explains its inevitability and not its rightness: if that is the sole justification for interest, it seems more reasonable to allow next year's economic conditions to determine the extent of the reward, as opposed to predetermining it in the form of interest (Mirakhor 1989).

After *riba*, contractual ambiguity is the most important element in financial contracts. In simple terms, *gharar* refers to any uncertainty created by the lack of information or control in a contract. It can be thought of as ignorance in regard to an essential element in a transaction, such as the exact sale price or the ability of the seller to deliver what is sold. The presence of ambiguity makes a contract null and void.

Gharar can be defined as a situation in which either party to a contract has information regarding some element of the subject of the contract that is withheld from the other party or in which neither party has control over the subject of the contract. Classic examples include transactions involving birds in flight, fish not yet caught, an unborn calf in its mother's womb, or a runaway animal. All such cases involve the sale of an item that may or may not exist. More modern examples include transactions whose subject is not in the possession of one of the parties and over which there is uncertainty even about its future possession.

Keeping in mind the notion of fairness in all Islamic commercial transactions, *Shariah* considers any uncertainty as to the quantity, quality, recoverability, or existence of the subject matter of a contract as evidence of *gharar*. However, *Shariah* allows jurists to determine the extent of *gharar* in a transaction and, depending on the circumstances, whether it invalidates the contract. By prohibiting *gharar*, *Shariah* prohibits many pre-Islamic contracts of exchange, considering them subject to either excessive uncertainty or opaqueness to one or both parties to the contract. In many cases, *gharar* can be eliminated simply by stating the object of sale and the price. A well-documented contract eliminates ambiguity as well.

Considering *gharar* as excessive uncertainty, one can associate it with the element of "risk." Some argue that prohibiting *gharar* is one way of managing risks in Islam, because a business transaction based on the sharing of profit and loss encourages parties to conduct due diligence before committing to a contract. Prohibition of *gharar* forces parties to avoid contracts with a high degree of informational asymmetry and with extreme payoffs; it also makes parties more responsible and accountable. Treating *gharar* as risk may preclude the trading of derivative instruments, which is designed to transfer risks from one party to another.

Another area where prohibition of *gharar* has raised concerns in contemporary financial transactions is the area of insurance. Some argue that writing an insurance (*takaful*) contract on the life of a person falls within the domain of *gharar* and thus invalidates the contract. The issue is still under review and not fully resolved.

DEVELOPMENT AND GROWTH OF ISLAMIC FINANCE

Islamic finance was practiced predominantly in the Muslim world through-out the Middle Ages, fostering trade and business activities with the development of credit. Islamic merchants in Spain, the Mediterranean, and the Baltic states became indispensable middlemen for trading activities. In fact, many concepts, techniques, and instruments of Islamic finance were later adopted by European financiers and businessmen.

An interest in the Islamic mode of banking emerged in several Muslim countries during the postcolonial era as part of an effort to revive and strengthen an Islamic identity. Independent but parallel attempts in Egypt and Malaysia led to the establishment of financial institutions in the early 1960s that were designed to operate on a non-interest basis so as to comply with Islamic economic principles.[4] The first wave of oil revenues in the 1970s and the accumulation of petrodollars gave momentum to this idea, and the growth of Islamic finance coincided with the current account surpluses of oil-exporting Islamic countries. The Middle East saw a mush-rooming of small commercial banks competing for surplus funds. At the same time, interest grew in undertaking theoretical work and research to understand the functioning of an economic and banking system without the institution of "interest." The first commercial bank was established in 1974 in the United Arab Emirates, followed by establishment of the Islamic Development Bank in 1975.

Western analysts quickly challenged the feasibility of a financial system operating without interest and debt. Here, we summarize their arguments in six propositions:[5]

- Zero interest would mean infinite demand for loanable funds and zero supply.
- Such a system would be incapable of equilibrating demand for and supply of loanable funds.
- Zero interest would mean no savings.
- Zero savings would mean no investment and no growth.
- There could be no monetary policy since instruments for managing liquidity could not exist without a predetermined, fixed rate of interest.
- In countries adopting such a system, there would be one-way capital flight.

By 1988 these arguments were countered when research, based on modern financial and economic theory, showed the following:

- A modern financial system can be designed without the need for an ex ante positive nominal fixed interest rate. In fact, as Western researchers showed, no satisfactory theory could explain the need for an ex ante positive nominal interest rate.
- The failure to assume an ex ante positive nominal fixed interest rate—that is, no debt contract—does not necessarily mean that there has to be zero return on capital.
- The return on capital is determined ex post, and the magnitude of the return on capital is determined on the basis of the return to the economic activity in which the funds are employed.
- The expected return is what determines investment.
- The expected rate of return—and income—is what determines savings. Therefore, there is no justification for assuming that there will be no savings or investment.
- Positive growth is possible in such a system.
- Monetary policy would function as in the conventional system, its efficacy depending on the availability of instruments designed to manage liquidity.
- Finally, in an open-economy macroeconomic model without an ex ante fixed interest rate, but with returns to investment determined ex post, the assumption of a one-way capital flight is not justified.

Therefore, a system that prohibits an ex ante fixed interest rate and allows the rate of return on capital to be determined ex post, based on returns to the economic activity in which the funds are employed, is theoretically viable.

In the process of demonstrating the analytical viability of such a system, research also clearly differentiated it from the conventional system. In the conventional system, which is based on debt contracts, risks and rewards are shared asymmetrically, with the debtor carrying the greatest part of the risk and with governments enforcing the contract. Such a system has a built-in incentive structure that promotes moral hazard and asymmetric information. It also requires close monitoring, which can be delegated to an institution acting on behalf of the collectivity of depositors and investors; hence the need for banking institutions.

In the late 1970s and early 1980s, it was shown, mostly by Minsky (1982), that such a system is inherently prone to instability because there will always be maturity mismatch between liabilities (short-term deposits) and assets (long-term investments). Because the nominal value of liabilities is guaranteed, while the nominal value of assets is not, when the maturity mismatch becomes a problem, banks will attempt to manage liabilities by offering higher interest rates to attract more deposits. There is always the possibility that this process will not be sustainable but instead will erode confidence and lead to a run on banks. Such a system, therefore, needs a lender of last resort and bankruptcy procedures, restructuring processes, and debt workout procedures to mitigate the contagion.

During the 1950s and 1960s, Lloyd Metzler of the University of Chicago proposed an alternative system in which contracts are based on equity rather than debt and in which the nominal value of liabilities is not guaranteed, since this is tied to the nominal value of assets.[6] Metzler showed that such a system does not have the instability characteristic of the conventional banking system. In his now classic article, Mohsin Khan showed the affinity of Metzler's model with Islamic finance (Khan 1987). Using Metzler's basic model, Khan demonstrated that this system produces a saddle point and is, therefore, more stable than the conventional system.

By the early 1990s, it was clear that an Islamic financial system not only is theoretically viable, but also has many desirable characteristics. The phenomenal growth of Islamic finance during the 1990s demonstrated the empirical and practical viability of the system (see table 1.1).

The 1980s proved to be the beginning of a period of rapid growth and expansion of the Islamic financial services industry. This growth became steady through the 1990s. The major developments of the 1980s include continuation of serious research at the conceptual and theoretical level, constitutional protection in three Muslim countries, and the involvement of conventional bankers in offering *Shariah*-compliant services. The Islamic Republic of Iran, Pakistan, and Sudan announced their intention to make their financial systems compliant with *Shariah*. Other countries such as Bahrain and Malaysia introduced Islamic banking within the framework of the existing system. The International Monetary Fund (IMF) initiated research in understanding the macroeconomic implications of an economic system operating without the concept of interest. Similar research was conducted to understand the issues of profit- and loss-sharing partnership contracts and the financial stability of such a system.

During the early growth of Islamic financial markets in the 1980s, Islamic banks faced a dearth of quality investment opportunities, which created business opportunities for the conventional Western banks to act as intermediaries, deploying Islamic banks' funds according to guidelines provided by the Islamic banks. Western banks helped Islamic banks to place

TABLE 1.1   Development of Islamic Economics and Finance in Modern History

Time period	Development
Pre-1950s	• Barclays Bank opens its Cairo branch to process financial transactions related to construction of the Suez Canal in the 1890s. Islamic scholars challenge the operations of the bank, criticizing it for charging interest. This criticism spreads to other Arab regions and to the Indian subcontinent, where there is a sizable Muslim community. • The majority of *Shariah* scholars declare that interest in all its forms amounts to the prohibited element of *riba*.
1950s–60s	• Initial theoretical work in Islamic economics begins. By 1953, Islamic economists offer the first description of an interest-free bank based on either two-tier *mudarabah* (profit- and loss-sharing contract) or *wakalah* (unrestricted investment account in which the Islamic bank earns a flat fee). • Mitghamr Bank in Egypt and Pilgrimage Fund in Malaysia start operations
1970s	• The first Islamic commercial bank, Dubai Islamic Bank, opens in 1974. • The Islamic Development Bank (IDB) is established in 1975. • The accumulation of oil revenues and petrodollars increases the demand for *Shariah*-compliant products.
1980s	• The Islamic Research and Training Institute is established by the IDB in 1981. • Banking systems are converted to an interest-free banking system in the Islamic Republic of Iran, Pakistan, and Sudan. • Increased demand attracts Western intermediation and institutions. • Countries like Bahrain and Malaysia promote Islamic banking parallel to the conventional banking system.
1990s	• Attention is paid to the need for accounting standards and a regulatory framework. A self-regulating agency, the Accounting and Auditing Organization of Islamic Financial Institutions, is established in Bahrain. • Islamic insurance (*takaful*) is introduced. • Islamic equity funds are established. • The Dow Jones Islamic Index and the FTSE Index of *Shariah*-compatible stocks are developed.
2000–the present	• The Islamic Financial Services Board is established to deal with regulatory, supervisory, and corporate governance issues of the Islamic financial industry. • *Sukuks* (Islamic bonds) are launched. • Islamic mortgages are offered in the United States and United Kingdom.

Source: Khan (1996); IDB (2005).

funds in commerce and trade-related activities by arranging a trader to buy goods on behalf of the Islamic bank and resell them at a markup. Gradually, Western banks recognized the importance of the emerging Islamic financial markets and started to offer Islamic products through "Islamic windows" in an attempt to attract clients directly. Islamic windows are not independent financial institutions; rather, they are specialized setups within conventional financial institutions that offer *Shariah*-compliant products. Meanwhile, due to the growing demand for *Shariah*-compliant products and fear of losing depositors, non-Western conventional banks also started to offer Islamic windows. In general, Islamic windows are targeted at high-net-worth individuals who want to practice Islamic banking: approximately 1–2 percent of the world's Muslim population.

The number of conventional banks offering Islamic windows is growing, as several leading conventional banks, such as the Hong Kong and Shanghai Banking Corporation (HSBC), are pursuing this market very aggressively. HSBC has a well-established network of banks in the Muslim world and, in 1998, launched HSBC Global Islamic Finance with the objective of promoting Islamic asset securitization, private equity, and banking in the industrial countries. The list of Western banks keeping Islamic windows includes, among others, ABN Amro, American Express Bank, ANZ Grindlays, BNP-Paribas, Citicorp Group, and Union Bank of Switzerland (UBS). The leading non-Western banks with a significant presence of Islamic windows are National Commercial Bank of Saudi Arabia, United Bank of Kuwait, and Riyadh Bank. Citibank is the only Western bank to have established a separate Islamic bank: Citi Islamic Investment Bank (Bahrain) in 1996.

By the early 1990s, the market had gained enough momentum to attract the attention of public policy makers and institutions interested in introducing innovative products. The following are some of the noteworthy developments.

Recognizing the need for standards, a self-regulatory agency—the Accounting and Auditing Organization for Islamic Financial Institutions (AAOIFI)—was established. AAOIFI was instrumental in highlighting the special regulatory needs of Islamic financial institutions. AAOIFI defined accounting and *Shariah* standards, which were adopted or recognized by several countries. However, as the market grew, the regulatory and supervisory authorities, with the help of the IMF, established a dedicated regulatory agency, the Islamic Financial Services Board (IFSB), in the early 2000s to address systemic stability and various governance and regulatory issues relating to the Islamic financial services industry. IFSB took on the challenge and started working in the area of regulation, risk management, and corporate governance.

Further progress was made in developing capital markets. Islamic asset-backed certificates, *sukuks*, were introduced in the market. Different structures of *sukuks* were launched successfully in Bahrain, Malaysia, and other financial centers. Among the issuers were corporations, multilaterals, and sovereign entities such as the Islamic Development Bank, the International Bank for Reconstruction and Development (World Bank), and the governments of Bahrain, Pakistan, and Qatar. During the equities market boom of the 1990s, several equity funds based on *Shariah*-compatible stocks emerged. Dow Jones and Financial Times launched Islamic indexes to track the performance of Islamic equity funds.

Several institutions were established to create and support a robust financial system, including the International Islamic Financial Market, the International Islamic Rating Agency, the General Council of Islamic Banks and Financial Institutions, and the Arbitration and Reconciliation Centre for Islamic Financial Institutions. Today, Islamic finance is no stranger to leading financial centers of the world. With the recent wave of high oil revenues in the Middle East, demand for *Shariah*-compliant products on both the buy and sell sides has increased sharply. It is expected that as leading market makers embrace and begin to practice Islamic finance, the market will grow further, and new products and services will be introduced in the near future.

NOTES

1. A billion is 1,000 million.
2. For further details see Mirakhor (1989); Iqbal and Mirakhor (2007).
3. www.study.quran.co.uk/LLhome.htm.
4. In Malaysia, a pilgrimage fund was established in the late 1950s to facilitate savings to pay for the pilgrimage trip to Makkah. The Pilgrimage Fund became a full-fledged interest-free investment bank in 1962. Around the same time, a cluster of small interest-free savings banks emerged in northern rural Egypt, starting in Mitghamr in 1963.
5. For further details, see Iqbal and Mirakhor (2007).
6. See http://cepa.newschool.edu/het/profiles/metzler.htm.

2

Theory and Practice of Islamic Financial Intermediation

Financial systems are crucial for the efficient allocation of resources in a modern economy. Their landscape is determined by the nature of financial intermediation—that is, how the function of intermediation is performed and who intermediates between suppliers and users of the funds. The acquiring and processing of information about economic entities, the packaging and repackaging of financial claims, and financial contracting are common elements that differentiate financial intermediation from other economic activities.

The main functions of a financial intermediary are asset transformation, conduct of orderly payments, brokerage, and risk transformation. Asset transformation takes place in the form of matching the demand for and supply of financial assets and liabilities (for example, deposits, equity, credit, loans, and insurance) and entails transformation of the maturity, scale, and location of the financial assets and liabilities of the ultimate borrowers and lenders. The administration of an accounting and payment system (for example, check transfer, electronic funds transfer, settlement, clearing) is another important function of intermediation. Typically, financial intermediaries also offer pure brokerage or matchmaking between borrowers and lenders and facilitate the demand for and supply of intangible and contingent assets and liabilities, such as collateral, guarantees, financial advice, and custodial services.

Financial intermediaries not only channel resources from capital-surplus agents (generally households) to capital-deficit ones (businesses) but also allow intertemporal smoothing of households' consumption and businesses' expenditures, enabling both firms and households to share

---

Key Messages

- The Islamic financial system is based on a set of contracts. These contracts include contracts for real economic activities, financing, intermediation, and social welfare.
- The *mudarabah* (trust financing) contract is the cornerstone of financial intermediation by Islamic banks. The owner of capital (depositors) forms a partnership with a manager (financial intermediary) on a profit- and loss-sharing basis.
- Both the assets and liabilities side of an Islamic bank balance sheet are based on *Shariah*-compatible financial instruments. Depositors are considered investors and are known as investment account holders.
- The assets of Islamic banks consist of trade financing, commodity trading, leasing, partnerships, and equity-based partnerships.
- Islamic products are offered by dedicated Islamic banks and several non-Islamic banks through special "Islamic windows."
- The number of Islamic investment banks, mortgage companies, Islamic insurance (*takaful*), and Islamic funds is growing.

---

risks. Increased financial market complexity and volatility have led financial intermediaries to offer products that mitigate, transfer, and share financial risks. Other factors stimulating financial innovations are the liberation of capital accounts, deregulation, and breakthroughs in technology.

Financial intermediation in Islamic history has an established historical record and has made significant contributions to economic development over time. Financiers in the early days of Islam—known as *sarrafs*—undertook many of the traditional, basic functions of a conventional financial institution, such as intermediation between borrowers and lenders, operation of a secure and reliable domestic as well as cross-border payment system, and provision of services such as the issuance of promissory notes and letters of credit. Commercial historians have equated the function of *sarrafs* with that of banks. Historians like Udovitch consider them to have been "bankers without banks" (Udovitch 1981). *Sarrafs* operated through an organized network and well-functioning markets, which established them as sophisticated intermediaries, given the tools and technology of their time. It is claimed that financial intermediaries in the early Islamic period also helped one another to overcome liquidity shortages on the basis of mutual help arrangements. There is evidence that some of the legal concepts, contracts, practices, and institutions developed in the late eighth century provided the foundations for similar instruments in Europe several centuries later (Chapra and Khan 2001).

The *Shariah* provides a set of *intermediation contracts* that facilitate an efficient and transparent execution and financing of economic activities. This set of contracts is comprehensive enough to provide a wide range of typical intermediation services such as asset transformation, a payment system, custodial services, and risk management. Intermediation contracts can be classified into three groups. The first is the most significant: it deals with intermediation through the formation of a partnership of capital and entrepreneurial skills. The second group, which is based on the concept of trust, deals with the placement of assets in the hand of intermediaries for the sake of protection or security. The third group facilitates explicit and implicit guarantees of financial performance between economic agents. These contracts play a critical role by providing stability and mitigating risk in the financial system.

STRUCTURE OF FINANCIAL STATEMENTS

For Islamic financial institutions, the nature of financial intermediation, including the function of banking, is different from that of conventional financial institutions. This difference is the key to understanding the difference in the nature of risks in conventional and Islamic banking. For Islamic banks, the *mudarabah* contract is the cornerstone of financial intermediation and thus of banking. In a *mudarabah* contract, the owner of capital forms a partnership with an entrepreneur or manager who has certain business skills, and both agree to share the profits and losses of the venture undertaken. Such a contract can be applied by an Islamic bank to raise funds in the form of deposits as well as to deploy funds on the assets side.

The basic concept is that both the mobilization and (in theory) the use of funds are based on some form of profit sharing among the depositors, the bank, and the entrepreneurs (users of funds). A typical Islamic bank performs the functions of financial intermediation by screening profitable projects and monitoring the performance of projects on behalf of the investors who deposit their funds with the bank.

Table 2.1 presents a stylized balance sheet of an Islamic bank, displaying different activities and financial instruments. It serves as a good starting point for understanding the dynamics of the risks inherent in Islamic banks. Panel A classifies both assets and liabilities based on the maturity profile of different instruments. Although some instruments, such as *ijarah* and *istisnah*, can be used across different maturity groups, this demarcation is based on the most common use of the instruments. Panel B provides an alternative view based on the functionality and purpose of

TABLE 2.1 A   Theoretical Balance Sheet of an Islamic Bank Based on Maturity Profile

Assets	Liabilities
Based on maturity profile	
Short-term trade finance (cash, *murabahah, salaam*)	Demand deposits (*amanah*)
Medium-term investments (*ijarah, istisnah*)	Investment accounts (*mudarabah*)
Long-term partnerships (*musharakah*)	Special investment accounts (*mudarabah, musharakah*)
Fee-based services (*joalah, kifalah,* and so forth)	Reserves
Non-banking assets (property)	Equity capital

TABLE 2.1 B   Theoretical Balance Sheet of an Islamic Bank Based on Functionality

Assets	Liabilities
Based on functionality	
Cash balances	Demand deposits (*amanah*)
Financing assets (*murabahah, salaam, ijarah, istisnah*)	Investment accounts (*mudarabah*)
Investment assets (*mudarabah, musharakah*)	Special investment accounts (*mudarabah, musharakah*)
Fee-based services (*joalah, kifalah,* and so forth)	Reserves
Non-banking assets (property)	Equity capital

different instruments. Although several Islamic banks organize their financial statements on the basis of functionality, a maturity-based view of the balance sheet is important to keep in mind as it helps to understand exposure at the institutional level.

Liabilities

The liabilities side of the balance sheet is based on the "two-window" theoretical model of an Islamic bank. In addition to equity capital, this model divides the "liability" or funding side of the bank balance sheet into two deposit windows, one for demand deposits and the other for investment or special investment accounts. The choice of window is left to the depositors. Unlike conventional commercial banking, the investment accounts of an Islamic bank are not liabilities in a strict sense because depositors in a conventional bank create immediate claims on the bank, whereas investors-depositors in Islamic banks are like partners.

In addition, special or restricted investment accounts are often shown as off-balance-sheet funds under management. A 100 percent reserve is required for demand deposits (but no reserve requirement is stipulated for the second window). This 100 percent requirement is based on the presumption that the money deposited as demand deposits is placed as *amanah* (demand deposits): they yield no returns and are repayable on demand and at par value; therefore, money creation through the multiplier effect is limited.

Money deposited in investment accounts, in contrast, is placed with the depositors' full knowledge that their deposits will be invested in risk-bearing projects; no guarantee is needed or justified. Investment account holders are investors or depositors who enter into a *mudarabah* contract with the bank, where investors act as the supplier of funds (*rab al-mal*) to be invested by the bank on their behalf, as the agent (*mudarib*). The investors share in the profits accruing to the bank's investments on the assets side. Therefore, such profit-sharing investment deposits are not liabilities. Investors' capital is not guaranteed, and they incur losses if the bank does; the form is closer to that of a limited-term, non-voting equity or a trust arrangement. Some Islamic banks also offer special investment accounts developed on the basis of a special-purpose or restricted *mudarabah* or on profit and loss sharing (*musharakah*). These special investment accounts, which are similar to close-end mutual funds, are highly customized and targeted toward high-net-worth individuals.

Assets

On the assets side, Islamic banks have more choice of instruments with different maturities and risk-return profiles. For short-term maturities, trade financing or financial claims resulting from a sales contract—that is, *murabahah*, *salaam*, and so forth—are available. For medium-term investments, leasing (*ijarah*), manufacturing contracts (*istisnah*), and various partnerships are possible; for long-term investments, partnerships in the form of *musharakah* can be undertaken. An Islamic financial intermediary may also engage an external entrepreneur on a *mudarabah* basis in which the bank acts as principal and the entrepreneur (user of the funds) acts as agent. In this capacity, an Islamic bank can form a syndicate with other financial or nonfinancial institutions to provide entrepreneurs with medium- to long-term capital. Finally, like any conventional bank, Islamic banks also provide customized services, guarantees, and underwriting services for a fee.

The risks of a financial intermediary can be better understood when the sources and applications of funds under management by the financial intermediary are viewed as subportfolios of distinct risk-return and maturity profiles. Table 2.2 provides an overview of the sources and application of funds for a typical Islamic bank. The composition and mix of different maturity buckets on the assets side depend on each financial institution, which may select a mix to match its needs to those of its depositors.

BASIC CONTRACTS AND INSTRUMENTS

Contracts play a vital role in the Islamic financial system, and all financial transactions are based on contractual agreements. Figure 2.1 provides an overview of different contracts and their intended role in Islamic financial systems. Following is a brief explanation of select basic contracts serving as financial instruments classified by their functionality.

Financing Instruments

Financing instruments are used primarily to finance obligations arising from the trade and sale of commodities or property. Financing instruments also include instruments generating rental cash flows against exchange of rights to use the assets such as *ijarah* and *istisnah*. Financing instruments are closely linked to a sale contract and therefore are collateralized by the product being financed. These instruments are the basis of short-term assets for the Islamic banks. *Murabahah*, a cost-plus sales contract, is one of the most popular contracts for purchasing commodities and other products on credit. The concept is that a financier purchases a product— that is, a commodity, raw materials, and so forth—for an entrepreneur who does not have his or her own capital to do so. The financier and the entrepreneur agree on a profit margin, often referred to as markup, which is added to the cost of the product. The payment is delayed for a specified

TABLE 2.2 Sources and Application of Funds

Sources of funding (liabilities and equity)	Application of funding (assets)
Equity capital and shareholders' reserves	Short-term trade finance (*murabahah, salaam*)
Demand and safekeeping deposits (*amanah*)	Regulatory cash reserve requirement
	Medium-term investment (*ijarah, istisnah*)
Investment accounts (*mudarabah*)	Long-term partnerships (*musharakat*)
Special investment accounts (*mudarabah, musharakah*)	Fee-based services (*joalah, kifalah*, and so forth)

FIGURE 2.1 **Contracts and Instruments**

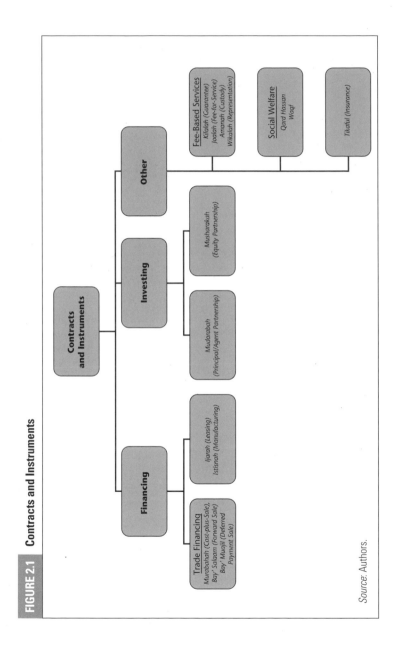

Source: Authors.

period of time during which the entrepreneur produces the final product and sells it in the market. To be a valid contract, *Shariah* requires that a *murabahah* contract be the result of an original sale and not a means of financing existing inventory. In addition, the financier must take ownership of the item on sale.

Murabahah was originally a sales transaction in which a trader would purchase a product and then sell it to the end user at a price calculated using an agreed profit margin over the costs incurred by the trader. Today, banks have taken over the trader's role of financier.

Bay al-muajjil, or sale with deferred payment, allows the sale of a product on the basis of a deferred payment in installments or a lump sum. The price of the product is agreed upon by the buyer and the seller at the time of the sale and cannot include any charges for deferring payments. *Bay' al-salaam,* or purchase with deferred delivery, is similar to conventional forward contracts in terms of function but is different in terms of the payment arrangements. In the case of *bay' al-salaam,* the buyer pays the seller the full negotiated price of a specific product that the seller promises to deliver at a specified future date. The main difference between *bay' al-salaam* and a conventional forward contract is that the full negotiated price is payable at the time of the contract, as opposed to the latter, where the full payment is not due in advance. This forward sale benefits both the seller and the buyer. The seller gets cash to invest in the production process, and the buyer eliminates uncertainty in the future price.

Several medium-term financing instruments are available: *ijarah* (a leasing contract) and *istisnah* (a manufacturing contract).

An *ijarah* contract gives something in return for rent. Technically, it is a contract of sale, but it is not the sale of a tangible asset; rather, it is a sale of the *usufruct* (right to use the object) for a specified period of time. The word *ijarah* conveys the sense of both hire and lease. In general, it refers to the lease of tangible assets such as property and merchandise, but it also denotes the hiring of personal services for a fee. Compared with the conventional form of financing, which is generally in the form of a debt, leasing provides financing in relation to a particular asset. In a sense, it combines financing and collateral, because the ownership of the asset serves as collateral and security against any future loss.

One of the major advantages of *ijarah* is that it resembles the conventional lease agreement. There are some differences between the two, but they function in largely the same way. One difference is that in *ijarah* the leasing agency must own the leased object for the duration of the lease. Another difference is the absence of compound interest that may be charged under conventional leases in the event of default or delay in the installment payments. Similarities with conventional leasing make this contract attractive to conventional investors and borrowers as well.

An *istisnah* contract facilitates the manufacture or construction of an asset at the request of the buyer. Once the manufacturer undertakes to manufacture the asset or property for the buyer, the transaction of *istisnah* comes into existence. Both parties—namely, the buyer and the manufacturer—agree on a price and on the specification of the asset to be manufactured. At the time of delivery, if the asset does not conform to the specifications, the party placing the order has the right to retract the contract.

An important feature of *istisnah* relates to the mode and timing of payment. There is flexibility in regard to the payment, and it is not necessary for the price to be paid in advance. It is also not necessary for it to be paid at the time of delivery. Both parties can agree on a schedule of payment convenient to both, and the payment can be made in installments.

Like *ijarah*, *istisnah* has great potential for application in the area of project finance in different sectors and industries. Successful applications include the manufacture of aircraft, locomotives, ships, and heavy-duty machinery. The *istisnah* contract also is suitable for building infrastructure such as roads, dams, housing, hospitals, and schools.

Investing Instruments

Investing instruments are vehicles for capital investment in the form of a partnership. There are two types of investing instruments: fund management (*mudarabah*) and equity partnerships (*musharakah*).

Mudarabah, which can be short, medium, or long term, is a trust-based financing agreement whereby an investor entrusts capital to an agent to undertake a project. Profits are based on a prearranged, agreed ratio. A *mudarabah* agreement is akin to a Western-style limited partnership in which one party contributes capital, while the other runs the business; profit is distributed based on a negotiated percentage of ownership. The investor bears the loss, but the agent does not share in any financial loss unless there is evidence of misconduct or negligence. *Mudarabah* is used on both the liabilities and the assets side.

Musharakah, which can be either medium or long term, is a hybrid of *shiraka* (partnership) and *mudarabah*, combining the act of investment and management. In the absence of debt security, the *Shariah* encourages this form of financing. The *Shariah* is fairly comprehensive in defining different types of partnerships, in identifying the rights and obligations of the partners, and in stipulating the rules governing the sharing of profits and losses. *Musharakah* is a form of partnership in which two or more persons combine either their capital or their labor, share the profits and losses, and have similar rights and liabilities. Within *musharakah* there are further subclassifications of partnerships with respect to the level of the partners' authority and obligations and the type of his or her contribution, such as management skills or goodwill.

ISLAMIC FINANCIAL INSTITUTIONS IN PRACTICE[1]

While early forms of Islamic financial institutions were highly concentrated in commercial banking activities, more diverse forms have emerged in the last two decades to cater to the demands of different segments of the market. Although the Islamic mode of banking has been mandated and adopted by the governments of the Islamic Republic of Iran, Pakistan, and Sudan, the supply of *Shariah*-compliant products has been led primarily by the private sector. In fact, private Islamic banks as a group are becoming some of the largest private sector financial institutions in the Islamic world, with growing networks through branches or subsidiaries. There is no standard way of grouping Islamic financial institutions, but based on the services rendered, today's Islamic financial institutions can be divided into the following broad categories: Islamic banks, Islamic windows, Islamic investment banks and funds, Islamic mortgage companies, Islamic insurance companies, and *mudarabah* companies.

Islamic Banks

Islamic banks represent the majority of Islamic financial institutions; they are spread around the globe in both the public and private sectors. Islamic banks typically are a hybrid of a conventional commercial bank and an investment bank and resemble a universal bank. After the state sponsorship of Islamic banking in the Islamic Republic of Iran, Pakistan, and Sudan, all commercial banks were transformed to comply with *Shariah* rules and principles. Islamic banks in other countries, especially in the Middle East, are in the private sector, where ownership is by shareholders in public companies, by holding companies, or by wealthy families or individuals. There are two major holding companies: Dar-al-Mal Islami Group and Al Barakah Group, which have an extended network of Islamic financial institutions.

Islamic banks have grown in numbers, but the average size of assets is still small compared with that of a conventional bank. No Islamic bank is on the list of the top 100 banks in the world. According to some estimates, more than 60 percent of Islamic banks have assets that are below the level

($500 million) that theoretical studies suggest as being the minimum to be viable. Aggregate assets of all Islamic banks are still less than those of any of the top 60 banks in the world. Finally, the size of assets of the largest Islamic bank amounts to a meager 1 percent of the assets of the largest bank in the world (see table 2.3).

Islamic Windows

As discussed in chapter 1, Islamic windows are specialized setups that offer *Shariah*-compliant products. During the 1980s, conventional Western banks acted as intermediaries, deploying funds according to guidelines defined by the Islamic banks. Western banks helped Islamic banks to place funds in commerce and trade-related activities by arranging for a trader to buy goods on behalf of the Islamic bank and to resell them at a markup. Gradually, Western banks began to offer Islamic products and to attract clients directly without having to use an Islamic bank as intermediary.

The number of conventional banks offering Islamic windows is growing. Hong Kong Shanghai Banking Corporation launched HSBC Global Finance in 1998, and numerous Western banks offer Islamic windows, including ABN Amro, American Express Bank, ANZ Grindlays, BNP Pariba, Citicorp Group, Morgan Stanley, and Union Bank of Switzerland (UBS).

Islamic Investment Banks and Funds

Islamic investment banks and investment funds emerged during the 1990s, when the market reached a threshold where large transactions and

TABLE 2.3 Size of Islamic Financial Institutions in 1999

Region	Number of Islamic financial institutions	Average capital (US$ million)	Average assets (US$ million)
South Asia	51	17	770
Africa	35	6	45
South East Asia	31	5	75
Middle East	47	116	2,204
Europe and the Americas	9	70	101
Asia and Australia	3	3	6
Total	176	42	839

Source: Kahf (1999).

investment banking became attractive. Whereas a typical Islamic bank's services are retail and consumer centered, Islamic investment banks are aiming to capitalize on large investment syndication, market-making, and underwriting opportunities. Islamic investment banks have been successful in developing innovative large-scale transactions for infrastructure financing in conjunction with conventional project finance for projects such as the Hub Power project in Pakistan.

Islamic investment funds are not new but are making a comeback after initial experimentation during which many of them did not survive. The 1990s witnessed real growth in Islamic funds, and by the start of the new millennium, there were more than 150 Islamic funds with a wide range of offerings, including equity (more than 85), commodity, leasing, and trade-related funds. Funds other than equity are considered to be low risk because of the nature of the underlying instrument. Both leasing and commodity funds provide investors a low return with minimum risk of loss. In the case of leasing, the fund is a securitized pool of lease contracts dealing with collateralized assets generating a steady stream of cash flow. Since a lease contract is more familiar to conventional bankers, lease funds have wider acceptability with conventional investors. Similarly, commodity funds have a short-term exposure in markets that are efficient and have developed forward markets, thus reducing the level of risk. In contrast, equity funds are similar to conventional mutual funds and are exposed to a higher degree of risk.

Islamic equity funds gained popularity during the 1990s when global equity markets experienced historical growth. Such funds are designed to ensure that equity stocks included in the fund are not only well diversified but also fully compliant with the *Shariah*'s guidelines. The selection of a stock goes through a strict screening or filtering process, which ensures that (a) the company's capital structure is predominantly equity based (only a limited proportion of debt is accepted in certain circumstances); (b) the nature of the business does not involve any prohibited activity such as gambling, interest-based transactions, and the production or consumption of alcohol, and (c) only a negligible portion of income is derived from interest on securities. Since the majority of Muslim countries do not have well-developed capital and stock markets, fund managers focus mostly on equity markets in the developed countries, where the domain of qualified stocks is limited, which constrains the opportunities to hold a well-diversified portfolio.

Dow Jones has recognized the significance and potential of Islamic equity funds by setting up an equity benchmark index—the Dow Jones Islamic Market Index (DJIM). DJIM tracks *Shariah*-compliant stocks from the 2,700 stocks in the Dow Jones Global Index. FTSE followed, announcing its own version of an index to track the performance of stocks qualified for Islamic investment. During the boom in equity markets, several institutions arranged investment in *Shariah*-compliant stocks through the Internet, but the timing of launch was not ideal, as equity markets started to decline by the end of the 1990s. Nevertheless, there is still a great potential for Islamic funds to expand across the globe through new technology.

Islamic Mortgage Companies

Islamic mortgage companies are another recent development. Targeted at the housing market for Muslim communities in Western countries (Canada, United Kingdom, and United States) with developed conventional mortgage markets, four models of Islamic mortgage are currently in practice. The first model is based on the *ijarah* (lease) contract and is the closest to the structure of a conventional mortgage. The second model is based on equity partnership (diminishing *musharakah*), where the mortgagee (lender) and mortgagor (borrower) jointly share ownership, which over a period of time is transferred to the mortgagor, who buys shares of ownership by contributing each month toward buying out the mortgagee's share in the property. Return to the lender is generated out of the fair rental value of the property. The third model is based on *murabahah* (sales transaction) and is practiced in the United Kingdom, where the property transfer tax (stamp duty) discriminates against the *ijarah*- or *musharakah*-based mortgage. The fourth model is designed along the lines of cooperative societies, where members buy equity (*musharakah*) membership and help each other to purchase property from the pool of the society's funds. Recently, the U.S. agency Freddie Mac recognized the importance of Islamic mortgages and began to underwrite and securitize them. The chances of success for Islamic mortgages are bright in Western markets, where capital markets are liquid, transparent, and well regulated. In particular, there is great potential for Islamic mortgages in the North American markets, where there is a sizable Muslim community in the middle- and upper-income brackets.

Islamic Insurance Companies

The closest Islamic instrument to the contemporary system of insurance is *takaful*, which literally means mutual or joint guarantee. Typically, *takaful* is carried out in the form of solidarity *mudarabah*, where the participants agree to share their losses by contributing periodic premiums in the form of investments. They are then entitled to redeem the residual value of profits after fulfilling the claims and premiums. A critical difference between contemporary insurance models and *takaful* is the participant's right to receive surplus profits. The participants in a given solidarity (that is, *takaful*) *mudarabah* have the right to share the surplus profits generated, but at the same time they are liable, in addition to the premiums, for amounts they have already distributed, if the initial premiums paid during a period are not sufficient to meet all the losses and risks incurred during that period. Another distinct feature of *takaful* is that the premiums and reserves can be invested only in *Shariah*-compliant instruments. *Takaful* companies can constitute reserves (like conventional mutual insurance companies), which means that the insured may have to make supplemental contributions if claims exceed premiums. At present, there is very limited application of *takaful* in Islamic financial markets, as very few institutions offer insurance services on a large scale.

Mudarabah Companies

The concept of a *mudarabah* company is very similar to that of a close-end fund managed by a specialized professional investment management company. Like a mutual fund, a *mudarabah* company is incorporated as a separate legal entity with a fund management company responsible for its operations. Unlike an Islamic bank, a *mudarabah* company is not permitted to accept deposits; it is funded by equity capital, provided by the sponsor's own subscribed capital and by *mudarabah* investment certificates, which are open to general investors through a public offering. Profits on investments are distributed among subscribers on the basis of their contribution, with the manager of the funds earning a proportion of the profits.

There can be two types of *mudarabah*: multipurpose—that is, a *mudarabah* having more than one investment purpose or objective—and specific purpose. All *mudarabahs*, however, are independent of each other, and none is liable for the liabilities of, or is entitled to benefit from the assets of, any other *mudarabah* contract or *mudarabah* company.

Considering that the *mudarabah* contract is the cornerstone of Islamic finance, *mudarabah* companies can play a critical role in the financial landscape of a developing economy, especially for small- and medium-size enterprises. For them to do so requires a financial sector that inspires investor confidence and facilitates the transparency and operational efficiency of *mudarabah* companies.

NOTES

1. Iqbal and Mirakhor (2007).

3

Corporate Governance: A Partnership

The issue of corporate governance has recently received considerable attention in conventional economic literature and public policy debates. This attention can be attributed to several factors: (a) the growth of institutional investors—that is, pension funds, insurance companies, mutual funds, and highly leveraged institutions—and their role in the financial sector, especially in major industrial economies; (b) widely articulated concerns and criticism to the effect that the contemporary monitoring and control of publicly held corporations in English-speaking countries, notably the United Kingdom and United States, are seriously defective, leading to suboptimal economic and social development; (c) the shift away from a traditional view of corporate governance as centered on "shareholder value" in favor of a corporate governance structure extended to a wide circle of stakeholders; and (d) the impact of increased globalization of financial markets, a global trend toward deregulation of financial sectors, and liberalization of institutional investors' activities.

The activities of Islamic banks and banking may affect the welfare of more than 20 percent of the world's population, mostly concentrated in developing countries, and their corporate governance arrangements matter for economic development. Sound corporate governance can create an enabling environment, which rewards banking efficiency, mitigates financial risks, and increases systemic stability. Lenders and other providers of funds are more likely to extend financing when they feel comfortable with the corporate governance arrangements of the funds'

Key Messages

- Corporate governance provides a disciplined structure through which a bank sets its objectives, determines the means of attaining them, and monitors the performance of those objectives.
- Effective corporate governance encourages a bank to use its resources more efficiently.
- Financial risk management is the responsibility of several key players in the corporate governance structure. Each key player is accountable for a dimension of risk management.
- The key players are regulators or lawmakers, supervisors, shareholders, directors, executive managers, internal auditors, external auditors, and the general public.
- To the extent that any key player does not, or is not expected to, fulfill its function in the risk management chain, other key players have to compensate for the gap created by enhancing their own role. More often than not, it is the bank supervisor who has to step into the vacuum created by the failure of certain players.

---

recipient and with the clarity and enforceability of creditor rights. Good corporate governance tends to lower the cost of capital, as it conveys a sense of lower risk that translates into shareholders' readiness to accept lower returns. Corporate governance is proven to improve operational performance. Finally, it reduces the risks of contagion from financial distress. Besides mitigating the internal risk of distress by positively affecting investors' perception of risk and their readiness to extend funding, it increases firms' robustness and resilience to external shocks. While Islamic scholars argue that Islamic corporate governance induces ethical behavior and is immune to the flaws of conventional banking, Islamic banks and banking are no less prone than conventional banks to suffer breaches of fiduciary responsibility or the consequences of asymmetric information. Research in corporate governance issues can benefit from understanding the relevance of corporate governance to the Islamic financial services industry and the governance issues that are unique to it.

Corporate governance relates to the manner in which the business of the bank is governed, including setting corporate objectives and the bank's risk profile, aligning corporate activities and behaviors with the expectation that the management will operate in a safe and sound manner, running day-to-day operations within an established risk profile, while protecting the interests of depositors and other stakeholders. It is defined by a set of relationships between the bank's management, its board, its shareholders, and other stakeholders.

The following are the key elements of sound corporate governance in a bank:

- A well-articulated corporate strategy against which the overall success and the contribution of individuals can be measured;
- The assignment and enforcement of clear responsibilities, decision-making authority, and accountabilities that are appropriate for the bank's risk profile;
- A strong financial risk management function (independent of business lines), adequate internal control systems (including internal and external audit functions), and a functional process with the necessary checks and balances;
- Adequate corporate values, codes of conduct, and other standards of appropriate behavior and effective systems for ensuring compliance, including special monitoring of a bank's risk exposures where conflicts of interest are expected to appear (for example, relationships with affiliated parties);
- Financial and managerial incentives for the board, management, and employees to act in an appropriate manner, including compensation, promotion, and penalties (that is, compensation consistent with the bank's objectives, performance, and ethical values).

Figure 3.1 portrays a risk management partnership in which each key player has clearly defined accountability for a specific dimension of every area of risk.

SUPERVISORY AUTHORITIES: MONITORING RISK MANAGEMENT

The primary role of bank regulators and supervisors is to facilitate the process of risk management and to enhance and monitor the statutory framework in which it is undertaken. Bank regulators and supervisors cannot prevent bank failures. However, by creating a sound enabling environment, they have a crucial role to play in influencing the other key players.

Bank supervision is sometimes applied incorrectly as a legal or administrative function focused largely on regulations related to the business of banking. Such regulations are often prescriptive in nature and impose onerous requirements on banks, which seek to circumvent them by developing innovative products.

Once regulators and supervisors understand that they cannot bear sole responsibility for preventing bank failures, they need to identify clearly

FIGURE 3.1 **Partnership in Corporate Governance of Banks**

Key Players and Responsibilities	Balance sheet structure	Income statement structure and profitability	Solvency risk and capital adequacy	ALM: balance sheet and income statement structure	Credit risk	Treasury management	Market risk	Other IFI risks	Operational risk
	Accountability (dimension of risk for which key player is responsible)								
Systemic									
Legal and regulatory authorities	Set regulatory framework, including risk exposure limits and other risk management parameters, which will optimize risk management in the banking sector								
Supervisory authorities	Monitor financial viability and effectiveness of risk management; check compliance with regulations								
Shariah board	Ensure that financial institutions comply with the rules of *Shariah* in financial intermediation activities and managerial behavior and protect the rights of depositors and other stakeholders								
Institutional									
Shareholders	Appoint "fit and proper" boards, management, and auditors								
Board of directors	Set risk management and other bank policies; have ultimate responsibility for the entity								
Executive management	Create systems to implement board policies, including risk management, in day-to-day operations								
Audit committee and internal auditors	Test compliance with board policies and provide assurance regarding corporate governance, control systems, and risk management processes								
External auditors	Express opinion and evaluate risk management policies								
Public or consumer (require transparency and full disclosure)									
Investors or depositors	Understand responsibility and insist on full disclosure; take responsibility for own decisions								
Rating agencies and media	Insist on transparency and full disclosure; inform the public and emphasize ability to service debt								
Analysts	Analyze quantitative and qualitative risk-based information and advise clients								

what they are capable of achieving and then focus on that specific mission. This process is currently taking place in most industrial countries. The role of a bank's supervisory authority is moving away from monitoring compliance with banking laws and old-style prudential regulations. A more appropriate mission statement today would be "to create a regulatory and legal environment in which the quality and effectiveness of bank risk management can be optimized in order to contribute to a sound and reliable banking system."

The task of bank supervision becomes monitoring, evaluating, and, when necessary, strengthening the risk management process that is undertaken by banks. However, the supervisory authority is only one of the many contributors to a stable banking system. Other players also are responsible for managing risk, and prudential regulations increasingly stress the accountability of top-level management. Recognizing the high cost of voluminous reporting requirements without corresponding benefits, many countries are moving toward a system of reporting that encourages and enables supervisors to rely more extensively on external auditors in the ordinary course of business, subject to having a clear understanding of their role in the risk management chain.

THE SHAREHOLDERS: APPOINTING
RISK POLICY MAKERS

Shareholders are in a position to appoint the people in charge of the corporate governance process and should screen their conduct carefully to ensure that they do not intend to use the bank solely to finance their own or their associates' enterprises. By electing the supervisory board and approving the board of directors, the audit committee, and external auditors, shareholders are in a position to determine the direction of a bank. Banks are different from other companies in that management and the board are responsible not only to shareholders but also to depositors, who provide leverage to the owners' capital. Depositors are different from normal trade creditors because the entire intermediation function in the economy, including payments and clearance (and therefore the stability of the financial system), is at stake.

The modern market-oriented approach to bank regulation is placing increasing emphasis on the fiduciary responsibility of shareholders. This is reflected in several ways, including more stringent bank licensing requirements and standards that a bank's founder and larger shareholders must meet in order to be considered fit and proper. Actions that may be taken against shareholders who fail to ensure the appointment of fit and proper persons have also become broader. Bank licensing procedures normally include the mandatory identification of major shareholders and require a minimum number of shareholders (which varies among jurisdictions).

Shareholders should play a key role in overseeing a bank's affairs. They are expected to select a competent board of directors whose members are experienced and qualified to set sound policies and objectives. The board of directors must be able to adopt a suitable business strategy for the bank, supervise the bank's affairs and its financial position, maintain reasonable capitalization, and prevent self-serving practices among themselves and throughout the bank as a whole.

In reality, shareholders may not be able to exercise the oversight function in a large bank with a dispersed ownership structure. While the founders of a bank must meet certain standards, as a bank becomes larger and shares are held more widely, the shareholding may become so diffused that individual shareholders have no voice in the bank's management and have little recourse but to sell their shares if they do not like the way the bank is being managed. In such cases, effective supervisory oversight becomes critical.

Another issue is whether shareholders are carrying out their fiduciary responsibilities effectively and whether they have taken advantage of their ownership position in the bank. In practical terms, this can be ascertained by reviewing select aspects, including the frequency of shareholder meetings, the number of shareholders who are normally present, and the percentage of total shares they represent. The level of direct involvement, if any, that the shareholders have with the bank, the supervisory board (directors), and the management board (executive management) should also be taken into account. Such an assessment should include a review of the current composition of the management and supervisory board, their remaining terms of office, and connections among board members, shareholders, and bank customers. A review should be conducted of the bank's level of exposure to shareholders who have more than 1 percent of holdings and are bank customers, including an examination of instruments such as loans and deposits that specifies the amounts, terms, conditions, and funding extended to shareholders.

THE BOARD OF DIRECTORS: ULTIMATE RESPONSIBILITY FOR A BANK'S AFFAIRS

Ultimate responsibility for the way in which a bank's business is conducted lies with the board of directors. The board sets the strategic direction, appoints management, establishes operational policies, and, most important, takes responsibility for ensuring the soundness of a bank. The board is answerable to depositors and shareholders for the lawful, informed, efficient, and able administration of the institution. The members of the board usually delegate the day-to-day management of banking to officers and employees, but board members are responsible for the consequences of unsound or imprudent policies and practices concerning lending, investing, protecting against internal fraud, or any other banking activity.

The composition of a board of directors is crucial. Studies have found that nearly 60 percent of failed banks had board members who either lacked banking knowledge or were uninformed and passive regarding supervision of the bank's affairs. A board with a strong chairman who is not the chief executive is more likely to provide objective inputs than a board whose chairman is also the chief executive. Banks need a board that is both strong and knowledgeable. It is essential for the board to encourage open discussion and, even more important, to tolerate conflict well, since conflict indicates that both sides of the coin are being considered.

Failed banks almost invariably suffer from deficiencies in their board and senior management. The leadership provided by the board of directors of many troubled institutions is often found to be ineffective. One of the chief functions of independent (nonexecutive) directors should therefore be to avoid economic and legal mistakes that could threaten the life of the bank. When problems are discovered by internal controls or external auditors, they should be brought to the immediate attention of the board of directors.

The most important duty of the board is to ensure that the management team has the necessary skills, knowledge, experience, and sense of judgment to manage the bank's affairs in a sound and responsible manner. The management team should be directly accountable to the board, and this relationship should be supported by robust structures. During good times, a board sets the tone and direction. It oversees and supports management efforts, testing and probing recommendations before approving them, and makes sure that adequate controls and systems are in place to identify and address concerns before they become major problems. During bad times, an active, involved board can help a bank to survive if it is able to evaluate problems, take corrective actions, and, when necessary, keep the institution on track until effective management can be reestablished and the bank's problems resolved.

An effective board should have a sound understanding of the nature of the bank's business activities and associated risks. It should take reasonable steps to ensure that management has established strong systems to monitor and control those risks. Even if members of the board are not experts in banking risks and risk management systems, they should ensure that such expertise is available and that the risk management system undergoes appropriate reviews by suitably qualified professionals. The board should take timely actions to ensure a level of capitalization that reasonably matches the economic and business environment of the bank as well as its business and risk profile.

The board should ensure that the bank has adequate internal audit arrangements in place and that risk management systems are applied properly at all times. Directors need not be experts in these control and audit mechanisms, but they should consult experts inside and, if necessary, outside the bank to ascertain that such arrangements are robust and being implemented properly. The board should also ensure that the banking laws and regulations applicable to a bank's business are followed. It should take all reasonable steps to ensure that the information in the bank's disclosure statements is transparent and accurate and that adequate procedures are in place, including external audits or other reviews, where appropriate, to ensure that the information disclosed is not false or misleading.

MANAGEMENT: RESPONSIBILITY FOR BANK OPERATIONS AND THE IMPLEMENTATION OF RISK MANAGEMENT POLICIES

Executive management of a bank has to be fit and proper, meaning not only that managers subscribe to standards of ethical behavior, but also that they have the competence and experience to run the bank. Because the management is responsible for implementing the board's policies in the bank's day-to-day operations, intimate knowledge of the financial risks being managed is vital.

As summarized in box 3.1, the financial soundness and performance of a banking system ultimately depend on the board of directors and on the senior management of member banks. The strategic positioning of a bank, the nature of a bank's risk profile, and the adequacy of the systems for identifying, monitoring, and managing the profile reflect the quality of both the management team's and the directors' oversight. For these reasons, the most effective strategy to promote a sound financial system is to strengthen the accountability of directors and management and to enhance the incentives for them to operate banks prudently. The role of senior management is therefore a fundamental component of a risk-based approach to regulation and supervision. Regulators increasingly aim to strengthen the participation and accountability of senior management, which are key responsibilities for maintaining a bank's safety and soundness.

BOX 3.1 **Accountability of Bank Management**

The U.S. Comptroller of the Currency has studied bank failures between 1979 and 1988 in an effort to determine the root causes of those failures. The ultimate message of this study is that not all banks in a depressed environment fail; rather, the banks with weak management were the ones that succumbed when times became difficult. The final word on this trend has been spoken by a governor of the U.S. Federal Reserve System: "It is important to recognize that bank stockholders suffer losses on their investments, and senior bank management is almost always replaced, regardless of the resolution technique used."

Quality and Experience

The quality and experience of the individuals on a senior management team are of great importance. In a financial institution, the process of risk management does not start at the strategy meeting, in the planning process, or in any other committee; it starts when a prospective employee is screened for appointment to the organization or for promotion to a senior position.

Regulators take several approaches to ensuring that management is fit and proper. Most regulators have established standards for managers, as illustrated in box 3.2. Jurisdictions with such standards often require that the central bank confirm the experience, technical capacity, and professional integrity of senior management before its members assume their duties. However, some jurisdictions do not, as a matter of policy, get involved in the appointment of senior management unless a bank is deemed unsafe due to incompetent management.

Management Responsibilities

While the board and management need to support one another, each has its own distinct role and responsibilities to fulfill. The chief executive officer and the management team should run the bank's day-to-day activities in compliance with board policies, laws, and regulations and should be supported by a sound system of internal controls. Although the board should leave day-to-day operations to management, it should retain overall control. The dictation of a board's actions by management indicates that the board is not fulfilling its responsibilities, ultimately to the detriment of the institution.

Management should provide directors with the information they need to meet their responsibilities and should respond quickly and fully

BOX 3.2 **Fit and Proper Standards for Bank Management**

Regulators in certain jurisdictions require banks' majority shareholders, directors, and managers to furnish information or adhere to standards regarding the following:

- Previous convictions for any crime involving fraud, dishonesty, or violence;
- The contravention of any law that, in the opinion of the regulator, is designed to protect the public against financial loss due to the dishonesty or incompetence of or malpractice by the person concerned. This standard applies when the person is involved in the provision of banking, insurance, investment, and financial services or in the management of juristic persons;
- Indication that a director has caused a particular company's inability to pay its debts;
- Whether or not, in the opinion of the regulator, the person concerned has ever been involved in any business practice that was deceitful or prejudicial or cast doubt on his competence and soundness of judgment;
- Whether or not any previous application to conduct business has been refused, or whether or not any license to conduct business has been withdrawn or revoked;
- Whether or not, while the person was a director or an executive officer of an institution, the institution was censured, warned, disciplined, or made the subject of a court order by any regulatory authority locally or overseas;
- Whether or not the person concerned has been associated with an institution that has been refused a license or has had its license to conduct business revoked;
- Any dismissal or barring of or disciplinary proceedings toward any professional or occupation, as initiated by an employer or professional body;
- The nonpayment of any debt judged due and payable locally or elsewhere;
- Whether or not the person concerned has ever been declared insolvent;
- Convictions for any offense, excluding traffic violations, political offenses, or offenses committed when the person in question was under the age of 18 years;
- Any litigation that the person in question has been involved with or related to the formation or management of any corporate body;
- Any related-party transactions with the institution concerned.

to board requests. In addition, management should use its expertise to generate new and innovative ideas and recommendations for consideration by the board. A bank should have adequate policies in place to increase the accountability of its managers. As the persons responsible for bank stewardship, managers should be given incentives to maintain a well-informed overview of business activities and corresponding risks. The duties and responsibilities of a bank's senior management include appointment to middle-level management positions of persons with adequate professional skills, experience, and integrity; the establishment of adequate performance incentives and personnel management systems; and staff training. Management should ensure that the bank has an adequate management information system and that the information is transparent, timely, accurate, and complete.

The key managerial responsibility is to ensure that all major bank functions are carried out in accordance with clearly formulated policies and procedures and that the bank has adequate systems in place with which to monitor and manage risks effectively. Managerial responsibilities for financial risk management are summarized in box 3.3.

Management's role in identifying, appraising, pricing, and managing financial risk is described well by the Basel Committee on Banking Supervision. The Basel Committee has stated that any corporation that uses new financial instruments has a critical need for all levels of management to acquire knowledge and understanding of their inherent risks and to adapt internal accounting systems to ensure adequate control. Risk management should be an integral part of the day-to-day activities of each and every line manager, in order to ascertain that risk management systems are applied properly and that procedures are followed. Management should also ensure that the bank has adequate internal controls, including appropriate audit arrangements, because risk management often fails as a result of an ineffective decision-making process and weak controls, not of unanticipated or extraordinary risks.

Recent changes in international banking have made the management process considerably more demanding. Financial innovation transfers price

---

BOX 3.3   **The Responsibilities of Management**

Management has the following responsibilities with regard to financial risk:

- Develop and recommend strategic plans and risk management policies for board approval;
- Implement strategic plans and policies after approval by the board;
- Establish an institutional culture promoting high ethical and integrity standards;
- Ensure development of manuals containing policies, procedures, and standards for the bank's key functions and risks;
- Implement an effective internal control system, including continuous assessment of all material risks that could adversely affect the achievement of the bank's objectives;
- Ensure the implementation of controls that enforce adherence to established risk limits;
- Ensure immediate reporting of noncompliance to management;
- Ensure that the internal auditors review and assess the adequacy of controls and compliance with limits and procedures;
- Develop and implement management reporting systems that adequately reflect business risks.

or market risk from one agent to another; it does not eliminate the risk itself. The pace of innovation, the growth of off-balance-sheet transactions, and the unbundling of different types of risk have rendered the analysis of financial statements and the management of a bank's financial position more complex. Management increasingly faces important questions about how best to account for, monitor, and manage risk exposure and how to integrate off-balance-sheet activities into other exposures.

Assessment Process

It is important to appraise the quality of management. The main objective of such an appraisal is to evaluate whether a bank's senior management personnel have the following:

- Adequate technical capacity, experience, and integrity to manage a bank, aspects that can be evaluated based on the bank's personnel practices in the area of management continuity;
- Systems in place to monitor and control the bank's material risks, including credit, exposure concentration, interest rate, currency, solvency, liquidity, and other risks and systems for evaluating whether or not these systems are applied properly and whether or not management takes appropriate actions, if and when necessary;
- Proper managerial guidance and systems for determining whether they have made adequate decisions in all key aspects of the bank's business, complied with all conditions of registration applicable to the bank, and maintained contact with those persons who are capable of controlling or significantly influencing the bank in a manner that is contrary to the bank's interests.
- Policies that call for the disclosure of directors' conflicts of interest.

THE AUDIT COMMITTEE AND INTERNAL AUDITORS: AN ASSESSMENT OF THE BOARD'S RISK MANAGEMENT IMPLEMENTATION

The audit committee and the internal auditors should be regarded as an extension of the board's risk management policy function. Internal auditors traditionally have performed an independent appraisal of a bank's compliance with its internal control systems, accounting practices, and information systems. Most modern internal auditors would, however, describe their task as providing assurance regarding the bank's corporate governance, control systems, and risk management processes. Although audit committees play a valuable role in identifying and addressing areas of risk, the prime responsibility for risk management cannot be abdicated to them; rather it should be integrated into all levels of management.

The mission statement of an audit committee that is organized according to modern principles should be "to enhance the management of operational risks on a groupwide basis." Following from this, the goals of an internal audit function are to accomplish the following:

- Enable management to identify and manage business risks;
- Provide an independent appraisal;
- Evaluate the effectiveness, efficiency, and economy of operations;
- Evaluate compliance with laws, policies, and operating instructions;
- Evaluate the reliability of information produced by accounting and computer systems;
- Provide investigative services to line management.

Contrary views exist regarding the value of audit committees. Such committees have been likened to a straw of hope that boards cling to in an attempt to show that they are managing risk. It is logical that a board facing risk management problems will rush to the historical source of information about problems in the company, namely the auditors. The proponents of this view often point out that the auditors are simply checklist experts, while risk management has never been such a simple pursuit and should not be delegated to a committee, department, or team.

They also have been the object of unflattering comment, such as the following:

- Audit committees are as ineffective in handling risk management as external auditors. They have no hope of ensuring timely and well-informed risk management decisions in a company. Their value lies in retrospective risk control.
- Audit committees create the impression that risk management is something that can be audited until it becomes right. By and large, auditors focus on numbers and figures, while risk management failures are often due to internal and individual shortcomings or bad decisions.
- Audit committees are ineffective because risk management is a dynamic process. The complex nature of present-day financial risks makes it impossible for audit committees to do anything more than look after auditable risks, and these are only one part of total risk.

■ The problems of internal auditors are exacerbated when they follow an inspection approach—they never become a partner in the risk management process, but remain an outsider not to be trusted to assist management in their operational risk management task—through sound advice coming from the macro view that internal auditors should have of an organization.

The monitoring and directing of the internal audit function are an integral part of the audit committee's overall responsibilities. Both the board and management must have a tool to ensure that policies are being followed and risks are being managed. Under a market-oriented approach, an audit extends beyond matters related directly to administrative controls and accounting. It comprises all methods and measures adopted by the business to safeguard its assets and manage its risks, check the accuracy and reliability of accounting and management information, promote operational efficiency, and encourage adherence to management policies. In short, the internal audit is an independent appraisal function and, since it is established within an organization to examine and evaluate its activities, performs a valuable service for the organization.

The most important duties of internal auditors are to "provide assurance regarding corporate governance, control systems, and risk management processes." Internal auditors should also review annual financial statements prior to their submission to the board of directors and ensure that appropriate accounting policies and practices are used in the development of financial statements. The review of financial statements must be detailed enough to allow internal auditors to be able to report on a range of aspects, including the accuracy of the balance sheet and income statement. The internal auditors also consider compliance with regulatory and legislative requirements, identify all significant discrepancies and disclosure problems, highlight differences between the annual report and management accounts, point to major fluctuations, and check management's compliance with statutory and other requirements.

Internal auditors and audit committees therefore make a vital contribution to the risk management process. They monitor the institution's financial risk profile and review management's procedures. Further details regarding the internal auditing function and audit are summarized in box 3.4. Internal auditors also evaluate the external audit function and ensure follow-up by management of problems identified in auditors' reports. However, in reality internal auditors and audit committees have limited ability to satisfy all of these requirements.

BOX 3.4	The Responsibilities of Audit Committees and Internal Auditors

Regarding the management of financial risk, the audit committees and internal auditors are responsible for the following:

- Review management's adherence to board policies and procedures;
- Provide assurance regarding corporate governance, control systems, and risk management processes;
- Perform a financial analysis of key risk indicators in order to assess operational risk management effectiveness;
- Verify the adequacy and accuracy of the information reported to the board by management;
- Report periodically to the board regarding adherence to policies and procedures;
- Improve communication between the board and management;
- Evaluate risk management measures for their appropriateness in relation to exposures;
- Test all aspects of risk activities and positions;
- Ensure effective management controls over positions, limits, and actions taken when limits are exceeded;
- Assess operations and suggest improvements.

EXTERNAL AUDITORS: A REASSESSMENT OF THE TRADITIONAL APPROACH OF AUDITING BANKS

The primary objectives of an audit are to express an opinion on whether or not the bank's financial statements fairly reflect its financial condition and the results of its operations for a given period. The external audit report is normally addressed to shareholders, but it is used by many other parties, such as supervisors, financial professionals, depositors, and creditors. The traditional approach to an external audit according to the requirements of generally accepted auditing standards (International Standards of Auditing, or ISA) typically includes a review of internal control systems. This assessment is undertaken to determine the nature and extent of substantive testing, provide an analytic review or trend analysis, and undertake a certain amount of detailed testing. Apart from the audit of the income statement, certain line items on the balance sheet are audited through the use of separate programs, for example, fixed assets, cash, investments, or debts. External auditors traditionally look for fraud and mismanagement in the lending function. Audits rarely include a detailed credit analysis of borrowers, as this has traditionally been performed by bank supervisors.

External auditors, as an integral part of the risk management partnership, have a specific role to fulfill. If market discipline is to promote stability of the banking system, markets must first have information and

| BOX 3.5 | The Responsibilities of External Auditors |

External auditors have the responsibility to undertake the following:

- Evaluate risks inherent in the banks they are auditing;
- Analyze and evaluate information presented to them to ensure that it makes sense;
- Understand the essence of transactions and financial engineering (structures) used by the client bank;
- Review management's adherence to board policies and procedures;
- Review the information supplied to the board, shareholders, and regulators;
- Review adherence to statutory requirements;
- Report to the board, shareholders, and regulators on the fair presentation of information submitted to them.

the capacity to hold directors and management accountable for the sound operation of a bank. External auditors play a key role in improving the market's ability to determine which banks to do business with.

The philosophy of and approach to external auditing clearly are crucial to the success or failure of a coordinated strategy of risk management. The work of the external auditor offers added protection for the consumer. It is therefore important for the profession to shift from a mere balance sheet audit to an evaluation of the risks inherent in the financial services industry. When such an approach has been adopted by all auditors of financial institutions, the risk management process will be significantly enhanced, which will benefit all users of financial services. Box 3.5 summarizes the risk management responsibilities of external auditors.

The role of the accounting and auditing profession has gained importance as part of the bank supervision process. Management letters and long-form reports submitted by auditors can provide supervisors with valuable insights into various aspects of a bank's operations. This is especially important when auditors become aware of facts that may endanger the stability of a particular bank or of the banking system. In many countries, especially those where supervisory resources are scarce, supervisors should avoid repeating the work of external auditors. In such situations, auditors have a broader mandate prescribed by law, but at a minimum it is important to establish adequate liaison mechanisms.

THE ROLE OF THE GENERAL PUBLIC

The investors-depositors as market participants have to accept responsibility for their own investment decisions. Perhaps the greatest disservice that the authorities have done to investors—particularly in jurisdictions where explicit deposit insurance does not exist—is to create the illusion that regulators can guarantee the safety of the public's deposits. When all is said and done, investors must understand that no amount of management or regulatory protection can take away their own responsibility for decisions regarding their investments. Investors and depositors retain responsibility for applying sound principles in the diversification of risk and in the assessment of a financial institution. In situations where consumers cannot protect themselves, a limited deposit insurance scheme for banks and simplified contractual disclosure for insurance companies and other portfolio managers may be considered.

The only way for the public to protect itself is to understand who is taking the risk: individuals as investors acting through agents (investment managers and brokers) or financial intermediaries pooling their funds and acting as principals (banks). When this distinction is clear and the public understands the risks that investment entails, the principal role of financial intermediaries will be to ensure that consumers are protected. This will be particularly true if the fit and proper requirement is applied to all providers of financial services.

The concept of "public" should be expanded to include the financial media and analysts, such as stockbrokers, other advisers, and rating agencies. In addition, the market's ability to provide a basis for informed decisions must be improved through full disclosure of the financial statements of banks as well as by informed and competent analysis in the media. Investors' interests can be safeguarded in more than one way, but disclosure of what is actually happening is essential.

As a general principle, much of the justification for banking regulation rests on imperfections in information disclosure. A policy of adequate information provision would help to mitigate this underlying problem and possibly allow for the removal of many of the quantitative constraints that are prevalent in banking today. Emphasis on transparency and accountability of management would also reduce the compliance costs and regulatory distortions that are often associated with conventional approaches to banking regulation.

Probably the most promising solution to these problems is legally mandated public disclosure. Louis Brandeis, a U.S. Supreme Court justice, observed in 1913 that sunlight is the best of disinfectants and electric light the most efficient policeman. This quaint-sounding aphorism still holds true. Brandeis made another crucial point: to be effective, disclosure must be made public. One of the most important benefits of mandating public disclosure is that the knowledge that information has to be disclosed publicly affects the conduct of financial institutions. Boards of directors and management know that, after being assimilated by the financial press and competitors, even the most highly technical information will filter through to the public. In the United States and other countries with strict information disclosure requirements, the threat of private litigation increases the incentive for management and boards to avoid problems.

Another form of public disclosure occurs when entities such as Standard and Poor's, Moody's Investors Service, and AM Best publish their ratings of companies. Ideally, these private rating agencies balance the need for public disclosure and for confidentiality, since they receive a great deal of information that is made public only in the form of ratings. Through published ratings, they have the ability to act quickly and have a more subtle effect than regulators commonly do. If rating agencies can build a reputation for reliability among financial analysts, senior management in banking institutions, and the broader public, they can provide an additional form of risk management for banks.

Market discipline could, therefore, be encouraged as an effective means to reduce the burden on regulators with regard to large, sophisticated investors. The role of financial analysts in assisting the public with risk management should not be underestimated. Financial analysts provide investment advice to clients and are therefore accustomed to presenting financial data from the perspective of investment risk. Investors who buy bank-negotiable certificates of deposit and other wholesale money market instruments should bear risk along with the creditors of bank holding companies. Faced with the possibility of losing their investments, such investors will police banks in order to protect their interests. Although all regulation can be left to the market, a policy of sharing resources between authorities and the private sector is bound to be more effective than a policy of having the parties act alone.

Nonetheless, institutions are sometimes downgraded only when extensive problems have already developed and when substantial, sometimes fatal, damage has been done. The question remains whether the market at large could have recognized deterioration or excessive risk taking at a sufficiently early stage if more information had been available. It will likely take a long time to develop techniques for the evaluation of risk and to standardize them in such a way as to capture them in published data. Market players are therefore limited in their ability to see credit problems as they develop. The experience of the 1980s, when each major credit problem surprised the market, is likely to remain the general pattern for the foreseeable future.

If market analysts cannot identify and properly evaluate credit and other problems until substantial harm has been done, market discipline will be insufficient to protect the overall safety of the banking system or of deposit insurance funds. In fact, the belated imposition of market pressure may complicate the task that supervisors have in dealing with problems. Consequently, the need for mechanisms to protect small and less-sophisticated investors will continue to exist.

4

Key Stakeholders

As emphasized in the previous chapter, corporate governance is a collective effort and the process itself functions optimally only when different stakeholders work collectively. As the Islamic banking industry has developed, several institutions have played important roles. New institutions to support further growth are emerging and becoming stakeholders in the fast-growing industry. This chapter focuses on the role of relevant stakeholders in the public and private sectors and discusses the significance of each. The players in the Islamic finance industry include the internal stakeholders, the different interest groups, and the institutions created to regulate, promote, and monitor their activity (see table 4.1).

INTERNAL STAKEHOLDERS

This section presents the key players within Islamic financial institutions and their general roles in the industry.

Bank regulators and supervisors act as facilitators in the process of risk management. As such, they enhance and monitor the statutory framework in which risk management is undertaken. By creating a sound enabling environment, they have a crucial role in influencing the other key players.

Ultimate responsibility for the way in which a bank's business is conducted lies with the *board of directors*. The board sets the strategic direction, appoints management, establishes operational policies, and, which is most important, is responsible for ensuring that the bank is sound.

Key Messages

- Effective stakeholder participation is integral to good corporate governance. The stakeholders in the Islamic finance industry include the internal stakeholders, the different interest groups, and the institutions created to regulate, promote, and monitor their activities.
- *Shariah* boards are a distinct feature of Islamic banks. Operating at the institutional and systemic level, *Shariah* boards have a great responsibility to protect the rights of all stakeholders according to the principles of *Shariah*.
- *Shariah* boards play a critical role in the introduction of new products and the provision of an oversight function.
- Multilateral institutions have played an important role in the development and growth of Islamic markets and banks. The Islamic Development Bank is dedicated to that purpose. The International Monetary Fund and the World Bank have contributed through research.
- Several key institutions such as Islamic Financial Services Board and the Accounting and Auditing Organization of Islamic Financial Institutions were established to strengthen regulatory framework.
- New stakeholders are emerging to develop financial infrastructure, including institutions dedicated to developing capital markets, rating agencies, and institutions that help to manage liquidity.

Executive management of a bank has to be "fit and proper," meaning not only that managers subscribe to standards of ethical behavior, but also that they have the competence and experience to run the bank. Because the management is responsible for implementing the board's policies on a day-to-day basis, it is vital that managers have intimate knowledge of the financial risks being managed.

The *audit committee and the internal auditors* should be regarded as an extension of the board's risk management policy function. Internal auditors traditionally perform an independent appraisal of a bank's compliance with its internal control systems, accounting practices, and information systems. Most internal auditors provide assurance regarding the bank's corporate governance, control systems, and risk management processes. Although audit committees play a valuable role in identifying and addressing areas of risk, the prime responsibility for risk management cannot be abdicated to them; rather, it should be integrated into all levels of management.

External auditors have come to play an important role in evaluating the quality of risk-based financial information. Since bank supervisors neither can nor should repeat the work done by external auditors, proper mechanisms are necessary to facilitate communication between bank supervisors and external auditors and between them and bank management. The

TABLE 4.1   Importance of Key Stakeholders in the Islamic Finance Industry

Key players	Responsibility for risk management	Importance	
		Policy level	Operational level
Systemic			
Legal and regulatory authorities	Optimize	Critical	n.a.
Bank supervisors	Monitor	Indirect (monitoring)	Indirect
Institutional			
Shareholders	Appoint key players	Indirect	Indirect
Board of directors	Set policy	Critical	Indirect
Executive management	Implement policy	Critical (implementation)	Critical
Audit committee, internal audit	Test compliance with board policies and provide assurance regarding corporate governance, control systems, and risk management processes	Indirect (compliance)	Critical
External auditors	Evaluate and express opinion	Indirect (evaluation)	n.a
Shariah boards	Protect rights and interests of stakeholders in light of *Shariah* principles	Critical	Critical
Consumer	Be accountable for own actions	n.a.	Indirect
Outside stakeholders, public	Act responsibly	n.a.	Indirect

Note: n.a. = Not applicable.

audit should be risk oriented rather than based on the traditional balance sheet and income statement. Relying too heavily on external auditors weakens the partnership, especially if doing so weakens the management and supervisory roles.

Shariah boards at the institutional and systemic level have a great responsibility to protect the rights of all stakeholders according to the principles of *Shariah*. Investors, depositors, and users of the funds trust the *Shariah* board to ensure that the institution is fully compliant with the *Shariah* in all of its activities.

The *Shariah* board is composed of religious scholars. Islamic banks cannot introduce a new product without prior permission and approval of their *Shariah* board, and, depending on the affiliation of the religious scholars on the board with any particular school of jurisprudential thought, this can determine the success or failure of a product with its target clients. Due to a shortage of *Shariah* scholars well versed in both *Shariah* and modern banking, many *Shariah* scholars sit on multiple boards and exert a great deal of influence.

The *public and depositors* are responsible for their own investment decisions, and this requires transparent disclosure of financial information and informed financial analyses. Widening the definition of public to include the financial media, financial analysts such as stockbrokers, and rating agencies would improve the ability of the public to judge the appropriateness of different instruments. However, small or unsophisticated depositors normally need more protection than simply transparent disclosure.

Shareholders are in a position to appoint the people in charge of the corporate governance process, and their conduct should be screened carefully to ensure that they do not intend to use the bank solely to finance their own or their associates' enterprises.

MULTILATERAL INSTITUTIONS[1]

Multilateral institutions have played an important role in the development and growth of Islamic markets and banks. Multilateral institutions interact with the Islamic banking industry in various capacities, and it is important to understand and evaluate the relationship—past, present, and potential.

Islamic Development Bank (IDB)

Established by the Articles of Agreement in October 1975, the Islamic Development Bank is a multilateral financial institution designed to foster economic development and social progress in the 53 member countries of the Organization of Islamic Countries (OIC) and in Muslim communities in nonmember countries. IDB provides financial assistance by way of equity and lease financing (*ijarah*), installment sale financing (*murabahah*), and grant (interest-free) loans for projects and assistance in promoting foreign trade among member countries. Projects are financed from ordinary capital resources through interest-free loans, leasing, installment sale, and equity participation. More recently, the IDB has introduced the use of *istisnah* (construction and manufacturing) contracts. In addition, technical assistance is available for facilitating the preparation and implementation of projects, particularly in the least developed member countries by way of grants (from a special assistance account) or through a combination of (interest-free) loans and grants.

IDB has concentrated on the public sector, but the trends of globalization, the integration of international trading and financial systems, and the dwindling of foreign funding for government-sponsored projects have prompted the need for the private sector to play an active role in economic development. Recognizing this need, in 1999 IDB established an independent entity, Islamic Corporation for the Development of the Private Sector (ICD), to deal with the private sector in its member countries. The new institution is expected to complement the role being played by IDB in supporting economic development by helping to strengthen the private sector in its member countries.

IDB has also established the Islamic Research and Training Institute (IRTI) with the objectives of providing training facilities for professionals engaged in development activities in member countries and undertaking research in the areas of Islamic economics, finance, and banking. IRTI serves as an information center, collecting and disseminating information in related fields. In addition to publication of an academic journal on Islamic economics, IRTI arranges both professional and academic seminars and conferences to promote research on Islamic economics and banking.

In 2005 the IDB Board of Governors approved the establishment of the International Islamic Trade Finance Corporation (ITFC) to finance trade activities of its member countries. Its main functions are as follows:

- To promote and facilitate among OIC member countries the use of *Shariah*-compliant instruments;
- To become a leader in the development and diversification of financial instruments and *Shariah*-compliant products for trade financing;
- To facilitate access of member countries and enterprises to international capital markets;
- To stimulate development of investment opportunities and enhance export capabilities of member countries;
- To provide technical assistance and training to local banks in member countries in trade finance-related areas;
- To offer advisory services to member countries and institutions on matters relevant to its core objectives.

The practices and performance of IDB have been rather different from what was originally envisaged, as its critics argue that the benefits to poorer Muslim countries have been limited. Although trade credit has grown, equity financing has languished despite all the efforts made to promote it. For IDB, exiting from its equity investments and recovering its capital have been virtually impossible in the absence of developed stock markets in most Muslim countries. Consequently, a considerable portion of its equity assets are tied up and illiquid.

It has been argued that IDB's performance, with respect to coordinating the activities of the banking sector and taking on certain central bank functions, has been below expectations. Member countries with balance-of-payments difficulties have not been able to convince IDB to act as a lender of last resort. Further, IDB has been slow to recognize the need for investment in development and infrastructure projects, even though most of its member countries are in desperate need of them. The initial expectations were that ICD would perform at a high level, but its setup and operations have been slow, which has dampened hopes that it may play the role originally envisioned. Due to limited market-based resource mobilization, the institution is unable to lend at competitive terms. IDB has issued two *sukuks* (Islamic bonds) to tap into capital markets, and it is hoped that, with more frequent access to capital markets, the institution will be able to expand its operations.

There is validity in some of these criticisms, which raises serious concerns about the effectiveness of the institution in light of its objectives. From the IDB's point of view, its constituent countries represent a wide spectrum of economies, from the richest to the poorest and from the least to the most indebted, making it difficult to achieve its original objectives. Nevertheless, to be effective, the IDB needs to take a leadership role in the wake of growing globalization and integration of financial markets and to develop strategies for promoting the development of institutions, markets, and financial infrastructure conducive to Islamic financial institutions. The IDB also has a role to play in serving as a forum for the formulation of common positions for OIC countries and advancing them in major international forums. It needs to make its voice heard on major issues concerning the new international financial architecture, ranging from international trade to globalization. IDB also needs to coordinate with other development institutions and to participate in sustainable development in member countries.

Bretton Woods Institutions

The International Monetary Fund (IMF) has demonstrated a degree of interest in creating an Islamic financial system since the early 1980s, when two of its member countries, the Islamic Republic of Iran and Pakistan, decided to change their banking systems to comply with the tenets of Islam. The IMF's involvement and contributions have evolved through three distinct phases since 1984. In the first phase (1984–88), the IMF initiated a modest program of research, which helped to establish the theoretical foundations of an Islamic financial system, the operations of Islamic banking, and the conduct of monetary policy within an Islamic system. In the second phase, which began in the 1990s, the IMF began working with the central banks of Islamic countries where Islamic banking was being practiced, providing technical assistance and sharing knowledge with respect to monetary policy, central bank financial operations, regulations, and supervision. The IMF's work in Sudan is noteworthy, as IMF worked closely with the Central Bank of Sudan to transform the central banking operations to conform with the *Shariah*. During the third phase (beginning in the late 1990s), the IMF began to assist Muslim countries in establishing multilateral institutions and to facilitate cooperation among them, notably on issues such as establishing an Islamic money market, an Islamic capital market, and an international Islamic banking and financial supervisory and standard-setting institution.

The World Bank's direct involvement with Islamic financial institutions has been minimal, as the institution deals primarily with the public sector. The World Bank has been involved in the development of financial systems, which has led to greater emphasis on financial sector and private sector development in developing countries. With this perspective, the Bank is working closely with its member countries where Islamic banking institutions are operating, sharing knowledge and experience in the development of legal, regulatory, accounting, and supervisory infrastructure. The World Bank's political risk guarantee, extended to participating commercial banks in the form of an extended co-financing operation (ECO) guarantee facility, was instrumental to the success of the private financing of the Hub River project in Pakistan. The project was the first to feature an Islamic markup-based, limited-recourse facility and the first to receive mobilization finance in the form of an *istisnah* facility, which was provided by the Al Rajhi Banking Corporation to finance the purchase and installation of power turbines. The ECO guarantee specifically protected foreign commercial lenders in the event that their claims were prejudiced by any change made in the Islamic *Shariah*. This so-called "*Shariah* event" protection was deemed to be critical in the project and was instrumental in achieving a mix of conventional and Islamic financing in a single project structure. More recently, the World Bank has made a valuable contribution by conducting research in Islamic finance in the area of regulation, governance, risk management, and standards.

The International Finance Corporation (IFC), a private sector arm of the World Bank Group, has transaction-oriented experience with Islamic financial institutions. IFC not only promotes capital market development but also supports project-oriented infrastructure investment, which constitutes one-third of its total worldwide financial portfolio in sectors like power, telecommunications, transportation, utilities, roads, ports, and water. IFC has been involved in the financing of more than $7 billion for conventional infrastructure projects costing more than $30 billion in developing countries. There are some commonalities between IFC's business model and Islamic finance, such as a preference for equity modes of financing, higher risk tolerance when entering new and innovative products, and familiarity with the emerging markets, which Western and conventional investors often consider to be higher risk.

The roles of the World Bank and IFC in Islamic finance need revisiting, as there is significant potential for cooperation and collaboration between the parties. The IFC, which would like to play a catalytic role in attracting international institutions and thus boost confidence and growth in the local market, needs to be involved more actively with developing Muslim countries, some of which are perceived to be high risk. IFC's capital market operations and advisory services could share their extensive experience with conventional finance, emerging markets, credit assessment setups, transparency, and liquidity enhancement techniques with Islamic countries interested in fostering Islamic financial institutions. Similarly, Islamic financial institutions could benefit from the IFC's cooperation in the area of project and infrastructure finance, where IFC has considerable experience. However, this cooperation cannot take place unless the necessary financial infrastructure and framework are developed in Muslim countries, a task where the involvement of IMF, IDB, and the World Bank is badly needed. Collectively, multilateral institutions could contribute to the development of Islamic financial systems by providing advisory services and technical assistance, by becoming market makers, and by working with the central banks to develop the needed infrastructure.

Countries that are determined to establish Islamic financial institutions need to exercise their rights as members of multilateral institutions to tap into the experience and expertise of such institutions. This would give multilateral institutions the incentive to invest time and resources in understanding Islamic financial markets and helping these countries to devise solutions to the challenges they face.[2] Another area of cooperation between the World Bank and Islamic financial institutions is the transfer of knowledge in treasury operations, asset management, and risk controls, areas where Islamic financial institutions have a shortage of technical expertise.

REGULATORY BODIES

Market participants' anticipation of the growth of the Islamic finance industry as well as its potential impact has raised public policy issues in the jurisdictions in which it operates. Accordingly, Islamic financial intermediation has attracted increasing attention from international organizations, international standard setters, national regulatory authorities, policy makers, and academia. Attention has been directed most notably on the Islamic financial institution's risk management practices, the broad institutional environment in which they operate, and the regulatory framework that governs them. Several institutions have been established as focal points on major issues, in particular the Accounting and Auditing Organization for Islamic Financial Institutions, the Islamic Financial Services Board, the International Islamic Financial Markets, the International Islamic Rating Agency, and the Liquidity Management Center.

Accounting and Auditing Organization for Islamic Financial Institutions (AAOIFI)

The objective of the Bahrain-based AAOIFI is to develop a core set of accounting, auditing, governance, and (recently) *Shariah* standards for Islamic financial institutions. There are clear differences between the balance sheet structure of an Islamic financial institution and that of a typical conventional bank. The latter deals mainly with spread-based fixed-income instruments, whereas the major component of an Islamic bank's liabilities and assets consists of investment accounts on a profit-sharing basis. Such differences have important implications for accounting and financial reporting. AAOIFI is attempting to resolve these differences and considers its accounting standards as being complementary to, rather than in conflict with, International Accounting Standards (IAS), aiming to fill the gaps in IAS, which do not have specific standards dealing with Islamic banking transactions.

Similar to accounting standards, Islamic financial institutions are exposed to differing prudential and supervisory standards depending on the country in which they operate. This is mainly due to the lack of proper understanding of the work of Islamic financial institutions and also to the implementation of different accounting standards. This was evident in the results of a study carried out by a committee comprising, among others, a number of central banks and AAOIFI that was formed to develop appropriate capital adequacy guidelines for Islamic financial institutions. This committee promulgated the Statement on the Purpose and Calculation of the Capital Adequacy Ratio for Islamic Banks, which takes into account the differences between deposit accounts in conventional banking and investment accounts in Islamic banking. This statement has built on the capital adequacy principles laid down by the Basel Committee on Banking Supervision.

Notable are AAOIFI's efforts to inform and encourage banking supervisors around the world to adopt the AAOIFI standards as the benchmark for Islamic financial institutions in their jurisdiction. These efforts to improve the transparency and comparability of the financial reporting of Islamic financial institutions are bearing fruit. The banking supervisors in a number of countries such as Bahrain and Sudan either require Islamic banks to comply with AAOIFI's standards or, as in the case of Qatar and Saudi Arabia, are specifying AAOIFI's standards as guidelines. In the Middle East, this leaves out Egypt, Kuwait, Tunisia, and the United Arab Emirates, where there are substantial Islamic banks. However, in European and Western markets, supervisors have not yet given these standards serious consideration. Countries such as Bahrain, Malaysia, and Sudan have led the drive toward developing specific regulatory guidelines for the Islamic banking industry. Recently, the central bank governors of those states where Islamic banks operate—mainly in Southeast Asia, the Middle East, and North Africa—met to approve the establishment of a new international body, the Islamic Financial Services Board, which will have a role similar to that of the Basel Committee on Banking Supervision.

Islamic Financial Services Board (IFSB)

The IFSB was established in Kuala Lumpur, Malaysia, in 2002 as a result of the efforts of AAOIFI, Islamic Development Bank, International Monetary Fund, and the central banks of several Islamic countries. The IFSB has 110 members, including 27 regulatory and supervisory authorities as well as 78 financial institutions from 21 countries. The government of Malaysia has enacted the Islamic Financial Services Board Act 2002, which gives the IFSB the immunities and privileges usually granted to international organizations and diplomatic missions

The primary objective of IFSB is to develop uniform regulatory and transparency standards to address characteristics specific to Islamic financial institutions, keeping in mind the national financial environment, international standards, core principles, and good practices. The IFSB also is promoting awareness of issues that are relevant to or have an impact on the regulation and supervision of the Islamic financial services industry. These efforts mainly take the form of international conferences, seminars, workshops, trainings, meetings, and dialogues staged in many countries. In December 2005, the Council of the IFSB adopted two standards—the Guiding Principles of Risk Management and the Capital Adequacy Standard—for institutions offering only Islamic financial services. This was followed by Corporate Governance in December 2006 and guidelines on the supervisory review process, transparency, market discipline, capital adequacy, and governance are at various stages of development.

International Islamic Financial Market (IIFM)

The major objectives of the IIFM are (a) to enhance cooperation among regulatory authorities of Islamic banks, (b) to address the liquidity problem by expanding the maturity structure of instruments, and (c) to explore the possibility of sovereign asset-backed securities. As part of this initiative, Malaysia has been working to establish a center to provide liquidity-enhancing products with the long-term objective of developing an Islamic interbank money market. More recently, IIFM has signed a memorandum of understanding with the International Capital Markets Association (ICMA) to collaborate on the development of primary and secondary markets for Islamic bonds (*sukuks*). Both associations have established working groups to coordinate efforts to facilitate standardized documentation and industry practices for floating and trading Islamic bonds.

International Islamic Rating Agency (IIRA)

The IIRA aims to assist in the development of regional financial markets by providing an assessment of the risk profile of entities and instruments that can be used for investment decisions. IIRA is sponsored by multilateral finance institutions, several leading banks and other financial institutions, and rating agencies from different countries. The organization has a board of directors and an independent rating committee as well as a *Shariah* board. The IIRA's mission is to support development of the regional capital market and to improve its functioning.

The *Shariah* quality rating provided does not aim to give a *Shariah* opinion on Islamic financial products, to comment on the decisions of the *Shariah* committees of banks and financial institutions, or to correct their *fatwas* (proclamations). IIRA's role is to assess the level of compliance by the institutions with the stipulations adopted by their *Shariah* committee in good faith, both in letter and in spirit. They also examine whether there is a mechanism within the institution to evaluate its compliance with the *Shariah* and whether the *Shariah* committee has enough authority, information, and resources to perform the examination and evaluation.

Liquidity Management Center

The Liquidity Management Center was established to facilitate investment of the surplus funds of Islamic banks and financial institutions into quality short- and medium-term financial instruments structured in accordance with the *Shariah* principles. It assists Islamic financial institutions in managing their short-term liquidity and supports the interbank market. In addition, the center attracts assets from governments, financial institutions, and corporates in both the private and public sectors in many countries. The assets are securitized into readily transferable securities or structured into other innovative investment instruments. The center also offers Islamic advisory services dealing with structured, project, and corporate finance as well as equity raising. The equal shareholders include Bahrain Islamic Bank, Dubai Islamic Bank, Islamic Development Bank, and Kuwait Finance House.

The key objectives are as follows:

- Facilitate the creation of an interbank money market that will allow Islamic financial institutions to manage their asset-liability mismatch;
- Enable Islamic financial institutions to participate as both investors (providers of funds) and borrowers (providers of assets);
- Provide short-term liquid, tradable, asset-backed treasury instruments (*sukuks*) in which Islamic financial institutions can invest their surplus liquidity;
- Provide short-term investment opportunities that have greater *Shariah* credibility and are priced more competitively than commodity *murabahah* transactions;
- Enable Islamic financial institutions to assume term-risk securities and liquidate such assets to improve the quality of their portfolios;
- Endeavor to create secondary market activity with designated market makers where such instruments can be traded actively.

NOTE

1. Iqbal and Tsubota (2005).
2. The World Bank has been providing advisory services in the areas of regulation, governance, and financial disclosure to select Gulf Cooperation Council countries with reference to the prevailing conventional financial system.

PART Two

Risk Management

Framework for Risk Analysis

The goal of financial management is to maximize the value of a bank, as defined by its profitability and risk level. Financial management comprises risk management, a treasury function, financial planning and budgeting, accounting and information systems, and internal controls. In practical terms, the key aspect of financial management is risk management, which covers strategic and capital planning, asset-liability management, and the management of a bank's business and financial risks. The central components of risk management are the identification, quantification, and monitoring of the risk profile, including both banking and financial risks.

RISK EXPOSURE AND MANAGEMENT

Many types of risks may be present in an individual bank (see table 5.1). *Financial risks* are subject to complex interdependencies that may significantly increase a bank's overall risk profile. For example, a bank engaged in foreign currency business is normally exposed to currency risk, but it is also exposed to liquidity, credit, and repricing risks if it carries open positions or mismatches in its forward book. *Operational risks* are related to a bank's organization and functioning, including computer-related and other technologies, compliance with bank policies and procedures, and measures against mismanagement and fraud. *Business risks* are associated with a bank's business environment, including macroeconomic and policy concerns, legal and regulatory factors, and the financial sector's infrastructure, such as payment systems and auditing professions. *Event risks* include all types of

Key Messages

- Analytical techniques facilitate an understanding of interrelationships between risk areas internally and among different banks.
- Trend analysis provides information regarding the volatility and movement of an individual bank's financial indicators over different time periods.
- The percentage composition of the balance sheet, income statement, and various account groupings enables comparison between time periods but also between different banking institutions at a given point in time.
- Ratios are often interrelated and, when analyzed in combination, provide useful information regarding risk.
- Computation of ratios and trends provides an answer only as to *what* happened.
- Analysis of the results should be performed by asking *why* events occurred, the *impact* of those events, and what *action* management should take to rectify a situation or continue a desired trend.

TABLE 5.1   Banking Risk Exposures

Financial risks	Operational risks	Business risks	Event risks
Balance sheet structure	Internal fraud	Macro policy	Political
Income statement structure and profitability	External fraud	Financial infrastructure	Contagion
Capital adequacy	Employment practices and workplace safety	Legal infrastructure	Banking crisis
Credit	Clients, products, and business services	Legal liability	Other exogeneous risks
Liquidity	Damage to physical assets	Regulatory compliance	
Market	Business disruption and system failures (technology risk)	Reputational and fiduciary	
Interest rate	Execution, delivery, and process management	Country risk	
Currency			

exogenous risks that, if they were to materialize, could jeopardize a bank's operations or undermine its financial condition and capital adequacy.

Risk management normally involves several steps for each type of financial risk and for the risk profile overall. These steps include identifying the risk management objective, risk management targets, and measures of performance. Also important are the identification and measurement of specific risk exposures, including an assessment of the sensitivity of performance to expected and unexpected changes in underlying factors. Decisions must also be made regarding the acceptable degree of risk exposure, the methods and instruments available to hedge excessive exposure, and the choice and execution of hedging transactions. In addition, the responsibility for various aspects of risk management must be assigned, the effectiveness of the risk management process must be assessed, and the competent and diligent execution of responsibilities must be ensured.

Effective risk management, especially for larger banks and for banks operating in deregulated and competitive markets, requires a formal process. In developing economies, especially those in transition, unstable, economically volatile, and shallow market environments significantly expand the range and magnitude of exposure to financial risk. Such conditions render risk management even more complex and make the need for an effective risk management process even more acute. The key components of effective risk management that should be present in a bank and be assessed by the analyst normally include the following:

- An established line function at the highest level of the bank's management hierarchy that is specifically responsible for managing risk and possibly also for coordinating the operational implementation of the policies and decisions of the asset-liability committee. The risk management function should be on par with other major functions and be accorded the necessary visibility and leverage within the bank.
- An established, explicit, and clear risk management strategy and a related set of policies with corresponding operational targets. Various risk management strategies exist, having originated from different approaches to interpreting interdependencies between risk factors and differences of opinion concerning the treatment of volatility in risk management.
- Introduction of an appropriate degree of formalization and coordination of strategic decision making in relation to the risk management process. Relevant risk management concerns and parameters for decision making on the operational level should be incorporated for all relevant business and functional processes. Parameters for the main financial risk factors (normally established according to the risk management policies of a bank and expressed as ratios or limits) can serve as indicators to business units of what constitutes acceptable risk. For example, a debt-to-equity ratio for a bank's borrowers expresses a level of credit risk. Maximum exposure to a single client is a risk parameter that indicates credit risk in a limited form.

■ Implementation of a process that bases business and portfolio decisions on rigorous quantitative and qualitative analyses within applicable risk parameters. This process, including analysis of a consolidated risk profile, is necessary due to the complex interdependencies of and the need to balance various financial risk factors. Because the risk implications of a bank's financial position and changes to that position are not always obvious, details may be of critical importance.

■ Systematic gathering of complete, timely, and consistent data relevant for risk management and provision of adequate data storage and manipulation capacity. Data should cover all functional and business processes, as well as other areas such as macroeconomic and market trends that may be relevant to risk management.

■ Development of quantitative modeling tools to enable the simulation and analysis of the effects of changes in economic, business, and market environments on a bank's risk profile and their impact on the bank's liquidity, profitability, and net worth. Computer models used by banks range from simple personal computer–based tools to elaborate mainframe modeling systems. Such models can be built in-house or be acquired from other financial institutions with a similar profile, specialized consulting firms, or software vendors. The degree of sophistication and analytical capacity of such models may indicate early on the seriousness of the bank's efforts to manage risk.

The new Basel Capital Accord will heighten the importance of quantitative modeling tools and the bank's capacity to use them, as they will provide a basis for implementing the internal ratings-based (IRB) approach to measuring a bank's capital adequacy. It is hoped that the IRB approach will bring additional sensitivity to risk, in that it will be more sensitive to the drivers of credit risk and economic loss in a bank's portfolio and create incentives for the bank to continuously improve its internal risk management practices.

It has been said that risk rises exponentially with the pace of change, but that bankers are slow to adjust their perception of risk. In practical terms, this implies that the market's ability to innovate is often greater than its ability to understand and properly accommodate the accompanying risk. Traditionally, banks have seen the management of credit risk as their most important task, but as banking has changed and the market environment has become more complex and volatile, awareness has developed of the critical need to manage exposure to other operational and financial risks as well.

UNDERSTANDING THE RISK ENVIRONMENT

The changing banking environment presents major opportunities for banks but also entails complex, variable risks that challenge traditional approaches to bank management. In order to survive in a market-oriented environment, withstand competition by foreign banks, and support private sector–led economic growth, banks must be able to manage financial risk.

An external evaluation of the capacity of a bank to operate safely and productively in its business environment is normally performed once each year. All annual assessments are similar in nature, but they have slightly different focuses, depending on the purpose of the assessment. Assessments are performed by supervisory authorities, external auditors, and others.

Supervisory authorities assess whether the bank is viable, meets its regulatory requirements, and is capable of fulfilling its financial commitments to depositors and other creditors. They also verify whether or not the bank's operations are likely to jeopardize the safety of the banking system as a whole.

External auditors assess whether financial statements provide a true and fair view of the bank's actual condition. Normally retained by the bank's board of directors, they also assess whether or not management meets the objectives established by the board and evaluate whether or not it exposes the bank's capital to undue risks. Banks are normally required to undergo an external audit that involves at least year-end financial statements and that is considered satisfactory to supervisory authorities.

The financial viability and institutional weaknesses of a bank are also evaluated through financial assessments, extended portfolio reviews, or limited assurance reviews. Such evaluations often occur when a third party evaluates credit risk that the bank poses, for example, in the context of the following:

- Participation in a credit-line operation of an international lending agency or receipt of a credit line or loan from a foreign bank;
- Establishment of correspondent banking relationships or access to international markets;
- Equity investment by an international lending agency, private investors, or foreign banks;
- Inclusion in a bank rehabilitation program.

The bank appraisal process normally includes an assessment of the institution's overall risk profile, financial condition, viability, and future prospects. The appraisal comprises off- and on-site examinations to the extent considered necessary. If serious institutional weaknesses are found to exist, appropriate corrective actions are recommended. If the institution is not considered viable in its current condition, actions are presented that may lead to its viability being reasonably assured or to its liquidation and closure. The bank review also assesses whether the condition of the institution can be remedied with reasonable assistance or presents a hazard to the banking sector as a whole.

In the case of Islamic banks, added attention must be paid to the contractual role (see table 5.2) of the bank concerned, when analyzing the risks inherent in the bank's assets and liabilities.

TABLE 5.2   Contractual Role and Risk in Islamic Banking

		Risk: Contractual role of the Islamic bank		
Balance sheet	Contractual Basis	Trustee: Agency, brokerage	Partnership: Investment banking	Principal/Agent: Conventional commercial banking
Liabilities: Funding sources				
Demand deposits	Amanah (trust)	✓		
Investment accounts	Mudarabah			✓
Special investment accounts	Mudarabah			✓
	Musharakah (partnership)		✓	
Reserves	Amanah (trust)			
Equity: shareholders' funds	Musharakah (partnership)		✓	
Assets: Application of funds				
Cash balances	Cash balances			
Financing assets	Murabahah			✓
	Bay' al-salaam			✓
	Bay' al muajjil			✓
	Ijarah, istisnah		✓	✓
Investment assets	Mudarabah musharakah		✓	✓
Investment in real estate	Mudarabah musharakah			
Property ownership	Ownership			
Fee-based services	Joalah, kifalah	✓	✓	✓

The conclusions and recommendations of a bank appraisal are typically expressed in a letter to shareholders, in a memorandum of understanding, or as an institutional development program. The most common objective of the latter is to describe priorities for improvement, as identified in the analyst's review, that would yield the greatest benefit to the institution's financial performance. To the extent considered necessary, such recommendations are accompanied by supporting documentation, flow charts, and other relevant information about current practices. The institutional development program often serves as the basis for discussions among the institution's management, government officials, and international lending agencies, which in turn implement the recommended improvements and decide what technical assistance is needed.

The process of bank analysis also occurs within the context of monetary policy making. Central banks have a mission to maintain a stable currency and economy. Three interrelated functions are critical to monetary stability: the implementation of monetary policy, the supervision of banks, and the monitoring of the payments system. All three functions must take place to ensure stability. For this reason, banking supervision cannot be divorced from the wider mission of monetary authorities. Although the attention of central banking policy focuses on the macroeconomic aspect of general equilibrium and price stability, micro considerations regarding the liquidity and solvency of individual banks are key to attaining stability.

Analysis of the Overall Banking Sector

The banking sector as a whole provides important information regarding the provision of finance to the real sector. Sectoral analysis is important because it allows norms to be established for either the sector as a whole or for a peer group within the sector. The performance of individual banking institutions can then be evaluated on the basis of these norms. Deviations from expected trends and relationships may be analyzed further, as they may disclose not only the risk faced by individual banks but also changes in the financial environment of the banking sector as a whole. By examining sector statistics, analysts can gain an understanding of changes that are occurring in the industry and of the impact of such changes on economic agents and sectors.

Banking statistics also provide insight into conditions in both the domestic and international economies. Financial innovation normally results in changes to measured economic variables, and as a result of this dynamism the monetary models of macroeconomists may not reflect reality.

The impact of banking activities on monetary statistics, such as figures for the money supply and credit extended to the domestic private sector, is also of concern to policymakers. Reviews of banks can serve as a structured mechanism to ensure that monetary authorities recognize and quantify nonintermediated funding and lending as well as other processes that are important to policy makers in the central bank. Taking a structured approach to evaluating banks makes sector statistics readily available for macroeconomic monetary analysis, which helps bank supervisors to assist monetary authorities in a meaningful way.

Understanding banking risk in a competitive and volatile market environment is therefore a complex process. In addition to effective management and supervision, sound and sustainable macroeconomic policies are needed, as are well-developed and consistent legal frameworks. Adequate financial sector infrastructure, effective market discipline, and sufficient banking sector safety nets are crucial. To attain a meaningful assessment and interpretation of particular findings, estimates of future potential, diagnosis of key issues, and formulation of effective and practical courses of action, bank analysts must have extensive knowledge of the particular regulatory, market, and economic environment in which a bank operates. In short, to do the job well, analysts must have a holistic perspective of the financial system even when considering a specific bank.

Financial Analysis

Financial analysis assesses a company's performance and trends in that performance. In essence, analysts convert data into financial metrics that assist in decision making, seeking to answer various questions: How successfully has the company performed, relative to its own past performance and relative to its competitors? How is the company likely to perform in the future? Based on expectations about future performance, what is the value of this company or the securities it issues?

A primary source of data is a company's financial reports, including the financial statements, footnotes, and management's discussion and analysis. Whether financial reports are prepared under the Accounting and Auditing Organization for Islamic Financial Institutions (AAOIFI) or International Financial Reporting Standards (IFRS), they do not necessarily contain all the information needed to perform effective financial analysis. While financial statements do contain data about the past performance of a company (its income and cash flows) as well as its financial condition (assets, liabilities, and owners' equity) on the date of the financial statement (which might be a couple of months ago in some jurisdictions), such statements may not provide some important nonfinancial information and do not forecast future results. The financial analyst must be capable of using the financial statements in conjunction with other information. Accordingly, analysts will most likely need to supplement the information found in a company's financial reports with industry and economic data.

Projections of future financial performance are used in determining the value of a company or its equity component. Projections of future financial performance are also used in credit analysis, particularly in project finance or acquisition finance, to determine whether a company's cash flow will be adequate to pay the interest and principal on its debt and to determine whether a company will likely be in compliance with its financial covenants.

Sources of data for analysts' projections include some or all of the following: the company's projections, the company's previous financial statements, industry structure and outlook, and macroeconomic forecasts.

Adjustments of a company's financial statements are sometimes necessary, for example when comparing companies that use different accounting methods or assessing the impact of differences in key estimates. In practice, required adjustments vary widely.

A number of business activities give rise to obligations that, although they are economic liabilities of a company, are not required to be reported on a company's balance sheet. Including such off-balance-sheet obligations in a company's liabilities can affect ratios and conclusions based on such ratios. For example, in the case of an operating license, the rights of the lessee (the party leasing the asset) may be very similar to the rights of the owner, but for accounting purposes, an operating lease is treated like a rental contract. The lessee simply records the periodic lease payment as a period expense in its income statement. In contrast, if a company actually owns an asset, the asset is shown on the balance sheet along with any corresponding liability, such as financing for the asset. For this reason, international accounting standards state that the entities should record operating leases on the balance sheet and avoid structures that obscure the substance of the transaction.

RISK-BASED ANALYSIS OF BANKS

Whereas Islamic banks are different from conventional banks in their form of financial intermediation, financial instruments, and structure of financial statements, these institutions are nevertheless subject to a similar framework for analyzing their risk and exposures. The principles and procedures for measuring and controlling risk are similar, so the analytical framework for assessing risk should be similar as well.

The practices of bank supervisors and the appraisal methods of financial analysts continue to evolve. This evolution is necessary in part to meet the challenges of innovation and new developments and in part to accommodate the broader convergence of international supervisory standards and practices, which are themselves continually discussed by the Basel Committee on Banking Supervision. Traditional banking analysis is based on a range of quantitative supervisory tools for assessing a bank's condition, including ratios. Ratios normally relate to liquidity, the adequacy of capital, quality of the investment portfolio, extent of insider and connected lending, size of exposures, and open foreign exchange positions. While these measurements are extremely useful, they are not in themselves an adequate indication of the risk profile of a bank, the stability of its financial condition, or its prospects.

The central technique for analyzing financial risk is the detailed review of a bank's balance sheet. Risk-based bank analysis includes important qualitative factors and places financial ratios within a broad framework of risk assessment and management and the changes or trends in risks. It also underscores the relevant institutional aspects, such as the quality and style of corporate governance and management; the adequacy, completeness, and consistency of a bank's policies and procedures; the effectiveness and completeness of internal controls; and the timeliness and accuracy of management information systems and information support.

Where appropriate, a bank should be analyzed as both a single entity and on a consolidated basis, taking into account exposures of subsidiaries and other related enterprises at home and abroad. A holistic perspective is necessary when assessing a bank on a consolidated basis, especially if the institution is spread over a number of jurisdictions or foreign markets. A broad view accommodates variations in the features of specific financial risks that are present in different environments.

A risk-based analysis should also indicate whether an individual institution's behavior is in line with peer group trends and industry norms, particularly when it comes to significant issues such as profitability, structure of the balance sheet, and capital adequacy. A thorough analysis can indicate the nature of and reasons for such deviations. A material change in risk profile experienced by an individual institution could be the result of unique circumstances that have no impact on the banking sector as a whole or could be an early indicator of trends.

The picture reflected by financial ratios also depends largely on the timeliness, completeness, and accuracy of data used to compute them. For this reason, the issue of usefulness and transparency is critical, as is accountability, which has become an important topic due to both the growing importance of risk management for modern financial institutions and the emerging philosophy of supervision.

ANALYSIS VERSUS COMPUTATION

Financial analysis is the discipline whereby analytical tools are applied to financial statements and other financial data, in order to interpret trends and relationships in a consistent and disciplined manner. In essence, the analyst is in the business of converting data into information and thereby enabling the screening and forecasting of information. A primary source of information is the entity's financial statements.

The objective of financial statements prepared according to IFRS and Generally Accepted Accounting Principles (GAAP) is to provide information that is useful in making economic decisions. However, even financial statements prepared to exacting international norms do not contain all the information that an individual may need to perform all of the necessary tasks, since they largely portray the effects of past events and do not necessarily provide nonfinancial information. Nonetheless, IFRS statements do contain data about the *past* performance of an entity (income and cash flows) as well as its current financial condition (assets and liabilities) that are useful in assessing future prospects and risks. The financial analyst must be capable of using the financial statements in conjunction with other information in order to reach valid investment conclusions.

Financial statement analysis (analytic review) normally comprises a review of financial conditions and specific issues related to risk exposure and risk management. Such reviews can be done off-site, whereas an on-site review would cover a much larger number of topics and be more concerned with qualitative aspects, including quality of corporate governance, physical infrastructure, and management's use of sound management information.

Integrating the various analytical components and techniques discussed in this chapter will distinguish a well-reasoned analysis from a mere compilation of various pieces of information, computations, tables, and graphs. The challenge is for the analyst to develop a storyline, providing context (country, macroeconomy, sector, accounting, auditing, and industry regulation, as well as any material limitations on the entity being analyzed), a description of corporate governance, and financial and operational risk and then relating the different areas of analysis by identifying how issues affect one another.

Before starting, the analyst should attempt to answer at least the following questions:

- What is the purpose of the analysis?
- What level of detail will be needed?
- What factors or relationships (context) will influence the analysis?
- What are the analytical limitations, and will these limitations have the potential to impair the analysis?
- What data are available?
- How will data be processed?
- What methodologies will be used to interpret the data?
- How will conclusions and recommendations be communicated?

Too much of what passes for analysis is simply the calculation of a series of ratios and verification of compliance with preset covenants or regulations, without analysis and interpretation of the implications of the calculations, establishing "what happened" without asking the more important questions regarding why and its impact. Once the analyst is sure that the overall approach and reasoning are sound, the analytic review should focus on the following issues:

- What happened, established through computation or questionnaires;
- Why it happened, established through analysis;
- The impact of the event or trend, established through interpretation of analysis;
- The response and strategy of management, established through evaluation of the quality of corporate governance;
- The recommendations of the analyst, established through interpretation and forecasting of results of the analysis;
- The vulnerabilities that should be highlighted, included in the recommendations of the analyst.

An effective storyline—supporting final conclusions and recommendations—is normally enhanced through the use of data spanning between five and 10 years, as well as graphs, common-size financial statements, and company and cross-sectional industry trends.

TABLE 5.3   Stages of the Analytical Review Process

Analytical phase	Sources of information	Output
Structuring and collection of input data	Questionnaires, financial statements, and other financial data	Completed input data, questionnaires, and financial data tables
Processing of data	Completed input data (questionnaires and financial data tables)	Processed output data
Analysis of processed and structured output data	Input data and processed output data	Analytical results
Development of an off-site analysis report	Analytical results and previous reports	Report of off-site analysis and identification of items to follow up with management and an on-site visit
Follow-up through on-site review, audit, or other physical verification	Off-site analytical report and nonfinancial data obtained during physical visit and discussions with management	Recommendation as to whether investment or granting of credit should proceed

The experienced analyst will distinguish between a computation-based approach and an analytic approach. With certain modifications, this process is similar to the approach used by risk-orientated financial supervisors and regulators.

Table 5.3 illustrates the more general use of the tools discussed here. In principle, the tools can be used during the entire bank analysis cycle. They can help an analyst to diagnose thoroughly a bank's financial condition, risk exposures, and risk management, as well as to evaluate trends and project future developments.

ANALYTICAL TOOLS

There are many tools to assist with bank analysis, including questionnaires and Excel models that could easily be adapted to an Islamic banking environment. These often consist of a series of spreadsheet-based data-input tables that enable an analyst to collect and manipulate data in a systematic manner. This chapter does not discuss detailed steps regarding the use of such tools; rather it provides a conceptual framework to explain their background. The intention is to facilitate the development of similar tools for Islamic financial institutions.

Questionnaires

Questionnaires and data tables should be completed by the bank being evaluated. Questions should be designed to capture management's perspective on and understanding of the bank's risk management process. The background and financial information requested in the questionnaire will provide an overview of the bank as well as allow for assessment of the quality and comprehensiveness of bank policies, management and control processes, and financial and management information. Questions fall into several categories, as follows:

- Institutional development needs;
- Overview of the financial sector and regulation;
- Overview of the bank (history and group and organizational structure);
- Accounting systems, management information, and internal controls;
- Information technology;
- Corporate governance, covering key players and accountabilities;
- Financial risk management, including asset-liability management, profitability, credit risk, and the other major types of financial risk.

Data-Input Tables

To facilitate the gathering and provisioning of data, an analytical model should contain a series of input tables for collecting financial data. The data can then be used to create either ratios or graphs. Data tables are normally related to the major areas of financial risk management. The balance sheet and income statements serve as anchor schedules, with detail provided by all the other schedules. The output of an analytical model (tables and graphs) can assist executives in the high-level interpretation and analysis of a bank's financial risk management process and its financial condition.

Output Summary Reports

The framework described above envisages the production of tables, ratios, and graphs based on manipulated input data. The report allows an analyst to measure a bank's performance and to judge the effectiveness of its risk management process. Combined with the qualitative information obtained from the questionnaire, these statistical tables and graphs make up the raw material needed to carry out an informed analysis, as required in off-site (or macro level) reports. The ratios cover the areas of risk management in varying degrees of detail, starting with balance sheet and income statement schedules. The graphs provide a visual representation of some of the analytical results and a quick snapshot of both the current situation in banks (such as financial structure and the composition of investment portfolios) and comparisons over time.

Ratios

A ratio is a mathematical expression of one quantity relative to another. There are many relationships between financial accounts and between expected relationships from one point in time to another. Ratios are a useful way of expressing relationships in the following areas of risk:

- *Activity (operational efficiency).* The extent to which an entity uses its assets efficiently, as measured by turnover of current assets and liabilities and long-term assets;
- *Liquidity.* The entity's ability to repay its short-term liabilities, measured by evaluating components of current assets and current liabilities;
- *Profitability.* Relation between a company's profit margins and sales, average capital, and average common equity;
- *Debt and leverage.* The risk and return characteristics of the company, as measured by the volatility of sales and the extent of the use of borrowed money;
- *Solvency.* Financial risk resulting from the impact of the use of ratios of debt to equity and cash flow to expense coverage;
- *Earnings, share price, and growth.* The rate at which an entity can grow as determined by its earnings, share price, and retention of profits;
- *Other ratios.* Groupings representing the preferences of individual analysts in addition to ratios required by prudential regulators such as banking supervisors, insurance regulators, and securities market bodies.

Financial analysis provides insights that can assist the analyst in making forward-looking projections. Financial ratios serve the following purposes:

- Provide insights into the microeconomic relationships within a firm that help analysts to project earnings and free cash flow (necessary to determine entity value and creditworthiness);
- Provide insights into a firm's financial flexibility, which is its ability to obtain the cash required to meet financial obligations or to acquire assets, even if unexpected circumstances should develop;
- Provide a means of evaluating management's ability.

Although they are extremely useful tools, ratios must be used with caution. They do not provide complete answers about the bottom-line performance of a business. In the short run, many tricks can be used to make ratios look good in relation to industry standards. An assessment of the operations and management of an entity should therefore be performed to provide a check on ratios.

Graphs and Charts

Graphs are powerful tools for analyzing trends and structures. They facilitate comparison of performance and structures over time and show trend lines and changes in significant aspects of bank operations and performance. In addition, they provide senior management with a high-level overview of trends in a bank's risk. Graphs can illustrate asset and liability structures, sources of income, profitability, and capital adequacy, composition of investment portfolios, major types of credit risk exposures, and exposure to interest rate, liquidity, market, and currency risk. Graphs may be useful during off-site surveillance. In this context, they can serve as a starting point to help with on-site examinations and to present the bank's financial condition and risk management aspects succinctly to senior management. They also help external auditors to illustrate points in their presentation to management and other industry professionals to judge a bank's condition and prospects.

Figure 5.1 shows a bank experiencing significant growth in short-term trade finance *(murabahat)* and dramatic declines in cash. When the current period is compared to the prior period, the growth in short-term international *murabahat* appears to be quite dramatic, but when the current period is compared to the period two years ago, it becomes clear that the growth has not been unusual in percentage terms.

In the same manner, a simple line graph can illustrate the growth trends in key financial variables (see figure 5.2). The rapid rise and then flattening of growth in Islamic finance and investing assets are clearly illustrated alongside the reduction in cash, creating more concern regarding the entity's liquidity: the increase in mediusm-term trade finance and short-term trade finance could have caused the reduction in liquidity (depending on how these increases in working capital were financed).

ANALYTICAL TECHNIQUES

Data can be interpreted in many ways. Common analytical techniques include ratio analysis, common-size analysis, cross-sectional analysis, trend analysis, and regression analysis.

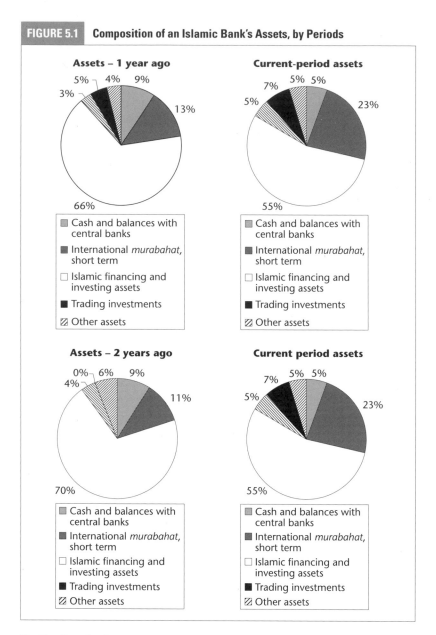

FIGURE 5.1 **Composition of an Islamic Bank's Assets, by Periods**

Assets – 1 year ago

5% 4% 9%
3%
13%
66%

- Cash and balances with central banks
- International *murabahat*, short term
- Islamic financing and investing assets
- Trading investments
- Other assets

Current-period assets

7% 5% 5%
5%
23%
55%

- Cash and balances with central banks
- International *murabahat*, short term
- Islamic financing and investing assets
- Trading investments
- Other assets

Assets – 2 years ago

0% 6% 9%
4%
11%
70%

- Cash and balances with central banks
- International *murabahat*, short term
- Islamic financing and investing assets
- Trading investments
- Other assets

Current period assets

7% 5% 5%
5%
23%
55%

- Cash and balances with central banks
- International *murabahat*, short term
- Islamic financing and investing assets
- Trading investments
- Other assets

Ratio Analysis

Financial ratios mean little when seen in isolation. Their meaning can only be interpreted in the context of other information. It is good practice to compare the financial ratios of a company with those of its major competitors. Typically, the analyst should be wary of companies whose financial

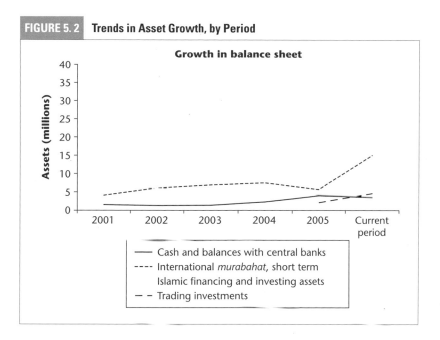

FIGURE 5. 2 Trends in Asset Growth, by Period

Growth in balance sheet

—— Cash and balances with central banks
---- International *murabahat*, short term
Islamic financing and investing assets
– – Trading investments

ratios are far above or below industry norms. In some cases, evaluating a company's past performance provides a basis for forward looking analyses. Such an evaluation may suggest that its performance is likely to continue at similar levels or that an upward or downward trend is likely to continue. Alternatively, for a company making a major acquisition or divestiture, for a new financial institution, or for a bank operating in a volatile environment, past performance may be less relevant to future performance.

An analyst should evaluate financial information based on the following:

- *Financial institution's goals.* Actual ratios can be compared with company objectives to determine if the objectives are being attained.
- *Banking industry norms (cross-sectional analysis).* A company can be compared with others in the industry by relating its financial ratios to industry norms or a subset of the companies in an industry. When industry norms are used to make judgments, care must be taken, because (a) many ratios are industry specific, but not all ratios are important to all industries; (b) companies may have several lines of business, which distorts aggregate financial ratios and makes it preferable to examine industry-specific ratios by lines of business; (c) differences in accounting methods can distort financial ratios; and (d) differences in corporate strategies can affect certain financial ratios.

- *Economic conditions.* Financial ratios tend to improve when the economy is strong and to weaken during recessions. Therefore, financial ratios should be examined in light of the phase of the business cycle in which the economy is traversing.
- *Experience.* An analyst with experience obtains an intuitive notion of the meaning of transformed data.

Common-Size Analysis

An analytical technique of great value is relative analysis, which is achieved by converting all financial statement items to a percentage of a given financial statement item such as total assets or total revenue. (see also figure 5.1).

Common-size analysis: Balance sheet structure

The structure of the balance sheet may vary significantly depending on the bank's business orientation, market environment, customer mix, or economic environment. The composition of the balance sheet is normally a result of risk management decisions.

The analyst should be able to assess the risk profile of the business simply by analyzing the relative share of various assets and changes in their proportionate share over time. For example, if short-term trade finance jumps from 33 to 43 percent of on-balance-sheet assets (see table 5.4), one would question whether the business's credit risk management systems are adequate to handle the increased volume of transactions and the short-term trade finance portfolio. In addition, such a jump could disclose a shift from another area of risk. Likewise, an increase or decrease in trading securities would indicate a change in the level of market risk to

TABLE 5.4   Balance-Sheet Composition of Assets
(Percent of total assets)

Assets	year 1	year 2
Cash and balances with central banks	10.1	6.6
International *murabahat,* short term	33.0	43.0
Islamic financing and investing assets	48.5	39.8
Real estate assets	5.9	7.1
Trading investments	0.0	0.0
Other assets	2.5	3.5
Total assets	100.0	100.0

which the institution is exposed. Such an assessment is possible prior to undertaking a detailed review of the management of either credit or market risk. When linked to the amount of net income yielded by each category of assets, this analysis increases in importance, enabling a challenging assessment of risk versus reward.

Common-size analysis: Income statement structure

Common-size analysis can be used effectively on the income statement as well. The emphasis in the income statement would be on the sources of revenue and their sustainability. A question worth asking pertains to the proportion of income earned in relation to the amount of energy invested through the deployment of assets. When analyzing the income structure of a business, analysts should give appropriate consideration to and acquire an understanding of the following aspects:

■ Trends in and the composition and accuracy of reported earnings;
■ The quality, composition, and level of income and expense components;
■ Dividend payout and earnings retention;
■ Major sources of income and the most profitable business areas;
■ Any income or expenditure recognition policies that distort earnings;
■ The effect of intergroup transactions, especially those related to the transfer of earnings and asset-liability valuations.

Cross-Sectional Analysis

Ratios are not meaningful when used on their own, which is why financial analysts prefer trend analysis (the monitoring of a ratio or group of ratios over time) and comparative analysis (the comparison of a specific ratio for a group of companies in a sector or for different sectors). This comparison becomes a useful tool in establishing benchmarks for performance and structure.

Cross-sectional (or relative) analysis of common-size financial statements makes it easier to compare an entity to other entities in the same sector, even though the entities might be of different sizes and operate in different currencies. If the examples given in figure 5.1 or table 5.3 referred to two different banks, rather than simply the same bank over more than one year, then the conclusions would compare the relative levels of liquidity, structure of assets, between the two banks.

However, the analyst has to be realistic when comparing entities, because size does influence business results, and entities are seldom exactly the same. Differences in currency are eliminated in the percentage presentation, but the analyst must keep in mind the macroeconomic environment that influences variables such as competition and inflation across currency and national boundaries.

Cross-sectional analysis is not the solution to all problems, as different accounting policies and methods will influence the allocation of transactions to specific line items on the financial statements. For example, some companies could include depreciation in the cost of sales, while others could show it separately. However, if all these aspects are kept in mind, cross-sectional analysis offers the analyst a powerful analytical tool.

Trend Analysis

The trend of an amount or a ratio, which shows whether it is improving or deteriorating, is as important as its current absolute level. Trend analysis provides important information regarding historical performance and growth and, given a sufficiently long history of accurate seasonal information, can be of great assistance as a planning tool for management. In table 5.5, the last two columns of the trend analysis incorporate both currency and percentage changes for the past two years. A small percentage change could hide a significant currency change and vice versa, prompting the analyst to investigate the reasons despite one of the changes being relatively small. In addition, past trends are not necessarily an accurate predictor of future behavior, especially if the economic environment changes. These caveats should be borne in mind when using past trends in forecasting.

Variations of Trend Analysis

Changes in currency and percentages focus the analysis on material items. A variation of growth in terms of common-size financial statements is to combine currency and percentage changes. Even when a percentage change might seem insignificant, the magnitude of the amount of currency involved might be significant and vice versa. Such combined analysis is therefore a further refinement of the analysis and interpretation of annual changes.

Annual growth (from year to year)

Any business that is well positioned and successful in its market can be expected to grow. An analysis of balance sheets can be performed to

TABLE 5.5 Balance-Sheet Growth, Year on Year
(Percent)

Assets	2001	2002	2003	2004	2005	2006	Change 2005–06
Cash and balances with central banks	Base	–16.0	6.6	65.6	74.2	–11.9	(476,251)
International *murabahat*, short term	Base	48.9	13.7	8.0	–24.6	165.0	9,333,398
Islamic financing and investing assets	Base	20.6	21.0	42.9	61.9	24.6	6,949,535
Real estate assets	Base	53.4	–9.9	8.2	–4.6	137.4	1,776,357
Trading investments	Base					119.2	2,502,443
Other assets	Base	76.9	40.2	106.8	–16.6	82.0	1,350,175
Total assets	Base	27.8	16.2	34.4	40.5	49.9	21,435,657

determine growth rates and the type of structural changes that have occurred in a business. Such an analysis indicates the general type of business undertaken by the enterprise and requires an understanding of the structure of its balance sheet and the nature of its assets and liabilities. Even when growth overall is not significant, individual components of the balance sheet normally shift in reaction to changes in the competitive market or economic or regulatory environment (as illustrated in table 5.4). As the balance sheet structure changes, inherent risks also change. The structure of a balance sheet should therefore form part of an assessment of the adequacy and effectiveness of policies and procedures for managing risk exposures. In normal situations, the growth of a business's assets is determined by an increase in the earnings base and access to stable external funding or investment, at a cost that is acceptable to the business.

Businesses that grow too quickly tend to take unjustified risks, and their administrative and management information systems often cannot keep up with the rate of expansion. Businesses that grow too slowly can likewise take risks that are unusual or poorly understood by them. Even well-managed businesses can run into risk management problems arising from excessive growth, especially concerning management of their working capital.

Cumulative growth from a base year

The analysis that can be performed using this technique is not significantly different from looking at year-on-year growth. Reviewing the cumulative effects of change over time, compared to a base year, dramatizes change and the need for remedial action when change outstrips the ability of risk management and administrative systems to keep up with growth or the enterprise's ability to finance its expansion.

Regression Analysis

Regression analysis uses statistical techniques to identify relationships (or correlation) between variables. An example of such a relationship could be sales and medium-term trade finance over time or hotel occupancies compared to hotel revenues. In addition to analyzing trends over time, regression analysis enables analytic review as well as identification of items or ratios that are not behaving as they should be, given the statistical relationships that exist between ratios and variables.

6

Balance-Sheet Structure

T he goal of financial risk management is to maximize the value of a bank, as determined by its level of profitability and risk. Since risk is inherent in banking and unavoidable, the task of the risk manager is to manage the different types of risk at acceptable levels and sustainable profitability. Doing so requires the continual identification, quantification, and monitoring of risk exposures, which in turn demands sound policies, adequate organization, efficient processes, skilled analysts, and elaborate computerized information systems. In addition, risk management requires the capacity to anticipate changes and to act in such a way that a bank's business can be structured and restructured to profit from the changes or at least to minimize losses. Regulatory authorities should not prescribe how business is conducted; instead they should maintain prudent over-sight of a bank by evaluating the risk composition of its assets and by insisting that an adequate amount of capital and reserves is available to safeguard solvency.

Until the 1970s, conventional banking business consisted primarily of the extension of credit—in other words, a simple intermediation of deposits that had been raised at a relatively low cost—and bank managers faced fairly simple decisions concerning loan volumes, pricing, and investments. The key managerial challenges of the past were controlling asset quality, loan losses, and overhead expenditures. In the context of recession, volatile interest rates, and inflation during the late 1970s and early 1980s, the management of both assets and liabilities became neces-sary in order to maintain satisfactory margin performance. Balance-sheet

---

Key Messages

- The composition of a bank's balance-sheet assets and liabilities is one of the key factors that determine the level of risk faced by the institution.
- Growth in the balance sheet and resulting changes in the relative proportion of assets or liabilities affect the risk management process.
- Changes in the relative structure of assets and liabilities should be a conscious decision of a bank's policy makers: the board of directors.
- Monitoring key components of the balance sheet may alert the analyst to negative trends in the relationships between asset growth and capital retention capability.
- It is important to monitor the growth of low, nonearning, and off-balance-sheet items.
- Balance-sheet structure lies at the heart of the asset-liability management process.

---

management became even more complex as a result of deregulation in the 1980s, with growing competition for funds becoming a primary concern of management.

The era of deregulation and increased competition continued in the 1990s, involving financial institutions other than banks. This environment underscored the need for competitive pricing and, in practical terms, for an increase in and engagement of liabilities in a manner that maximizes spreads between costs and yields on investments and controls exposure to related risks. Due to the inverse relationship of these two goals, a balancing act between maximizing the spreads and controlling risk exposures has become a focal point in the financial management, regulation, and supervision of banks.

This chapter highlights the importance of the structure and composition of liabilities and assets, as well as the related income statement items. In addition, it illustrates the ways in which a bank's risk managers and analysts can analyze the structure of balance sheets and income statements, as well as individual balance-sheet items with specific risk aspects, such as liquidity in the case of deposit liabilities or market risk in the case of traded securities. In this process, the interaction between various types of risk must be understood to ensure that they are not evaluated in isolation. Finally, the key principles of effective risk management are discussed.

Figure 6.1 and table 6.1 both illustrate the detailed composition of a typical bank's balance sheet. The structure of a typical balance sheet has demand deposits and investment accounts from customers on the liability side (see table 9.2) and Islamic financing and investing accounts (loans to

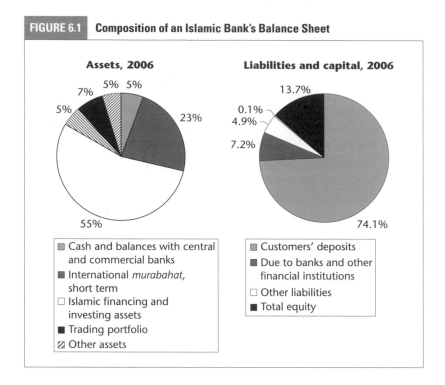

FIGURE 6.1 Composition of an Islamic Bank's Balance Sheet

Assets, 2006

- ▣ Cash and balances with central and commercial banks
- ▪ International *murabahat*, short term
- ☐ Islamic financing and investing assets
- ▪ Trading portfolio
- ▨ Other assets

Liabilities and capital, 2006

- ▣ Customers' deposits
- ▪ Due to banks and other financial institutions
- ☐ Other liabilities
- ▪ Total equity

TABLE 6.1 Composition of·an Islamic Bank's Balance Sheet

Balance-sheet item	2005	2006
Assets		
Cash and balances with central and commercial banks	3,995,220	3,518,969
International *murabahat*, short term	5,657,841	14,991,239
Islamic financing and investing assets–net	28,305,912	35,255,447
Real estate assets	1,292,445	3,068,802
Trading portfolio	2,099,402	4,601,845
Fixed and other assets	1,647,459	2,997,634
Total assets	42,998,279	64,433,936
Liabilities		
Customers' deposits (investment and current accounts)	33,391,950	47,732,482
Due to banks and other financial institutions	4,099,357	4,649,900
Other liabilities	1,628,155	3,155,269
Accrued *zakat* (charitable donations)	39,612	72,035
Total equity	3,839,205	8,824,250
Total liabilities and equity	42,998,279	64,433,936

customers in conventional banking terms) on the asset side. This pattern reflects the nature of banks as intermediaries, with ratios of capital to liabilities at such a low level that their leverage would be unacceptable to any business outside the financial services industry.

COMPOSITION OF ASSETS

The structure of individual balance sheets may vary significantly depending on business orientation, market environment, customer mix, or economic environment. Figures 6.2 to 6.4 illustrate different ways of observing or analyzing the structure and growth of the asset components of a bank over time.

The analyst should be able to assess the risk profile of the bank simply by analyzing the relative share of various asset items and changes in their proportionate share over time. For example, if the Islamic financing and investing asset portfolio drops from 66 to 55 percent, while international short-term commodity finance (*murabahat*) jumps from 13 to 23 percent (figure 6.2), one would question whether the bank's risk management systems are adequate to handle the increased volume of commodities transactions. Normally, such a jump would reflect a shift from another

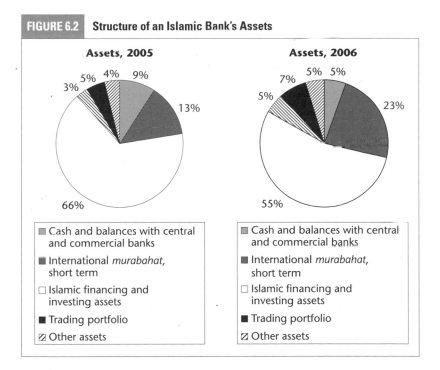

FIGURE 6.2 **Structure of an Islamic Bank's Assets**

Assets, 2005

Assets, 2006

Cash and balances with central and commercial banks

International *murabahat*, short term

Islamic financing and investing assets

Trading portfolio

Other assets

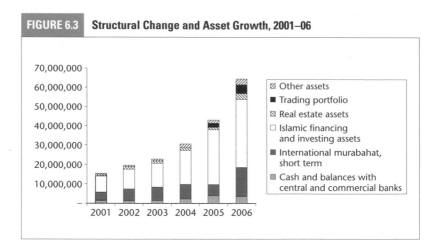

FIGURE 6.3 Structural Change and Asset Growth, 2001–06

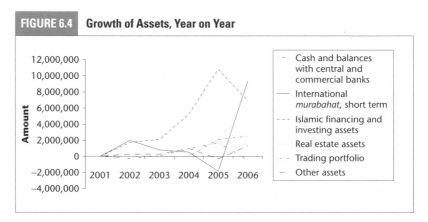

FIGURE 6.4 Growth of Assets, Year on Year

area of risk. In this case, cash also declined from 9 to 5 percent, affecting the liquidity of the bank. Likewise, an increase or decrease in trading securities would indicate a change in the level of market risk to which the institution is exposed. Such an assessment is possible at a macro level, prior to any detailed review of credit, liquidity, or market risk management. When linked to the amount of net income yielded by each category of assets, this analysis increases in importance, enabling a challenging assessment of risk versus reward.

Liquid Assets

Liquid assets are needed to accommodate expected and unexpected fluctuations in the balance sheet. In environments where markets are not developed and the liquidity of different claims still depends almost exclusively on their maturity rather than on the ability to sell them, banks tend to keep a relatively high level of liquid assets that yield little or no income. In such environments, liquid assets typically account for at least 10 percent, or in extreme situations as much as 20 percent, of total assets. Increasing market orientation, the growth of financial markets, and the greater diversity of financial instruments worldwide entail greater short-term flexibility in liquidity management, which in turn reduces the need to hold large amounts of liquid assets. In banking environments with developed financial markets, liquid assets typically account for only about 5 percent of total assets. However, realizing assets in times of liquidity crises might not be as easy in an Islamic as in a conventional banking environment. An appraisal of whether the level of liquid assets is satisfactory must therefore be based on a thorough understanding of money and banking market dynamics in the particular country, as certain assets that appear liquid in good times may not be liquid in more difficult periods.

Cash Balances

Cash balances represent the holdings of highly liquid assets, such as bank notes, gold coin, and bullion, as well as deposits with the central bank. A percentage of deposits is normally required to be held in order to meet the central bank's reserve requirements and to serve as a tool to reflect monetary policy. Flat-rate reserve requirements are used to control the amount of money that a bank is able to extend as credit. However, when banks are required to hold reserve assets in excess of the amount they normally would, particularly when the assets yield no income, the cost to banks increases. This creates incentives for banks to devise instruments that are not subject to reserve requirements, encourages intervention through new channels, and may give a competitive advantage to institutions that do not have reserve requirements. Such options tend to reduce the effectiveness and the importance of reserve requirements as a monetary policy tool.

Regulators have tried to make reserve requirements more difficult to circumvent and have reduced the incentives for doing so. For example, regulators have reduced the level, type, and volatility of reserve holdings or increased the various types of compensation made to banks for maintaining reserves.

Financing and Investing Assets

Islamic financing and investing assets are normally the most significant component of an Islamic bank's assets. In conventional banking, these include loans for general working capital (overdrafts), investment lending, asset-backed installment and mortgage loans, financing of debtors (accounts receivable and credit card accounts), and tradable debt such as acceptances and commercial paper. Islamic financing and investing assets are extended in domestic and foreign currency and are provided by banks as financing for public or private sector investments. Such investments could include the items listed in table 6.2.

In the past decade, innovation has increased the marketability of bank assets through the introduction of sales of assets such as mortgages, automobile loans, and export credits used as backing for marketable securities (a practice known as securitization and highly appropriate in an Islamic banking environment as providing a real underlying investment; see chapter 2).

An analysis of this trend may highlight investment or spending activity in various sectors of the economy, while an analysis of a foreign currency loan portfolio may indicate expectations regarding exchange rate and interest rate developments. Further, evaluation of trade credits may reveal important trends in competitiveness of the economy and its terms of trade.

TABLE 6.2   Islamic Financing and Investing Assets – Gross

Assets	2005	2006
Financing assets		
Commodities *murabahat*	5,322,281	7,091,886
International *murabahat*	3,763,437	3,598,780
Vehicles *murabahat*	3,006,849	3,877,829
Real estate *murabahat*	1,905,860	3,499,405
Total *murabahat*	13,998,427	18,067,900
Istisnah	2,636,913	4,452,347
Ijarah	5,154,076	6,038,210
Others		161,060
Total financing assets	21,789,416	28,719,517
Investing assets		
Sukuks	1,420,012	5,764,652
Musharakahs	5,827,754	2,832,292
Mudarabahs	2,100,232	3,053,780
Investment funds	0	0
Wakalah	153,749	185,257
Total investing assets	9,501,747	11,835,981

Trading Portfolios

Trading assets, such as *sukuks* (bonds), represent the bank's trading books in securities, foreign currencies, equities, and commodities.

Although similar securities are involved, trading portfolios are often divided into different liquidity tranches (portfolios with different liquidity and yield objectives). In conventional banking, proprietary trading is aimed at exploiting market opportunities with leveraged funding (for example, through the use of repurchase agreements), whereas a portfolio funded by deposit taking could be traded as a stable liquidity portfolio. The same principles could be applied equally to Islamic banks.

Trading portfolios are valued in terms of International Accounting Standard (IAS) 39 and can be classified as trading, available for sale, or held to maturity. However, trading assets would normally be disclosed at fair value (marked to market) in the bank's financial statements (see chapter 12 for IFRS and AAOIFI disclosure).

In many developing countries, banks have been or are obligated to purchase government bonds or other designated claims, usually to ensure that a minimum amount of high-quality liquidity is available to meet deposit demands. Frequently, requirements are intended to ensure a predictable flow of finance to designated recipients. Government is the most frequent beneficiary, often with an implicit subsidy. Such obligatory investments may diminish the availability and increase the cost of credit extended to the economy (and the private sector).

In developed countries and financial markets, an increase in bank trading portfolios generally reflects the growing orientation of a bank to nontraditional operations. In risk management terms, such an orientation would mean that a bank has replaced credit risk with market price risk.

Other Assets

Other assets could comprise a bank's longer-term ownership investments, such as equities held in the bank's long-term investment portfolio. These include equity investments in subsidiaries, associates, and other listed and unlisted entities. The percentage of a portfolio that is devoted to this type of instrument varies among countries, although not necessarily as a result of a bank's own asset-liability management decisions. Such assets are also valued in terms of IAS 39 and are normally classified as available for sale or held to maturity.

For equity investments, the balance sheet should be reviewed on a consolidated basis to ensure a proper understanding of the effect of such investments on the structure of the bank's own balance sheet and to assess the asset quality of the bank.

Fixed Assets

Fixed assets represent the bank's infrastructure resources and typically include the premises under which the bank operates, other fixed property, computer equipment, vehicles, furniture, and fixtures. In certain circumstances, banks may have a relatively high proportion of fixed assets, such as houses, land, or commercial space. These holdings would be the result of collections on collateral that, under most regulations, banks are required to dispose of within a set period of time. They may also reflect the deliberate decision of a bank to invest in real estate, if the market is fairly liquid and prices are increasing. In some developing countries, investments in fixed assets reach such high proportions that central banks may begin to feel obliged to limit or otherwise regulate property-related assets. A bank should not be in the business of investing in real estate assets, and therefore a preponderance of these assets would affect the assessment of the bank. In more developed countries, real estate assets not acquired in the normal course of banking business would be booked in a subsidiary at the holding company level in order to protect depositors from associated risks.

Other assets often include intangible assets. These vary with regard to the predictability of income associated with a particular asset, the existence of markets for such assets, the possibility of selling the assets, and the reliability of the assessments of the asset's useful life. The treatment of assets in evaluating capital adequacy can be controversial. For example, specific assets may include suspense accounts, which have to be analyzed and verified to ensure that the asset is indeed real and recoverable.

COMPOSITION OF LIABILITIES

The relative share of various components of the balance sheet—liabilities, in this instance—is a good indication of the levels and types of risk to which a bank is exposed.

An increase in the level of nonretail deposits or funding could expose a conventional bank to greater volatility in satisfying its funding requirements, requiring increasingly sophisticated liquidity risk management. Certain funding instruments also expose a bank to market risk.

The business of banking is traditionally based on the concept of low margins and high leverage. Consequently, a special feature of a bank's balance sheet is its low ratio of capital to liabilities, which would normally be unacceptable to any other business outside the financial services industry. The acceptable level of risk associated with such a structure is measured and prescribed according to risk-based capital requirements, which are, in turn, linked to the composition of a bank's assets.

While the types of liabilities present in an Islamic bank's balance sheet are nearly universal, their exact composition varies greatly depending on the particular bank's business and market orientation, as well as the prices and supply characteristics of different types of liabilities at any given point in time. The funding structure of a bank directly affects its cost of operation and therefore determines a bank's potential profit and level of risk. The structure of a bank's liabilities also reflects its specific asset-liability and risk management policies.

Customer Deposits

Customer deposits—*amanah* (trust), investment accounts, and special investment accounts—usually constitute the largest proportion of a bank's total liabilities. Deposits from customers—the amount due to other customers and investors—represent money accepted from the general public, such as demand and investment deposits, and funding products, such as savings, fixed and notice, and foreign currency deposits in conventional banks. The structure and stability of the deposit base are of utmost importance. Broader trends also come into play. An analysis of private sector deposits (including deposits from repurchase agreements and certificates of deposit) highlight economic trends related to the level of spending, as well as its effect on inflation. Furthermore, growth in money supply is calculated using total deposits in the banking system. A change in the level of deposits in the banking system is therefore one of the variables that influences monetary policy.

Within the deposit structure, some items are inherently more risky than others. For example, large corporate deposits are less stable than household deposits, not only because they are more concentrated but also because they are managed more actively. A large proportion of nonretail or nonstandard deposits can be unstable, which tends to indicate that the bank's investment and partnership accounts holders may be paying higher "rates" than they would at another bank or that depositors may be attracted by liberal credit policies. Cash collateral and various types of loan escrow accounts may also be counted as deposits, although these funds can only be used for their stated purpose.

Competition for funds is a normal part of any banking market, and depositors, both households and corporations, often aim to minimize idle funds. A bank should therefore have a policy for attracting and maintaining deposits and procedures for analyzing, on a regular basis, the volatility and character of the deposit and investment account structure so that funds can be used productively even when the probability of withdrawal exists. Analysts of the deposit structure should determine the percentage of hard-core, stable, seasonal, and volatile deposits.

Amounts Due to Banks and Other Financial Institutions

These include all deposits, loans, and advances extended between banks and are normally regarded as volatile sources of funding. An analysis of interbank balances may point to structural peculiarities in the banking system; for example, when funding for a group of banks is provided by one of its members.

International borrowing may occur in the same form as domestic banking, except that it normally exposes a bank to additional currency risk. Direct forms of international borrowing include loans from foreign banks, export promotion agencies in various countries, and international lending agencies, as well as nostro accounts. Indirect forms include notes, acceptances, import drafts, and trade bills sold with the bank's endorsement, guarantees, and notes or trade bills rediscounted with central banks in various countries. The existence of foreign funding is generally a good indicator of international confidence in a country and its economy.

Given the volatility of such funding sources, however, if a bank is an extensive borrower its activities should be analyzed in relation to other aspects of its operations that influence borrowing. The acceptable reasons for reliance on interbank funding include temporary or seasonal loan or cash requirements and the matching of large and unanticipated withdrawals of customer deposits. Money centers or large regional banks engaged in money market transactions tend to borrow on a continuous basis. Otherwise, heavy reliance on interbank funding indicates that a bank carries a high degree of funding risk and is overextended in relation to its normal volume of deposits.

Other Liabilities

Other liabilities would normally include trade creditors and other sundry items. In an Islamic bank, the unpaid portion of depositors' share of profits would be an important component. Amounts owed to the central bank may also appear among the bank's liabilities. The most frequent reason for borrowing from the central bank is that changes have occurred in the volume of required reserves as a result of fluctuations in deposits. These shifts occur when banks have not correctly forecasted their daily reserve position and have been forced to borrow to make up the difference—that is, they help banks to meet temporary requirements for funds. Longer-term credit from the central bank indicates an unusual situation that may be the result of national or regional difficulties or problems related to the particular bank in question. Historically, central bank financing was often directed toward a special purpose determined by government policies, for example, in the areas of agriculture or housing, but this type of activity is increasingly out of date.

EQUITY

The capital of a bank represents the buffer available to protect creditors against losses that may be incurred by managing risks imprudently. According to international norms, banks normally have primary and secondary capital components—tier 1 and tier 2 capital (see chapter 13 for further discussion of this point). The key components of bank capital are common shares or stock, retained earnings, and perpetual preferred stock, all of which are counted as primary capital. Otherwise, to qualify for tier 1 or tier 2 capital, a capital instrument should have long maturity and not contain or be covered by any covenants, terms, or restrictions that are inconsistent with sound banking. For example, instruments that result in higher dividends or interest payments when a bank's financial condition deteriorates cannot be accepted as part of capital. Secondary capital components will normally mature at some point, and a bank must be prepared to replace or redeem them without impairing its capital adequacy. When determining capital adequacy, the remaining maturity of the components of secondary capital should also be assessed.

BALANCE-SHEET GROWTH AND STRUCTURAL CHANGE

A bank that is well positioned and successful in its market can be expected to grow. An analysis of the balance sheet can be performed to determine growth rates and the type of structural changes that occur in a bank. Such an analysis indicates the general type of business undertaken by a bank and requires an understanding of the structure of its balance sheet and the nature of its assets and liabilities. Even when overall balance-sheet growth is not significant, individual components normally shift in reaction to changes in the competitive market or economic or regulatory environments (as illustrated by figures 6.3 and 6.4, as well as table 6.3). As the structure of the balance-sheet changes, inherent risks also change. Therefore, the structure of a balance sheet should be assessed along with the adequacy and effectiveness of policies and procedures for managing risk exposures.

Figure 6.5 illustrates the overall growth of a hypothetical bank's assets and capital. In addition, it highlights the extent to which a bank's growth is balanced or the extent to which the bank has been able to maintain regulatory capital requirements in relation to total assets and risk-weighted asset growth. A graph of this kind can indicate capital adequacy problems to come, perhaps as a result of rapid expansion.

In normal situations, the growth of a bank's assets is justified by an increase in the stable funding base at a cost that is acceptable to the bank as well as by profit opportunities. The spread between investment liability accounts and investment and long-term partnership accounts on the asset side should normally be stable or increasing. In a stable market environment, increasing margins may indicate the acceptance or presence of higher risk. In order to avoid increased lending risk, emphasis is often placed on fee-generating income, which does not involve the bank's balance sheet.

Banks that grow too quickly tend to take unjustified risks and often find that their administrative and management information systems

TABLE 6.3   Percentage Composition of the Balance Sheet, 2001–06 (Percent)

Composition of the balance sheet	2001	2002	2003	2004	2005	2006
Cash and balances with central and commercial banks	10.1	6.6	6.1	7.5	9.3	5.5
International *murabahat*, short term	26.8	31.2	30.5	24.5	13.2	23.3
Islamic financing and investing assets	54.7	51.6	53.7	57.1	65.8	54.7
Real estate assets	5.9	7.1	5.5	4.4	3.0	4.8
Trading portfolio	0	0	0	0	4.9	7.1
Other assets	2.5	3.5	4.2	6.5	3.8	4.7
Total assets	100	100	100	100	100	100
Customers' deposits	86.0	86.7	87.3	81.5	77.7	74.1
Due to banks and other financial institutions	1.4	1.2	1.4	4.6	9.5	7.2
Other liabilities	4.4	4.0	3.8	4.2	3.8	4.9
Accrued *zakat* (charitable donation)	0.1	0.1	0.1	0	0.1	0.1
Shareholder's equity	8.1	8.1	7.5	9.8	8.9	13.7
Total liabilities and capital	100	100	100	100	100	100

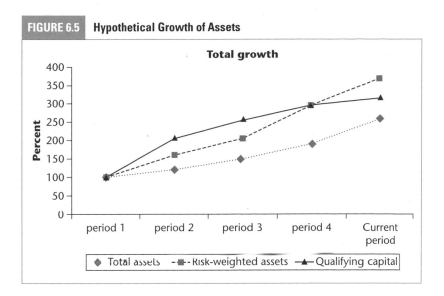

FIGURE 6.5 **Hypothetical Growth of Assets**

cannot keep up with the rate of expansion. Banks that grow too slowly can likewise take risks that are different or not clearly understood by them. Even well-managed banks can run into risk management problems arising from excessive growth, especially concerning their loan portfolios.

In some countries, the conduct of monetary policy may limit or significantly affect the rate of growth and the structure of a bank's assets. Despite the shift away from reliance on portfolio regulations and administrative controls, credit ceilings have been and still are a relatively common method of implementing monetary policy in some transitional economies, especially in countries with less developed financial markets. An alternative method of indirectly manipulating the demand for and level of credit in the economy has traditionally been to influence the cost of credit.

Changes in banking and finance mean that the scope for circumventing credit ceilings and interest rate regulations has increased significantly. A loss of effectiveness, and concerns over the distortions that credit ceiling and interest rate manipulations generate, are the reasons why these instruments are increasingly abandoned in favor of open-market interventions. The use of credit ceilings in countries where such monetary policies have been pursued for long periods of time may have reduced the competitive ability of banks, encouraged innovation, and fostered the creation of alternative instruments or channels of financial intermediation. In other words, they have inadvertently shaped the evolution of banking systems.

7

Income Statement Structure

Profitability, in the form of retained earnings, is typically one of the key sources of capital generation. A sound banking system is built on profitable and adequately capitalized banks. Profitability is a revealing indicator of a bank's competitive position in banking markets and of the quality of its management. It allows a bank to maintain a certain risk profile and provides a cushion against short-term problems.

The income statement, a key source of information on a bank's profitability, reveals the sources of a bank's earnings and their quantity and quality, as well as the quality of the bank's loan portfolio and the targets of its expenditures. Income statement structure also indicates a bank's business orientation. Traditionally, the major source of conventional banking income has been interest, but the increasing orientation toward nontraditional business is also reflected in income statements. For example, income from trading operations and fee-based income accounts for an increasingly high percentage of earnings in modern banks. This trend implies higher volatility of earnings and profitability. It also implies a different risk profile from that of a traditional bank.

Changes in the structure and stability of banks' profits have sometimes been motivated by statutory capital requirements and monetary policy measures such as obligatory reserves. In order to maintain confidence in the banking system, banks are subject to minimum capital requirements. The restrictive nature of this statutory minimum capital may cause banks to change their business mix in favor of activities and assets that entail a lower capital requirement. However, although such

---

Key Messages

- Profitability indicates a bank's capacity to carry risk or to increase its capital.
- Regulators should welcome profitable banks as contributors to stability of the banking system.
- Profitability ratios should be seen in context, and the potential yield on the "free" equity portion of capital should be deducted prior to drawing conclusions about profitability.
- The components of income could change over time, and core costs should be compared to assumed core income to determine whether such costs are indeed fully covered.
- Management should understand which assets they are spending their energy on and how this relates to the income generated from such assets.

---

assets carry less risk, they may earn lower returns. Excessive obligatory reserves and statutory liquidity requirements damage profits and may encourage disintermediation. They also may result in undesirable banking practices. For example, the balance sheets of banks in many developing and transitional economies contain large proportions of fixed assets, a trend that adversely affects profitability. Regulatory authorities should recognize the importance of profits and, to the extent possible, avoid regulations that may unduly depress profitability.

Taxation is another major factor that influences a bank's profitability as well as its business and policy choices, because it affects the competitiveness of various instruments and different segments of the financial markets. For example, taxation of investment and partnership income, combined with a tax holiday for capital gains, can make deposits and investment accounts less attractive than equity investments. In general, banks adjust their business and policy decisions to minimize the taxes to be paid and to take advantage of any loopholes in tax laws. Beyond the level and the transparency of profit taxation, key areas to consider when assessing the business environment and profit potential of a bank are if and how fiscal authorities tax unrealized gains and interest income and whether or not they allow provisions before taxation. Many fiscal authorities also apply direct taxes to banking transactions and margins.

A thorough understanding of the source of profits and changes in the income-profit structure of both an individual bank and the banking system as a whole is important to all key players in the risk management process. Supervisory authorities should, for example, view bank profitability as an indicator of stability and as a factor that contributes to depositor confidence. Maximum sustainable profitability should therefore be encouraged, since healthy competition for profits indicates an efficient and dynamic financial system.

COMPOSITION OF THE INCOME STATEMENT

A bank's income statement is a key source of information regarding the sources and structure of its income. An example of an analytical income statement is shown in table 7.1. In the last two columns of this example, the various components of income and expenses (even gross interest income and gross interest expenses) are disclosed as a percentage of the total income. In a conventional bank, the equivalent items would relate mostly to net interest income and trading income with the former often constituting a relatively minor component of overall income, especially when the volume of activity to generate the net interest income is taken into account (see also figure 7.1).

TABLE 7.1   Composition of the Income Statement, 2005–06

	Amount		Percent	
Composition	2005	2006	2005	2006
Income				
Income from Islamic financing and investing assets	1,733,647	2,441,532	64	53
Income from international *murabahat,* short term	196,409	525,153	7	11
Income from investment properties	149,906	153,203	6	3
Income from sale of properties under construction, net	141,626	412,710	5	9
Commissions, fees, and foreign exchange income	401,294	906,716	15	20
Sundry income	73,161	137,143	3	4
Total income	2,696,043	4,576,457	100	100
Expenses				
General and administrative expenses	(569,464)	(1,148,174)	21	25
Provisions and reversals of impairment	(130,173)	(76,467)	5	2
Depreciation of investment properties	(11,612)	(10,240)	0	0
Total expenses	(711,249)	(1,234,881)	26	27
Profit before depositors' share and tax	1,984,794	3,341,576	74	73
Depositors' share of profits	(918,405)	(1,757,611)	− 34	− 38
Profit for the year before tax	1,066,389	1,583,965	40	35
Income tax	(3,015)	(6,122)	− 00.28	− 00.39

Financing and Investing Income

Islamic financing and investing income originates from Islamic products intermediated by an Islamic financial institution. Such income is normally recognized on a time-apportioned basis over the period of the contract on the principal amounts outstanding, meaning that a bank calculates income due for each period of time covered by the income statement, regardless of whether or not the income has been received or paid. Accounting policies should normally require that an investment or partnership account be accorded nonaccrual status if a client is overdue by a specified period of time or deemed to be potentially unable to pay, at which point all previously accrued but unpaid income should be reversed out of income. In the absence of such a policy, banks end up overtstating their income and profits.

Significant income sources should be subdivided further. For example, investing and financing accounts can be analyzed by assets provided to the government, to state enterprises, and to private enterprises or by product revenue. This subdivision may be required for supervisory or statistical purposes. It may also be the result of a bank's internal organization, as modern, cost-conscious banks often develop elaborate pricing and costing systems for their various business and product lines to ensure that the contribution of each product to the bottom line is clearly understood.

Depositors' Share of Profits and Losses

Depositors' share of profits and losses comprises payments related to investments and partnership income received for customers' current savings and investment deposits. A breakdown of expenses provides an understanding of a bank's sources of funding and the corresponding funding cost. The subdivision of expenses is typically based on instruments as well as the maturity structure of funding instruments, such as demand deposits, investment accounts, and special investment accounts. A conventional bank with low expenses and thus low funding costs is clearly better positioned than one with high expenses, as it would be able to intermediate at market rates with a higher profit margin. The smaller deposit-related expenses, however, often involve higher operating expenses. For example, household deposits and investment accounts typically involve lower expenses, but branch networks are needed to collect them, and these are expensive to maintain. This is why some banks prefer funding by large corporate (wholesale) deposits, even if this implies higher profit-sharing costs.

Trading Income

Trading income comprises income from dealings and brokerage businesses as well as income from trading and from investments in securities, foreign currencies, equities, and commodities. This income is mostly due to the difference between the purchase and sale price of the underlying instruments but also includes dividend payments. The stability or sustainability of trading income affects the viability of a bank and is critically related to the quality of a bank's market risk management function, the effectiveness of the corresponding functional processes, and the proper information technology support. Trading assets would normally be disclosed at fair value (marked to market) in the bank's financial statements.

Investment Income

Investment income comprises income from a bank's longer-term equity-type investments, such as equities and interest-bearing (recapitalization or non-trading) bonds held in the bank's long-term investment portfolio, as well as dividend income from subsidiaries and similar types of investments. Proprietary investment income depends on the contractual rate and, for equity investments, on the financial performance of the respective companies. By its nature, the income from equity investments is difficult to predict accurately. Investment assets could be shown on the balance sheet as assets available for sale or assets held to maturity. Marked-to-market income on the revaluation of such assets would then not flow through the income statement but be taken directly to a reserve account in the balance sheet.

Sundry Other Banking-Related Operating Income

Other banking-related operating income could include the following:

- Knowledge-based or fee-based income received from nontraditional banking business such as merchant banking or financial advisory services.
- Fee-based income derived from various services to clients, such as account or fund management services and payment transaction services. This class of income is generally desirable, as it does not imply exposure to any financial risk and does not inherently carry any capital charges.

- Gains (losses) on revaluation of assets, which indicate changes in the value of assets held in a bank's trading book. The trading book includes the bank's position in financial instruments that are intentionally held for short-term resale. Banks take on such positions with the intention of benefiting in the short term from actual or expected differences between their buying and selling prices or from variations in the price or interest rate.
- Foreign exchange gains (losses), which often appear in the income statements of banks in developing countries, since such banks are frequently funded by foreign loans. Gains or losses result from changes in the exchange rate that, depending on whether a bank's net position is long or short and whether the domestic currency has depreciated or appreciated, result in a gain or loss to the bank.

Profit for the Year

Profit for the year is the difference between a bank's asset-related income and expenses. The aim of any bank would normally be to derive stable and growing operating income from its core business. In the case of an Islamic bank, table 7.1 can be rearranged to include "depositors' share of profits" under expenses, providing a more transparent view of operating expenditure.

General and Administrative Expenses

General and administrative expenses include costs related to staff, rent and utilities, auditing and consulting, computer and information technology systems, and general administration. Impairment provisions, included in operating expenses, have the most significant impact on the cost of intermediation and are one of the most controllable items. The level of operating expenses is generally related to a bank's efficiency. Efficient management of these expenses requires balancing short-term cost-minimization strategies with investments in human and physical resources—especially the banking technology necessary for effective management of banking risks and for long-term maintenance of the bank's competitive position.

Salaries and staff-related expenses, such as social security, pensions, and other benefits, are normally the largest cost item for a bank, because banking is a knowledge- and staff-intensive business. Computers and information technology–related expenses, such as software licenses and application system development and maintenance, are also becoming major expense items, especially in modern or internationally oriented banks that are critically dependent on information support for identifying market opportunities, for processing transactions, and for managing and reporting risk.

Provisions for Losses or Impairment

Provisions for losses or impairment are expenses related to the credit risk inherent in granting investing assets and long-term partnerships. Provisions are made to compensate for the impaired value of the related investing and financing assets and profits due. They may include write-offs and recoveries (that is, amounts recovered on assets previously written off), or these items may be shown as a separate line in the income statement. The exact position of investing and financing impairments on a bank's income statement depends on the tax treatment of provisions. In countries where the provisions before taxation are not allowed, loss provisions normally appear after taxation. This category also comprises loss provisions for all other assets where the value of the asset could be impaired; for example, the assets in a bank's investment portfolio. In many countries, prudential requirements mandate that a bank carry assets at the lower of the nominal value or the market value (in which case, loss provisions need to be made) and recognize any appreciation in value only when the investment is liquidated.

Depreciation

Depreciation is a cost due to the reduction in value of a bank's fixed assets. It is conceptually similar to provisions. Banks typically depreciate buildings over 25 to 50 years, movable assets and office equipment over three to five years, and computers over two to three years.

When analyzing a bank's income structure, an analyst should give appropriate consideration to and acquire an understanding of the following aspects:

- Trends in and the composition and accuracy of reported earnings;
- The quality, composition, and level of income and expense components;
- Dividend pay-out and earnings retention;
- Major sources of income and the most profitable business areas;
- The manner and extent to which accrued but uncollected interest is absorbed into income, in particular when such interest relates to loans that are or should be placed into risk categories of substandard or worse;

- The extent to which collateral values (rather than operating cash flows) are the basis for decisions to capitalize interest or roll over extensions of credit;
- Any income or expenditure recognition policies that distort earnings;
- The effect of intergroup transactions, especially those related to the transfer of earnings and asset-liability valuations.

INCOME STRUCTURE AND EARNINGS QUALITY

In today's environment, markets that have traditionally been the sole domain of conventional banks have opened up to competition from other institutions. Banks, in turn, have diversified into nontraditional markets and no longer perform a simple intermediation function—that is, deposit taking and lending. In fact, an overview of the industry's profit structure in most developed countries reveals that the traditional banking business is only marginally profitable and that income from other sources has become a significant contributor to the bottom line. Bank profitability appears to be largely attributable to fee income generated from knowledge-based activities, including merchant banking, corporate financing, and advisory services and from trading-based activities in securities, equities, foreign exchange, and money markets.

This change in the profit structure of banks has had the effect of improving profitability without increasing the traditional credit risk that results from investing and financing portfolios. For example, many blue-chip corporate clients are increasingly able to attract funding in their own name through the issuance of commercial paper. Instead of conventional banks maintaining large corporate loans on their balance sheets, banks increasingly underwrite or service issues of their large corporate clients or perform a market-making function. Doing so generates fee income without increasing credit risk exposure. However, income generated in this manner (for example, through securities trading and merchant banking) is by its nature less stable and predictable because it depends on market conditions and trading performance. The trading portfolio is also subject to market risk, which can be substantial.

Components of Income

The analysis of profitability starts by considering the structure of a bank's income and its components (see table 7.2)—investing and financing asset income, transactions-based fee income, trading income, and other sources of income—and the trends over the observation period.

TABLE 7.2   Percentage Composition of Islamic Products' Revenues over Time (Percent)

Financing and investing assets	2001	2002	2003	2004	2005	2006
Financing assets						
Commodities *murabahat*	39.07	36.74	35.18	26.91	23.73	28.85
Vehicles *murabahat*	15.13	17.14	18.72	14.87	10.66	9.46
Istisnah	27.94	25.84	20.94	13.42	8.04	5.85
Ijarah	1.41	3.83	6.04	9.80	11.15	12.94
Total financing assets	83.54	79.74	80.88	65.00	53.58	57.10
Investing assets						
Musharakah	10.06	11.03	8.20	7.39	8.71	9.36
Mudarabah	3.64	3.91	2.88	3.26	3.99	6.86
Wakalah	0.36	2.00	2.55	1.02	2.92	9.51
Sukuks	0	0	0	0	3.13	8.65
Investment funds	0	0.19	2.56	5.26	4.62	1.66
Others	0.76	1.59	0.89	1.21	0.55	2.30
Total investing assets	14.83	18.71	17.08	18.13	23.91	38.33
Investment in companies						
Dividend income	0.60	0.86	1.34	1.42	1.99	1.60
Loss on trading investments	0	0	0	0	−0.15	−1.45
Gain on sale of investments carried at fair value through income statement	1.03	0.69	0.69	15.45	5.98	6.57
(Loss) gain on revaluation of investments carried at fair value through income statement	0	0	0	0	14.70	−2.16
Total investment in companies	1.63	1.55	2.03	16.87	22.51	4.56
Total income from Islamic financing and investing assets	100.00	100.00	100.00	100.00	100.00	100.00

The information contained in a bank's income statement provides an understanding of the institution's business focus and the structure and stability of its profits. In order to facilitate a comparison between different types of banking institutions, various income statement items, such as profit margins, fee and investment income, and overhead are usually expressed as a percentage of total assets. By using the asset base as a common denominator, banks are able to compare themselves to the sector average and to other types of banks. When aggregated, such

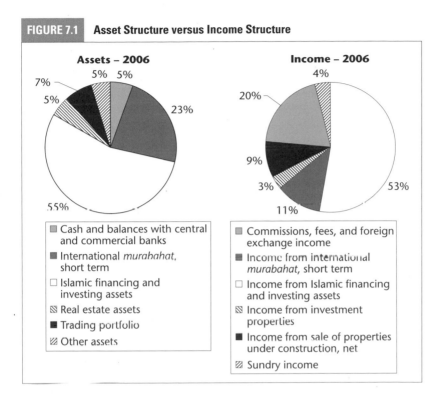

FIGURE 7.1   **Asset Structure versus Income Structure**

Assets – 2006

7% 5% 5% 5% 23% 55%

- ▣ Cash and balances with central and commercial banks
- ▪ International *murabahat,* short term
- ▢ Islamic financing and investing assets
- ▧ Real estate assets
- ▪ Trading portfolio
- ▨ Other assets

Income – 2006

4% 20% 9% 3% 11% 53%

- ▣ Commissions, fees, and foreign exchange income
- ▪ Income from international *murabahat,* short term
- ▢ Income from Islamic financing and investing assets
- ▧ Income from investment properties
- ▪ Income from sale of properties under construction, net
- ▨ Sundry income

information can also highlight changes taking place within a peer group or the banking sector.

Figure 7.1 illustrates the composition of a bank's gross income. Such a graph enables an analyst to determine the quality and stability of a bank's profit, including its sources and any changes in their structure. The purpose of this comparison is to determine exactly how the assets of a bank are engaged and whether or not the income generated is commensurate with the proportion of assets committed to each specific asset category (in other words, whether the income is earned where the energy is spent). Assets should normally be engaged in product categories that provide the highest income at an acceptable level of risk. The same analysis can be performed to identify categories of assets that might be generating proportionately lower yields.

Similarly, liabilities make up the source of funding to which various expenses are related. An analytical comparison of classes of expenses with related liability categories highlights a bank's exposure to specific sources of funding and reveals whether structural changes are taking place in its sources of funding. A similar type of graph and analysis can be used to assess whether or not the components of the total expenditures are of the same proportions as the related liabilities. Expensive categories of funding would be clearly highlighted on such a graph, and the reasons for the specific funding decisions would need to be explained. In the long term, this type of analysis would be able to highlight if and what sort of structural changes are taking place in the income and expenditure structure of a bank and whether or not they are justified from the profitability perspective.

Figure 7.2 illustrates the next step: the analysis of how a bank's income covers its operating expenses. In the case illustrated, as expected, the income from Islamic assets contributes significantly to the bank's profitability and its capacity to cover its operating costs. Both the gross income and the operating expenses have shown proportionate growth in the observation period, with expenses now almost equaling core Islamic asset income. The bank's core income has remained fairly stable (although the structure of which assets generated the income has changed). In conventional banking terms, non-core fee and trading income is generally considered to be less stable than core operating (that is, intermediation) income.

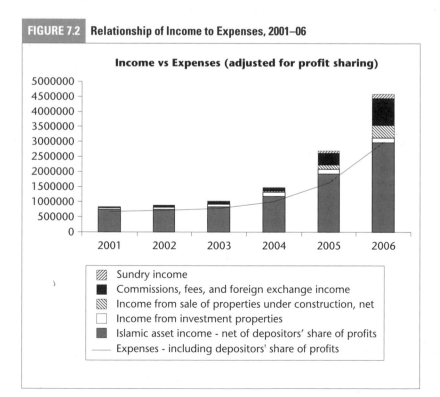

FIGURE 7.2 Relationship of Income to Expenses, 2001–06

Operating expenses are one of the items on a bank's income statement that can be controlled. One acceptable reason for the increase in operating expenses can always be that required investments in human resources and banking infrastructure are expected to pay off in the future. If no such reasons can be found, the bank should be asked to rethink its business strategy.

Internal Performance Measurement System

In such an intensively competitive business, modern banks can no longer afford to carry insufficiently profitable products, services, or lines of businesses. International banks and financial conglomerates especially must organize their internal relationships in a way that enables them to establish the exact contribution to the bottom line of their many constituent parts. In the last decade, more refined systems for measuring profitability and performance have been developed to address this need.

The conclusions drawn by internal performance measurement systems directly affect the products offered and their pricing and can shape the bank's decision to enter or exit particular products or services. Internal measurement techniques usually take into account the underlying risks (which may negatively affect the bank's expenses). Therefore, they enhance the bank's risk management techniques and the application of a consistent incentive compensation system based on achievement rather than on meritocracy.

A good performance measurement framework comprises a number of elements, including an effective organization that allows a clear allocation of income and expenses to business units related to different lines of a bank's business, products, or market segments; an internal transfer pricing system to measure the contribution of various business units to the bottom line; and an effective and consistent means to incorporate the elements of risk into the performance measurement framework. Once the net contributions are known, by business lines, products, or markets, it can be clearly established which customer segments are the most promising and which products should be scrutinized concerning their revenue-generating capacity. A good performance measurement framework also allows analysis of the net contribution that a relationship with a large customer makes to the bank's bottom line.

Internal Transfer Pricing System

The internal transfer pricing system refers to the cost of funds as they are moved from one business unit to another. A sophisticated internal transfer pricing system also covers the allocation of overhead costs to business units and includes transfer prices for internal services such as accounting or legal services. Internal transfer prices could, in principle, reflect market prices, including maturities, and the repricing characteristics of the corresponding assets or liabilities. In practice, most banks choose a weighted average based on their specific funding mix. For consistent application of such a system, a bank must also have a supporting management accounting system.

There are a number of ways to incorporate the risk element into this framework. For the lending function, as an example, the internal cost of funds could reflect the credit risk of the asset being funded, with a higher transfer price being allocated to lower-quality assets. Assets with higher risk could be expected to generate higher returns. Most banks apply a uniform transfer price for all assets, and the risk element is accommodated by requiring higher returns on lower-quality loans.

Another step is to determine how much equity should be assigned to each of the different business or product lines. The key issue is not to determine the right amount of capital to be assigned to each business unit, but to assign equity to all businesses in a consistent manner and based on the same principles. In practice, it is often unnecessary to measure risk using sophisticated modeling techniques for all bank business lines and products in order to determine the appropriate coefficients, and in any case it is nearly impossible to do it in a practical, consistent, and meaningful manner. Instead, banks typically use much simpler calculations of return on risk equity. A practical approach followed by some conventional banks is to use the weights provided under the Basel Accord (IFSB regulations can be substituted) as a basis for calculations.

Transfer pricing should be scrutinized when the bank belongs to a banking group or a holding company, especially if the group is domiciled abroad. In some cases, internal transfer prices have been set that allow the parent to take profits from a bank, for example, by charging more than the applicable market price for funds borrowed by the bank from other business units or members of the conglomerate or by paying less than the market price for funds provided by the same bank. Such cases are especially frequent in countries where there are limits to or complications with dividend repatriation.

PROFITABILITY INDICATORS AND RATIO ANALYSIS

Profit is the bottom line or ultimate performance result showing the net effects of bank policies and activities in a financial year. The trends in stability and growth of profit are the best indicators of a bank's performance

TABLE 7.3 Profitability Ratios, 2001–06
(Percent)

Profitability ratios	2001	2002	2003	2004	2005	2006
Profit as a percent of total assets (ROA)	1.0	0.9	1.0	1.5	2.5	2.4
Expenses as a percent of total assets	1.4	1.4	1.2	1.5	1.7	1.9
Gross income as a percent of total assets	5.4	4.5	4.5	4.8	6.3	7.1
Basic and diluted earnings per share attributable to shareholders of the parent	1.52	1.58	2.32	4.00	0.59	0.71
Profit as a percent of total equity (ROE)	12.3	10.6	14.0	15.4	27.7	17.9
Expenses as a percent of gross income	26.2	30.9	26.3	30.8	26.4	27.0
Provisions and impairments as a percent of expenses	16.5	9.5	−16.6	19.6	18.3	6.2
Expenses, including amounts owed to depositors, as a percent of total assets	4.4	3.6	3.5	3.3	3.8	4.6
Expenses, including amounts owed to depositors, as a percent of gross income	81.7	80.9	76.7	68.6	60.4	65.4
Amount						
Expenses, including amounts owed to depositors	681,525	713,580	785,949	1,008,985	1,629,654	2,992,492

in both the past and the future. Profitability is usually measured by all or part of a set of financial ratios, as shown in table 7.3.

Figures 7.3 and 7.4 illustrate another way of viewing trends in the level of operating expenses in relation to total assets and gross operating income. This approach could provide the analyst with information on the relationship between a bank's expenses and earning capacity, as well as on whether or not the bank has optimized its potential. Income and expenses are presented in relation to total assets. When compared with industry norms, such a view could yield important conclusions— for example, that a bank's expenses are high because it is overstaffed.

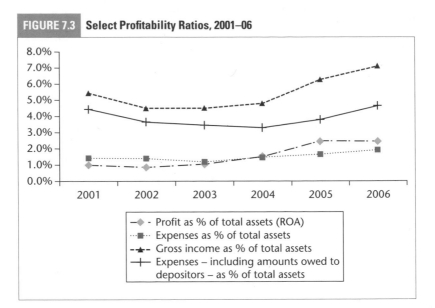

FIGURE 7.3 Select Profitability Ratios, 2001–06

FIGURE 7.4 Additional Profitability Ratios, 2001-06

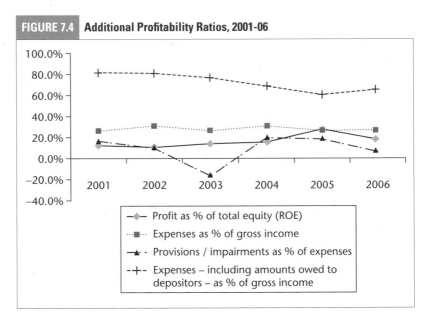

The ratio of operating expenses including amounts owed to depositors, to gross operating income is also very useful, as it clearly indicates the bank's profitability.

Key indicators include the return on average equity, which measures the rate of return on shareholder investment, and the return on assets, which measures the efficiency of use of the bank's potential. Other ratios measure the profitability of a bank's core business (for example, margin ratios), the contribution to profit of various types of activities, the efficiency with which the bank operates, and the stability of its profits. Ratios are observed over a period of time in order to detect trends in profitability. An analysis of changes of various ratios over time reveals changes in bank policies and strategies or in its business environment.

Numerous factors may influence a bank's profitability. In some cases, inflation may increase operating costs faster than income. Marking the value of assets to market requires that unrealized gains are recognized as income; since these gains are yet to be realized, this may negatively affect the quality of earnings. Given the traditional fixed margin on which banks operate, a change in the level of their profit rates will trigger changes in the gross profit. Because banks are influenced by the high level of competition in the banking sector, many have made significant investments in infrastructure-related assets, especially with regard to information technology. Investments such as these have both increased the overhead cost of banking and negatively affected profitability.

Viewed in the context of the financial items to which they are related, operating ratios enable an analyst to assess the efficiency with which an institution generates income. Industry efficiency norms facilitate a comparison between individual banks and the banking system. A review of investment and financing income allows an analyst to determine the return on the loan assets. Similarly, a comparison of investment account expenses indicates the relative cost of "funding."

The ratios also can be used in a broader context. The cost and revenue structure of the banking system can be assessed by calculating and analyzing provisions and the profit-loss margin to gross income; investment income to investments; and overhead to net funding income. The value added by the banking system can be determined by calculating net income after taxes in relation to total average assets (that is, the return on average assets) and net income after taxes in relation to owner equity (that is, the return on equity).

Modern bankers pay a great deal of attention to the message that is revealed by ratio analysis. Banks usually manage profitability by trying to beat market averages and keep profits steady and predictable; which in turn attracts investors. Ratios are therefore extremely useful tools, but as with other analytical methods, they must be used with judgment and caution, since they alone do not provide complete answers about the bottom-line performance of banks. In the short run, many tricks can be used to make bank ratios look good in relation to industry standards.

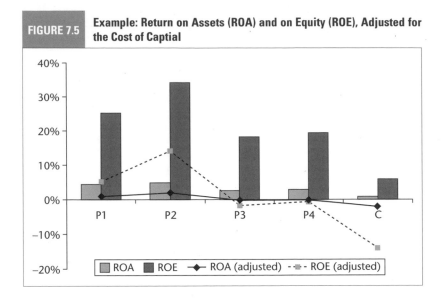

FIGURE 7.5 Example: Return on Assets (ROA) and on Equity (ROE), Adjusted for the Cost of Captial

An assessment of the operations and management of a bank should therefore be performed to provide a check on profitability ratios.

The need to generate stable and increasing profits also implies the need to manage risk. For that reason, asset-liability management has become an almost universally accepted approach to profitability (risk) management. Since capital and profitability are intimately linked, a major objective of asset-liability management is to ensure sustained profitability so that a bank can maintain and augment its capital resources.

Bottom-line profitability ratios—the return on equity and assets— indicate the net results of a bank's operations in a financial year or over a period of time. Figure 7.5 illustrates how to adjust these profitability ratios by deducting an assumed cost of capital to show the real profit of a bank. By comparing the return on equity to the after-tax return on risk-free government securities, one can determine whether equity invested in the bank has earned any additional returns, as compared to risk-free investments. The result may disclose that it is better for shareholders simply to invest in risk-free government securities or for the bank concerned to cease its intermediation function and close its doors.

8

Credit Risk Management

redit or counterparty risk is the chance that a debtor or issuer of a financial instrument—whether an individual, a company, or a country—will not repay principal and other investment-related cash flows according to the terms specified in a credit agreement. Inherent to banking, it means that payments may be delayed or not made at all, which can cause cash flow problems and affect a bank's liquidity. Despite innovation in the financial services sector, more than 70 percent of a bank's balance sheet generally relates to this aspect of risk management. For this reason, credit risk is the principal cause of bank failures.

The techniques used by Islamic banks to mitigate credit risk are similar to those used by conventional banks. However, in the absence of credit-rating agencies, banks rely on the client's track record with the bank and gather information about the creditworthiness of the client through informal sources and local community networks.

FORMAL POLICIES FOR MANAGING CREDIT RISK

Bank supervisors place considerable importance on formal policies laid down by the board of directors and diligently implemented or administered by management. A lending or financing policy should outline the scope and allocation of a bank's credit facilities and the manner in which a credit portfolio is managed—that is, how investment and financing assets are originated, appraised, supervised, and collected. A good policy

Key Messages

- Credit risk management lies at the heart of survival for the vast majority of banks.
- Credit risk can be limited by reducing connected-party lending and large exposures to related parties.
- Asset classification and subsequent provisioning against possible losses affect not only the value of the investing and financing asset portfolio but also the underlying value of a bank's capital.
- The profile of customers (*who* has been lent to) must be transparent.
- Risks associated with the key banking products (*what* has been lent) must be understood and managed.
- The maturity profile of investing and financing asset products (for *how long* the loans have been made) interacts strongly with liquidity risk management.
- A bank's capacity for risk management contributes significantly to the quality of its risk management practices.

is not overly restrictive and allows for the presentation of proposals to the board that officers believe are worthy of consideration but that do not fall within the parameters of written guidelines. Flexibility is needed to allow for fast reaction and early adaptation to changing conditions in a bank's mix of assets and the market environment.

Virtually all regulatory environments prescribe minimum standards for managing credit risk; see box 8.1 for the Islamic Financial Services Board (IFSB) principles of credit risk. These cover the identification of existing and potential risks, the definition of policies that express the bank's risk management philosophy, and the setting of parameters within which credit risk will be controlled.

Specific measures typically include three kinds of policies. One set aims to *limit or reduce credit risk.* These include policies on concentration and large exposures, diversification, lending to connected parties, and overexposure to sectors or regions. The second aims to *classify assets.* These mandate periodic evaluation of the collectibility of the portfolio of credit instruments. The third aims to *provision loss* or make allowances at a level adequate to absorb anticipated loss.

POLICIES TO REDUCE CREDIT RISK

In an effort to reduce or limit credit risk, regulators pay close attention to three issues: exposure to a single customer, related-party financing, and overexposure to a geographic area or economic sector.

BOX 8.1   **IFSB Principles of Credit Risk**

Principle 2.1. [Islamic financial institutions] shall have in place a *strategy* for financing, using the various Islamic instruments in compliance with *Shariah*, whereby they recognize the potential credit exposures that may arise at different stages of the various financing agreements.

Principle 2.2. [Islamic financial institutions] shall carry out a *due diligence review* in respect of counterparties prior to deciding on the choice of an appropriate Islamic financing instrument.

Principle 2.3. [Islamic financial institutions] shall have in place appropriate *methodologies* for measuring and *reporting the credit risk exposures arising* under each Islamic financing instrument.

Principle 2.4. [Islamic financial institutions] shall have in place *Shariah*-compliant *credit risk–mitigating techniques* appropriate for each Islamic financing instrument.

Single-Customer Exposure

Modern prudential regulations usually stipulate that a bank refrain from investing in or extending credit to any individual entity or related group of entities in excess of an amount representing a prescribed percentage of the bank's capital and reserves. Most countries impose a single-customer exposure limit of between 10 and 25 percent of capital. The threshold at which reporting to supervisory authorities becomes necessary should normally be set somewhere below the maximum limit. Supervisors can then devote special attention to exposures above the threshold and require banks to take precautionary measures before concentration becomes excessively risky.

The main difficulty in defining exposure is to quantify the extent to which less direct forms of credit exposure should be included within the exposure limit. As a matter of principle, contingent liabilities and credit substitutes, such as guarantees, acceptances, letters of credit, and all future commitments, should be included, although the treatment of specific instruments may vary. For example, a financial obligation guarantee may be treated differently than a performance risk guarantee. The treatment of collateral is another contentious issue, as the valuation of collateral can be highly subjective. As a matter of prudence, collateral should not be considered when determining the size of an exposure.

Another conceptual question is the definition of the term "single client." According to international practice, a single client is an individual, legal person, or a connected group to which a bank is exposed. Single clients are mutually associated or control other clients, either directly or indirectly, normally through a voting right of at least 15–20 percent, a dominant shareholding, or the capacity to control policy making and management. In addition, the exposure to a number of single clients may represent a cumulative risk if financial interdependence exists and their expected source of repayment is the same (see figure 8.1 for a hypothetical example).

In practical terms, a large exposure usually indicates a bank's commitment to support a specific client. Here the risk is that a bank that extends credit to a large corporate client may not be objective in appraising the risks associated with such credit.

The management of large exposures involves an additional aspect: the bank's ability to identify common or related ownership, to exercise effective control, and to rely on common cash flows to meet its own obligations. Particularly in the case of large clients, banks must pay attention to the completeness and adequacy of information about the debtor. Bank credit officers should monitor events affecting large clients and their performance on an ongoing basis, regardless of whether or not they are meeting their obligations. When external events present a cause for concern, credit officers should request additional information from the

FIGURE 8.1 **Exposure to 20 Largest Exposures (Hypothetical Example)**

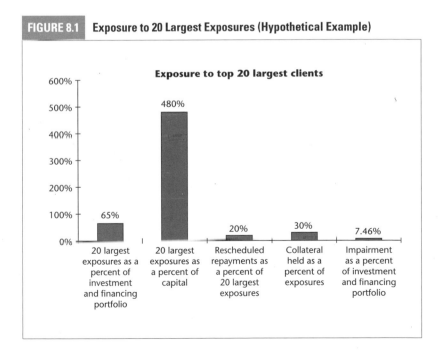

debtor. If there is any doubt that the person or group receiving the investment or financing might have difficulty meeting its obligation to the bank, the concerns should be raised with a higher level of credit risk management, and a contingency plan on how to address the issue should be developed.

Related-Party Financing

Dealing with connected parties is a particularly dangerous form of credit risk exposure. Related parties typically include a bank's parent, major shareholders, subsidiaries, affiliate companies, directors, and executive officers. Such parties are in a position to exert control over or influence a bank's policies and decision making, especially concerning credit decisions. A bank's ability to identify and track extensions of credit to insiders is crucial (see table 8.1).

The issue is whether credit decisions are made on a rational basis and according to the bank's policies and procedures. An additional

TABLE 8.1   Related-Party Lending

Type of related entity	Amount of loans	Amount of loans not in the A (pass) category	Amount of loans, as percentage of qualifying capital	Amount of loans not in the A (pass) category, as percentage of qualifying capital	Collateral held
Shareholders holding more than 5 percent of shares					
Shareholders holding less than 5 percent of shares					
Shareholders of any shareholders					
Board of directors					
Executive management					
Entities controlled by the bank					
Entities that have control over the bank					
Close relative to any of the above					
Total					

concern is whether credit is based on market terms or on terms that are more favorable with regard to amount, maturity, rate, and collateral than those provided to the general public.

Most regulators establish limits for related parties, typically stipulating that total credit to related parties cannot exceed a certain percentage of Tier 1 or total qualifying capital. If prudential regulations have not established such a limit, the bank should maintain one as a matter of board policy. Prudent banking practice would require board approval of all facilities extended to related parties.

Overexposure to Geographic Areas or Economic Sectors

Another dimension of risk concentration is the exposure of a bank to a single sector of the economy or a narrow geographic region. This makes a bank vulnerable to weaknesses in a particular industry or region and poses a risk that it will suffer from simultaneous failures among several clients for similar reasons. This concern is particularly relevant for regional and specialized banks or banks in small countries with narrow economic profiles, such as those with predominantly agricultural economies or exporters of a single commodity.

It is often difficult to assess the exposure of a bank to various sectors of the economy, as most bank reporting systems do not produce such information. For example, a holding company of a large diversified group could be used to finance projects in various industries in which the company operates. In any case, banks should have well-developed systems to monitor sector risks, assess the impact of adverse trends on the quality of their portfolio and income statements, and deal with increased risk.

Banks engaged in international lending face additional risks, the most important of which are country (or sovereign) and transfer risks. The country risks encompass the entire spectrum of risks posed by the macroeconomic, political, and social environment of a country that may affect the performance of clients. Transfer risks are the difficulties that a client might have in obtaining the foreign exchange needed to service a bank's obligations. The classification of international loans should normally include both country and transfer risks. A bank may be asked to provision for international loans on a loan-by-loan basis, whereby the level of necessary provisions is raised to accommodate additional risk. Alternatively, a bank may determine aggregate exposures to country and transfer risks on a country-by-country basis and provide special reserves to accommodate risk exposures.

CREDIT RISK SPECIFIC TO ISLAMIC BANKS

The unique characteristics of the financial instruments offered by Islamic financial institutions result in the following special credit risks (for a detailed explanation, please refer to IFSB Standard on Risk Management for Islamic Financial Institutions and Iqbal and Mirakhor 2007).

■ In *murabahah* transactions, Islamic banks are exposed to credit risks when the bank delivers the asset to the client but does not receive payment from the client in time. In case of a nonbinding *murabahah*, where the client has the right to refuse delivery of the product purchased by the bank, the bank is further exposed to price and market risks.

■ In *bay' al-salaam or istisnah* contracts, the bank is exposed to the risk of failure to supply on time, to supply at all, or to supply the quality of goods as contractually specified. Such failure could result in a delay or default in payment, or in delivery of the product, and can expose Islamic banks to financial losses of income as well as capital.

■ In the case of *mudarabah* investments, where the Islamic bank enters into the *mudarabah* contract as *rab al-mal* (principal) with an external *mudarib* (agent), in addition to the typical principal-agent problems, the Islamic bank is exposed to an enhanced credit risk on the amounts advanced to the *mudarib*. The nature of the *mudarabah* contract is such that it does not give the bank appropriate rights to monitor the *mudarib* or to participate in management of the project, which makes it difficult to assess and manage credit risk. The bank is not in a position to know or decide how the activities of the *mudarib* can be monitored accurately, especially if losses are claimed. This risk is especially present in markets where information asymmetry is high and transparency in financial disclosure by the *mudarib* is low

Credit risk management for Islamic banks is complicated further by additional externalities. Especially in the case of default by the counterparty, Islamic banks are prohibited from charging any accrued interest or imposing any penalty, except in the case of deliberate procrastination. Clients may take advantage by delaying payment, knowing that the bank will not charge a penalty or require extra payments. During the delay, the bank's capital is stuck in a nonproductive activity and the bank's investors-depositors are not earning any income. Another example is where the bank's share in the capital invested through a *mudarabah* or *musharakah* contract is transformed into a debt obligation in case of proven negligence or misconduct of the *mudarib* or the *musharakah's* managing partner. As a result, the rules to recover a debt are applied, and these are different from the rules of *mudarabah* and *musharakah* investment.

Using collateral and pledges as security against credit risk is a common practice among all Islamic banks. The bank might ask the client to post additional collateral before entering into a murabahah transaction. In some cases, the subject matter of murabahah is accepted as collateral. Posting collateral as security is not without difficulties, especially in developing countries. Typical problems include illiquidity of the collateral or inability of the bank to sell the collateral, difficulties in determining the fair market value on a periodic basis, and legal hindrances and obstacles in taking possession of the collateral. Due to weak legal institutions and slow processing, it becomes difficult for the bank to claim the collateral. In addition to collateral, personal and institutional guarantees are also accepted to minimize credit risk.

ANALYZING CREDIT RISK IN THE ASSET PORTFOLIO

The detailed composition of assets usually provides a good picture of a bank's business profile and business priorities as well as the type of intermediation risk that the bank is expected and willing to take. Any analysis should include an overview of *what* products have been invested in, to *whom*, and for *how long*. Figures 8.2 and 8.3 illustrate the customer profile and composition of investment and financing products, and tables 8.2 to 8.4 provide an overview of the customer and maturity profile.

Analysis of the aggregate portfolio should therefore include the following:

- A summary of the major types of investment and financing assets, including details of the number of customers or customer types, average maturity, and average earnings;
- A review of the distribution of the portfolio, including various perspectives on the number of investment and financing assets and total amounts, for example, according to currency, short-term (less than one year) and long-term (more than one year) maturities, industrial or other pertinent economic sectors, state-owned and private clients, and corporate and retail lending;
- A list of government or other guarantees;

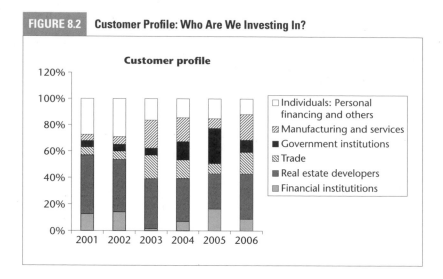

FIGURE 8.2 Customer Profile: Who Are We Investing In?

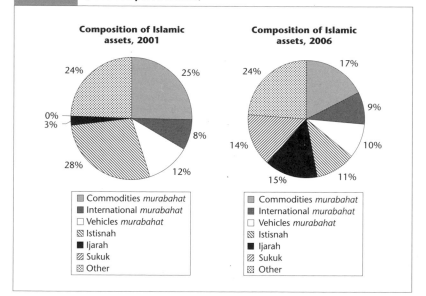

FIGURE 8.3 Composition of Islamic Products: What Are We Investing In? (2006 Compared to 2001)

TABLE 8.2   Customer Profile: Who Are We Investing In?

Customer assets	2001	2002	2003	2004	2005	2006
Financial institutitions	1,383,365	1,762,418	236,178	1,432,294	5,113,612	3,602,506
Real estate	4,839,918	4,900,108	5,456,906	6,439,081	8,362,403	13,869,026
Trade	667,627	810,398	2,609,638	2,812,415	2,406,786	6,633,344
Government	521,217	642,546	777,502	2,799,965	8,370,227	3,719,212
Manufacturing and services	513,257	730,259	3,106,754	3,626,226	2,314,940	7,933,024
Personal financing and others	2,999,433	3,621,295	2,380,118	2,896,943	4,723,195	4,798,386
Total	10,924,817	12,467,024	14,567,096	20,006,924	31,291,163	40,555,498

TABLE 8.3   Composition of Products: What Are We Investing In?
(Percent of total)

Assets	2001	2002	2003	2004	2005	2006
Financing						
Commodities *murabahat*	25	20	21	18	17	17
International *murabahat*	8	9	8	14	12	9
Vehicles *murabahat*	11	13	13	12	10	10
Real estate *murabahat*	7	7	5	5	6	9
Total *murabahat*	52	55	47	48	45	45
Istisnah	28	21	17	11	8	11
Ijarah	3	0	17	24	16	15
Others	1	1	0	0	0	0
Total financing assets	83	76	81	83	70	71
Investing						
Sukuk	0	0	0	0	5	14
Musharakat	10	9	9	9	19	7
Mudarabat	4	5	7	7	7	8
Investment funds	2	5	0	0	0	0
Wakalat	0	0	3	1	0	0
Gross investing assets	17	19	19	17	30	29
Projects in Progress	0.08	4.21				
Total	100	100	100	100	100	100

TABLE 8.4   Maturity Profile of Total Assets: For How Long Are We Investing?

Maturity profile of assets	2001	2002	2003	2004	2005	2006
Less than 3 months	8,440,268	9,306,606	10,272,647	11,497,545	15,203,780	31,725,644
3 months to 1 year	1,748,961	1,779,905	2,946,684	6,068,174	5,896,048	10,908,547
Over 1 year	5,144,749	8,511,279	9,558,988	13,047,642	21,898,451	21,799,745
	15,333,978	19,597,790	22,778,319	30,613,361	42,998,279	64,433,936

- A review of accounts by risk classification;
- An analysis of nonperforming accounts.

The portfolio reflects a bank's market position and demand, its business and risk strategy, and its credit extension capabilities. When feasible, the portfolio review (examination) should include a random sampling of accounts so that a major percentage of the total portfolio and a statistically significant number of accounts are covered. A detailed credit portfolio review should include the following:

- All customers with an aggregate exposure larger than 5 percent of the bank's capital;
- All exposures to shareholders and connected parties;
- All investment and financing assets for which the financing schedule has been rescheduled or otherwise altered since the granting of the facility;
- All investment and financing assets classified as substandard, doubtful, or loss.

In each case, a credit review should consider documentation in the client's file and be accompanied by a discussion of the client's business, near-term prospects, and credit history with the responsible credit officer (see box 8.2). When the total amount due exceeds 5 percent of a bank's capital, the analysis should also consider the client's business plans for the future and the potential consequences for debt service capacity and principal repayment.

The specific objective of these reviews is to assess the likelihood that the credit will be repaid, as well as whether or not the classification of the loan proposed by the bank is adequate. Other considerations include the quality of collateral held and the ability of the client's business to generate the necessary cash.

BOX 8.2	Content of an Investment and Financing Asset Review File

For each of the assets reviewed, a summary file should be made showing the following:

- Entrepreneur's name and line of business;
- Use of proceeds;
- Date credit granted;
- Maturity date, amount, currency, and terms of the investment;
- Principal source of repayment;
- The nature and value of collateral or security (or valuation basis, if a fixed asset);
- Total outstanding liabilities in cases where the bank is absorbing the credit risk;
- Delinquency or nonperformance, if any;
- Description of monitoring activities undertaken;
- Financial information, including current financial statements and other pertinent information;
- Specific provisions that are required and available

Interbank Deposits

Interbank deposits are an important category of bank assets. They may account for a significant percentage of a bank's balance sheet, particularly in countries that lack convertibility but allow citizens and economic agents to maintain foreign exchange deposits. Other reasons for interbank deposits are to facilitate fund transfers and the settlement of securities transactions or to take advantage of the ability of other banks to perform certain services more economically or efficiently due to their size or geographic location.

A review of interbank (lending) transactions typically focuses on the following aspects:

- The establishment and observation of counterparty credit limits, including a description of the existing credit limit policy;
- Any interbank credits for which specific provisions should be made;
- The method and accuracy of reconciliation of nostro and vostro accounts;
- Any interbank credits with terms of pricing that are not the market norm;
- The concentration of interbank exposure with a detailed listing of banks and amounts outstanding as well as limits.

Interbank deposits should be treated like any other credit risk exposure. A bank's policy should require that correspondent banks be reviewed carefully with regard to their exposure limits as well as their ability to provide adequate collateral. Banks from regulatory environments that are strict, well supervised, and in tune with international standards are customarily treated as a lesser risk than banks from developing countries.

Off-Balance-Sheet Commitments

All off-balance-sheet commitments that incur credit exposure should be reviewed. An assessment should be made of the adequacy of procedures for analyzing credit risk and the supervision and administration of off-balance-sheet credit instruments, such as guarantees. An off-balance-sheet portfolio review should be carried out with the same principles and in a manner similar to a portfolio review. The key objective is to assess the ability of the client to meet particular financial commitments in a timely manner.

Nonperforming Assets

Nonperforming assets are assets that are not generating income. As a first step, loans are often considered to be nonperforming when principal or interest on them is due and left unpaid for 90 days or more (this period may vary by jurisdiction). Asset classification and provisioning entail much more than simply looking at amounts overdue. The investment cash flow and overall ability to repay amounts owed are significantly more important than whether the payment is overdue or not.

For financial reporting purposes, the principal balance outstanding, rather than delinquent payments, is used to identify a nonperforming portfolio. The nonperforming portfolio indicates the quality of the total portfolio and ultimately of a bank's credit decisions. Another indicator is the bank's collection ratio.

When assessed within the context of nonperforming assets, the aggregate level of provisions indicates the capacity of a bank to accommodate credit risk. The analysis of a nonperforming portfolio should cover a number of aspects, as follows:

■ Classifications, broken down by type of customer and branch of economic activity, to determine overall trends and whether or not all customers are affected equally;
■ Reasons for the deterioration of the portfolio quality, which can help to identify possible measures to reverse a given trend;
■ A list of nonperforming accounts, including all relevant details, assessed on a case-by-case basis, to determine if the situation is reversible, exactly

what can be done to improve repayment capacity, and whether or not workout or collection plans have been used;

■ Provision levels, to determine the bank's capacity to withstand defaults;

■ The impact on profit- and loss-sharing accounts, to determine exactly how the bank will be affected by the deterioration in asset quality.

There can be a number of reasons for deteriorating portfolio quality. It is unavoidable that banks make mistakes in judgment. However, for most failed banks, the real problems are systemic in nature and rooted in the bank's credit culture. Box 8.3 illustrates the kinds of problems that indicate distortion in a bank's credit culture.

ASSET CLASSIFICATION AND LOSS PROVISIONING POLICIES

Asset classification is a process whereby an asset is assigned a grade for credit risk, which is determined by the likelihood that obligations will be serviced and liquidated according to the terms of the contract. In general, all assets for which a bank is taking a risk should be classified, including advances, accounts receivable, investment and financing assets, equity participations, and contingent liabilities.

Asset classification is a key tool of risk management. Assets are classified at the time of origination and then reviewed and reclassified as necessary (according to the degree of credit risk) a few times a year. The review should consider service performance and the client's financial condition. Economic trends and changes in the market for and the price of goods also affect evaluation of loan repayment. Assets classified as "pass" or "watch" are typically reviewed twice a year, while critical assets are reviewed at least each quarter.

Banks determine classifications by themselves but follow standards that are normally set by regulatory authorities. Box 8.4 outlines the standard rules for asset classification that are currently used in most industrial countries.

The primary emphasis is placed on the client's ability and willingness to meet obligations out of prospective operating cash flow. Some jurisdictions require that all credit extended to an individual client should be assigned the same risk classification, while differences in classification should be noted and justified. Other jurisdictions recommend that each asset be assessed on its own merits. In cases where assets may be classified differently depending on whether subjective or objective criteria are used, the more severe classification should generally apply. If supervisory authorities, and in many cases external auditors, assign more stringent classifications than the bank itself, the bank is expected to adjust the classification.

| Box 8.3 | Signs of a Distorted Credit Culture |

In its commercial bank examination manual, the U.S. Federal Reserve system cites the following problems as signs of a distorted credit culture. These principles could also be applied to discover signs of distortion in an Islamic financial institution:

Self-dealing arises when too much credit is extended to directors and large share-holders or to their interests, compromising sound credit principles under pressure from related parties. Self-dealing has been the key issue in a significant number of problem banks.

Compromise of credit principles arises when loans that have undue risk or are extended under unsatisfactory terms are granted with full knowledge that they violate sound credit principles. The reasons for the compromise typically include self-dealing, anxiety over income, competitive pressures in the bank's key markets, or personal conflicts of interest.

Anxiety over income arises when concern over earnings outweighs the soundness of lending decisions, underscored by the hope that risk will not materialize or lead to loans with unsatisfactory repayment terms. This is a relatively frequent problem since a loan portfolio is usually a bank's key revenue-producing asset.

Incomplete credit information indicates that loans have been extended without proper appraisal of borrower creditworthiness.

Complacency is a frequent cause of bad loan decisions. Complacency is typically manifested in a lack of adequate supervision of old, familiar borrowers, dependence on oral information rather than reliable and complete financial data, and an optimistic interpretation of known credit weaknesses because the borrower survived a distressed situation in the past. In addition, banks may ignore warning signs regarding the borrower, economy, region, industry, or other relevant factors or fail to enforce repayment agreements, including a lack of prompt legal action.

Lack of effective supervision invariably results in a lack of knowledge about the borrower's affairs over the lifetime of the loan. Consequently, initially sound loans may develop problems and losses because of a lack of effective supervision.

Technical incompetence includes a lack of technical ability among credit officers to analyze financial statements and obtain and evaluate pertinent credit information.

Poor selection of risks typically involves the following: (a) the extension of loans with initially sound financial risk to a level beyond the reasonable payment capacity of the borrower, which is a frequent problem in unstable economies with volatile interest rates; (b) loans where the bank-financed share of the total cost of the project is large relative to the equity investment of the owners and loans for real estate transactions where equity ownership is narrow; (c) loans based on the expectation of successful completion of a business transaction, rather than on the borrower's creditworthiness, and loans made for the speculative purchase of securities or goods; (d) loans to companies operating in economically distressed areas or industries; (e) loans made because of large deposits in a bank, rather than sound net worth of collateral; (f) loans predicated on collateral of problematic liquidation value or collateral loans that lack adequate security margins.

BOX 8.4   Asset Classification Rules

According to international standards, assets are normally classified in the following categories.

Standard or pass. When debt service capacity is considered to be beyond any doubt. In general, assets that are fully secured by cash or cash substitutes (for example, bank certificates of deposit and treasury bills and notes) are usually classified as standard regardless of arrears or other adverse credit factors.

Specially mentioned or watched. Assets with potential weaknesses that may, if not checked or corrected, weaken the asset as a whole or jeopardize the client's capacity to meet obligations in the future. This, for example, includes credit given through an inadequate loan agreement, a lack of control over collateral, or a lack of proper documentation. Clients operating under economic or market conditions that may affect them negatively in the future should receive this classification. This also applies to borrowers with an adverse trend in their operations or an unbalanced position in the balance sheet, but which have not reached a point where repayment is jeopardized.

Substandard. Well-defined credit weaknesses when the primary sources of repayment are insufficient and the bank must look to secondary sources, such as collateral, the sale of a fixed asset, refinancing, or fresh capital. Substandard assets are typically assets whose cash flow may not be sufficient to meet current cash flow commitments; or intermediation to borrowers that are significantly undercapitalized. They may also include short-term assets to borrowers for which the inventory-to-cash cycle is insufficient to repay the debt at maturity. Nonperforming assets that are at least 90 days overdue are normally classified as substandard, as are renegotiated loans and advances for which the borrower has paid delinquent interest from his own funds prior to renegotiations and until sustained performance under a realistic repayment program has been achieved.

Doubtful. Such assets have the same weaknesses as substandard assets, but their collection in full is questionable on the basis of existing facts. The possibility of loss is present, but certain factors that may strengthen the asset defer its classification as a loss until a more exact status may be determined. Nonperforming assets that are at least 180 days past due are also classified as doubtful, unless they are sufficiently secured.

Loss. Certain assets are considered uncollectible and of such little value that the continued definition as bankable assets is not warranted. This classification does not mean that an asset has absolutely no recovery or salvage value, but rather that it is neither practical nor desirable to defer the process of writing it off, even though partial recovery may be possible in the future. Nonperforming assets that are at least one year past due are also classified as losses, unless such assets are very well secured.

In some advanced banking systems, banks use more than one rating level for assets in the category of pass or standard. The objective of this practice is to improve the ability to differentiate among different types of credit and to improve the understanding of the relationship between profitability and rating level.

Asset classification provides a basis for determining the adequate level of provisions for possible losses. Such provisions, together with general loss reserves that are normally counted as Tier 2 capital in conventional banks and are not assigned to specific assets, form the basis for establishing a bank's capacity to absorb losses. In determining an adequate reserve, all significant factors that affect the collectibility of the portfolio should be considered. These factors include the quality of credit policies and procedures, prior loss experiences, quality of management, collection and recovery practices, changes in national and local economic and business conditions, and general economic trends. Assessments of asset value should be performed systematically, consistently over time, and in conformity with objective criteria. They should be supported by adequate documentation.

Loss provisioning may be mandatory or discretionary, depending on the banking system. The tax treatment of provisions also varies considerably from country to country, although many economists believe that provisions should be treated as business expenses for tax purposes. Tax considerations should not, however, influence prudent risk management policies. In some highly developed countries, it is left to the banks to determine the prudent level of provisions. While some merit exists in estimating loss potential on a case-by-case basis, particularly for large clients, it may be more practical to assign a level of required provisions based on each classification category. In many countries, in particular those with fragile economies, regulators have established mandatory levels of provisions that are related to asset classification.

The established level of mandatory provisions is normally determined by certain statistics. In countries where the legal framework for debt recovery is highly developed, such as the United States, approximately 10 percent of substandard assets eventually deteriorate into loss. The percentages for doubtful and loss classifications are approximately 50 and 100 percent, respectively. In developing countries where the legal framework and tradition of collection may be less effective, provisions in the range of 20 to 25 percent for substandard assets may be a more realistic estimate of loss potential. Table 8.5 presents the level of provisions in countries with less developed legal frameworks. Additional charts that the analyst might want to prepare include pie charts on asset classification, loss experience over time as a percentage of assets invested, and provisioning as a percentage of substandard assets.

Two approaches exist for dealing with loss assets. One is to retain them on the books until all remedies for collection have been exhausted. This is typical for banking systems based on the British tradition; in this

TABLE 8.5 Recommended Provisions

Classification	Recommended provisions	Qualification
Pass	1–2 percent	(Tier 2) General loss reserve, if disclosed
Watch	5–10 percent	Specific provision
Substandard	10–30 percent	Specific provision
Doubtful	50–75 percent	Specific provision
Loss	100 percent	Specific provision

case, the level of loss reserve may appear unusually large. The second approach requires all loss assets to be written off promptly against the reserve, that is, be removed from the books. This approach is typical of the U.S. tradition and is more conservative in that loss assets are considered to be not bankable but not necessarily *non*recoverable. By immediately writing off loss assets, the level of the reserve will appear smaller in relation to the outstanding portfolio. In evaluating the level of provisions established by a bank, the analyst must clearly understand whether the bank is aggressively writing off its losses or is simply providing for them.

Estimates of the level of necessary loss provisions include a degree of subjectivity. However, management discretion should be exercised in accordance with established policies and procedures (see appendix B for the IFSB standard on risk management). At a minimum, the following aspects of the overall allowance for losses should be taken into account:

- A survey of the bank's existing provisioning policy and the methodology used to carry it out, considering, in particular, the value attributed to collateral and its legal or operational enforceability;
- An overview of asset classification procedures and the review process, including the time allotted for review;
- Any current factors that are likely to cause losses associated with a bank's portfolio and that differ from the historical experience of loss, including changes in a bank's economic and business conditions or in its clients, external factors, or alterations of bank procedures since the last review;
- A trend analysis over a longer period of time, which serves to highlight any increases in overdue amounts and the impact of such increases;
- An opinion of the adequacy of the current policy and, on the basis of the loans reviewed, extrapolation of additional provisions necessary to bring the bank's total loan-loss provisions in line with International Accounting Standards (IAS).

Workout Procedures

Workout procedures are an important aspect of credit risk management. If timely action is not taken to address problem accounts, opportunities to strengthen or collect on these poor-quality assets may be missed, and losses may accumulate to a point where they threaten a bank's solvency. An assessment of workout procedures should consider the organization of this function, including departments and responsible staff, and assess the performance of the workout units by reviewing attempted and successful recoveries (in terms of both number and volume) and the average time for recovery. The workout methods used and the involvement of senior management should also be evaluated.

During a workout process, each account and client should be considered on its own merits. Typical workout strategies include the following:

- Reducing the credit risk exposure of a bank—for example, by having the client provide additional capital, funds, collateral, or guarantees;
- Working with the client to assess problems and find solutions such as the provision of advice, the development of a program to reduce operating costs or increase earnings, the selling of assets, the design of a restructuring program, or the change in account terms;
- Arranging for a client to be bought or taken over by a more creditworthy party or arranging for some form of joint-venture partnership;
- Liquidating exposure by settling out of court or by taking legal action, calling on guarantees, foreclosing, or liquidating collateral.

REVIEW OF RISK MANAGEMENT CAPACITY

An overall review of credit risk management evaluates a bank's policies and practices for managing credit risk. This entails evaluating a bank's capacity to assess, administer, supervise, enforce, and recover investment and financing assets, advances, guarantees, and other credit instruments. It also entails determining the adequacy of financial information used as the basis for investing in the financial instrument or extending credit.

Investing and Financing Islamic Products

When carrying out its duties on behalf of both depositors, investment account holders, and shareholders, the board of directors must ensure that a bank's investing function fulfills three fundamental objectives: (a) investment and financing assets should be intermediated on a sound and collectible basis; (b) funds should be invested profitably for the benefit of shareholders and the protection of depositors; and (c) the legitimate credit (intermediation) needs of economic agents or households should be satisfied.

The review of investing operations evaluates whether the process meets these criteria. In other words, it is crucial to assess whether investment and financing assets are well structured, policies are well reflected in internal procedures and manuals, staffing is adequate and diligent in following established policies and guidelines, and the information normally available to participants in the process is timely, accurate, and complete. An analyst should question management about any wild fluctuations in asset classes to determine what strategy is being followed. Table 8.6 and figure 8.4 facilitate such analysis.

The integrity and credibility of the process depend on objective credit decisions that ensure an acceptable level of risk in relation to the expected return. A review of the process should analyze credit manuals and other written guidelines applied by various departments of a bank and the capacity and performance of all departments involved in the credit function. It should also cover the origination, appraisal, approval, disbursement, monitoring, collection, and handling procedures for the various credit functions provided by the bank. Specifically, the review should encompass the following:

- A detailed credit analysis and approval process, including samples of client application forms, internal credit summary forms, internal credit manuals, and client files;
- Criteria for approving client's requests, for determining return policies and limits for assets at various levels of the bank's management, and for handling assets distributed through the branch network;
- Collateral policy for all types of financial instruments and actual methods and practices concerning revaluation of collateral and files related to collateral;
- Administration and monitoring procedures, including responsibilities, compliance, and controls;
- A process for handling exceptions.

Human Resources

Clearly defined levels of authority for credit approval help to ensure that decisions are prudent and within defined parameters. All staff involved in credit origination, appraisal, supervision, and other credit processes need to be trained in Islamic products and fundamental *Shariah* principles

TABLE 8.6   Year-on-Year Fluctuations in Growth of Portfolio Components

Asset	2001	2002	2003	2004	2005	2006
Financing						
Commodities *murabahat*	Base	−9%	23%	16%	49%	33%
International *murabahat*	Base	21%	2%	152%	36%	−4%
Vehicles *murabahat*	Base	28%	14%	30%	26%	29%
Real estate *murabahat*	Base	11%	−6%	19%	106%	84%
Total *murabahat*	**Base**	**7%**	**13%**	**42%**	**45%**	**29%**
Istisnah	Base	−14%	−6%	−8%	15%	69%
Ijarah	Base	180%	224%	85%	10%	17%
Others	Base	−18%	−73%	−15%	−100%	
Total financing assets	**Base**	**5%**	**24%**	**41%**	**31%**	**32%**
Less: Deferred income	Base	−6%	2%	4%	21%	75%
Down payments from *Istisnah* customers	Base	−80%	2948%	23%	−100%	
Contractors and consultants' *Istisnah*	Base	−19%	−95%	−42%	4785%	209%
Provisions for impairment	Base	9%	−8%	10%	13%	11%
	Base	**9%**	**32%**	**49%**	**33%**	**24%**
Investing	Base					
Sukuk	Base					306%
Musharakat	Base	5%	18%	33%	241%	−51%
Mudarabat	Base	34%	45%	40%	59%	45%
Investment funds	Base	140%	−100%			
Wakalat	Base	127%	1074%	−41%	−47%	20%
Gross investing assets	**Base**	**34%**	**13%**	**22%**	**186%**	**25%**
Less: Provisions for impairment	Base	−34%	14%	6%	52%	−17%
Net investing assets	**Base**	**37%**	**13%**	**22%**	**189%**	**25%**
Total Islamic financing and investing assets, net	**Base**	**21%**	**21%**	**43%**	**62%**	**25%**

pertaining to defaults, penalties, and investor rights. Specifically, their number, level, age, experience, and responsibilities should be identified and evaluated. Staff organization, skills, and qualifications should be analyzed in relation to policies and procedures. All ongoing training programs for a bank's credit staff should be reviewed and their adequacy

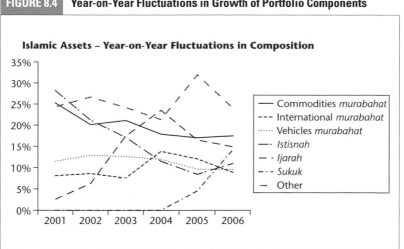

FIGURE 8.4 Year-on-Year Fluctuations in Growth of Portfolio Components

assessed. The quality and frequency of staff training are often a good indicator of the level of credit skills.

Information Flows and Disclosure

A bank must have efficient systems for monitoring adherence to established guidelines. This can best be accomplished through an internal review and reporting system that informs the board of directors and senior management of how policies are being carried out and that provides them with sufficient information to evaluate the performance of lower-echelon officers and the condition of the portfolio. Since information is the basic element of the investment and financing management process, its availability, quality, and cost-effectiveness should be analyzed. In addition, because the information needed may be dispersed in different parts of the bank, an analysis should pay attention to information flows, in particular, whether the information supplied is complete and available in a timely and cost-effective manner. Such an analysis is linked closely to a review of human resources, organizational and control structures, and information technology.

Different countries have different classification rules, provisioning requirements, and methods of treating problem accounts, and different banks exercise judgment to different degrees. This makes adequate disclosure essential, as it allows supervisors and other interested third parties to evaluate the true financial condition of a bank. Regulatory authorities need to mandate principles of disclosure related to sound credit risk, as recommended by the Basel Committee on Banking Supervision. Specifically, these include disclosure of information about the following:

- Policies and methods used to account for impairments (that is, provisions);
- Risk management and control policies and practices;
- Allowances (loss reserves) and specific allowances (provisions) by major categories of clients and geographic regions and reconciliation of movements in the allowances for impairment;
- Large exposures and concentration of exposures to connected parties;
- Balances and other pertinent information on accounts that have been restructured or are otherwise irregular with respect to the original agreement.

9

ALM, Liquidity, and Market Risks

As financial instruments and markets have become more complex and processing has been automated, the treasury function of financial intermediaries has been expanded and made more complex.[1] Typical treasury functions include, but are not limited to, the following:

- The overall policy framework, including (a) general policy guidance and directions, (b) ALM (asset-liability management), (c) strategic asset allocation, (d) benchmark approval, and (e) use of external portfolio managers;
- Funding and liquidity management;
- Investment and cash flow management, referred to as asset management;
- Risk analysis and compliance, which includes (a) model validation, (b) risk measurement (liquidity, counterparty or credit, market, commodity, and currency risk), (c) performance measurement, analysis, and reporting, (d) compliance with broad investment guidelines, and (e) quantitative strategies and risk research (model development, benchmark construction);
- Treasury operations, including (a) correspondent bank accounts (banking relations), (b) settlements, (c) accounting, and (d) information systems and services.

This list of treasury functions exposes the financial institution to a new breed of risks that have to be managed. These include asset-liability management, liquidity, and market risks. Generally, risk management is

---

Key Messages

- Islamic banks should theoretically be less exposed to asset-liability mismatches than their conventional counterparts. This comparative advantage is rooted in the "pass-through" and the "risk-sharing" nature of Islamic banks.
- Liquidity management is a key banking function and an integral part of the asset-liability management process.
- Banks are particularly vulnerable to liquidity problems, on an institution-specific level and from a systemic or market viewpoint.
- Liquidity management policies should comprise a risk management (decision-making) structure, a liquidity management and funding strategy, a set of limits for liquidity risk exposures, and a set of procedures for liquidity planning under alternative scenarios, including crisis situations.
- Market risk results from the volatility of positions taken in the four fundamental economic markets: return-sensitive debt securities, equities, currencies, and commodities.
- The volatility of each of these markets exposes banks to fluctuations in the price or value of marketable financial instruments.
- The treasury function is normally divided into a portfolio management unit (front office), a risk analytics and compliance unit (middle office), and an operations unit (back office).
- Allocation of tasks between the units may differ from bank to bank, but risk management *principles* for the various functions do not change.
- Compliance with laws, regulations, policies, and guidelines is paramount, as it is the culture of compliance that determines the environment within which trading decisions are made.
- The objective of risk management is to provide an independent measurement and monitoring of market risks and other risks being undertaken across various treasury businesses.

---

part of the treasury function of the financial institution, making the inability to manage risks properly a risk in and of itself. Due to the small size of the majority of Islamic financial institutions, the treasury function is limited to cash management. These institutions cannot benefit from economies of scale and therefore cannot afford to invest in the infrastructure required for a robust risk and treasury management framework. This is a source of further exposure.

Like conventional banks, Islamic banks are also exposed to some form of asset-liability mismatch risk. In addition, typical treasury risks for Islamic banks are liquidity, market, rate-of-return, equity-investment, and hedging risks. Market risks are similar to the market risks of conventional banks, except that there is no interest rate risk. Instead of interest rate risk, Islamic banks are exposed to markup (cost-plus margin charged in trade financing contracts) risks and are further exposed to the risks of changes in the benchmark indexes used to determine markup rates and other rates on return. Another risk specific to Islamic banks is exposure due to differences in the expected and actual rate of returns passed on to the investment account holders. By design, Islamic banks should be keeping a handsome portion of their assets in equity investments, but in practice this share is modest. Nevertheless, any investment in equity-based or profit- and loss-sharing partnerships exposes Islamic banks to equity investment risks that are not applicable to conventional banks. Finally, in the absence of any derivative products, Islamic banks are unable to hedge their exposures to price, rate-of-return, and foreign exchange risks.

This chapter discusses asset-liability mismatch, liquidity risk and market risk, before addressing the measurement and management of market risk.

ASSET-LIABILITY MANAGEMENT

Asset-liability management involves the raising and use of funds. More specifically, it comprises strategic planning, implementation, and control processes that affect the volume, mix, maturity, profit rate sensitivity, quality, and liquidity of a bank's assets and liabilities. The primary goal of asset-liability management is to produce a high-quality, stable, large, and growing flow of net interest income. This goal is accomplished by achieving the optimum combination and level of assets, liabilities, and financial risk.

Asset-liability management risk results from the difference in maturity terms and conditions of a bank's portfolio on its assets and liabilities sides. According to theory, Islamic banks should be less exposed to asset-liability mismatch and therefore to equity duration risk, than their conventional counterparts. This comparative advantage is rooted in the "pass-through" nature of Islamic banks, which act as agents for investors-depositors and pass all profits and losses through to them. In addition, the *risk-sharing* feature, in which banks participate in the risks of their counterparties and investors-depositors share the risks of the banking business, plays a critical role. Direct market discipline, one of the three main pillars recently emphasized by the Basel Committee on Banking Supervision in enhancing the stability of the international financial market, is embedded in this risk-sharing principle.

Following the theoretical model, any negative shock to an Islamic bank's asset returns is absorbed by both shareholders and investors-depositors. While depositors in the conventional system have a fixed claim on the returns to the bank's assets (receiving a predetermined interest rate in addition to their guaranteed principal, irrespective of the bank's profitability on its assets side), holders of *profit-sharing* investment accounts in the Islamic system share in the bank's profits and losses alongside the shareholders and are exposed to the risk of losing all or part of their initial investment. The assets and liabilities are matched as a result of the "pass-through" structure.

In practice, however, the risk-sharing and pass-through features are not fully followed. For example, rather than strictly sharing profits and losses with depositors, banks distribute profits, even if there are no or low profits, which creates distortions and puts strains on the equity shareholders (providers of capital). Further mismatches arise from the heavy dependence on short-term trade financing and limited use of partnership-based agreements. The outcome is the dominance of short-term, low-profit, and fixed-income assets, that is, markup-based trade financing, which limits the amount of funds that can be invested in longer-term, more profitable, riskier assets. In short, although in theory there should be no mismatch between assets and liabilities of an Islamic bank, current practices have introduced distortions that expose banks to asset-liability mismatch risk, especially when they have no liquid assets with which to hedge such risks.

Table 9.1 presents a theoretical balance sheet (see also table 2.1, panel B). On the "liabilities" side, it is common practice to accept deposits on the basis of profit and loss sharing; it is on the assets side that practice diverges from the theoretical model. At least three major deviations between the theory and the practice have direct or indirect implications for the overall riskiness of the banking environment, modifying the theoretical balance sheet shown in table 9.1.

TABLE 9.1   Theoretical Balance Sheet of an Islamic Bank Based on Functionality

Assets	Liabilities
Cash balances	Demand deposits (*amanah*)
Financing assets (*murabahah, salaam, ijarah, istisnah*)	Investment accounts (*mudarabah*)
Investment assets (*mudarabah, musharakah*)	Special investment accounts (*mudarabah, musharakah*)
Fee-based services (*joalah, kifalah*, and so forth)	Reserves
Non-banking assets (property)	Equity capital

Trend toward Less Risky Short-Term Assets

On the assets side, the majority of Islamic banks have limited themselves to trade financing assets, which tend to be less risky and of shorter maturity. This aspect is a significant deviation from what theoretical models and basic principles of Islamic finance posit that the structure should be. On the assets side of the balance sheet, Islamic banks clearly prefer asset-backed financial claims resulting from sale and trade. This preference is due to the fact that sales-related securities are considered low risk and resemble conventional fixed-income securities in terms of the risk-return profile. In addition to trade-based instruments, Islamic banks prefer leasing, considered to carry a lower risk and have less uncertain returns than partnership-based instruments. In a typical case, sale- and lease-based transactions dominate the assets portfolio and can exceed 80 percent, with the remainder allocated to profit-sharing arrangements. On average, as a mode of financing, *murabahah* (41 percent) is the first choice of Islamic banks, followed by *musharakah* (11 percent), *mudarabah* (12 percent), *ijarah* (10 percent), and others (26 percent).

Islamic banks' overdependence on trade- and commodity-financing instruments has limited their choice of maturity structure; as a result, a major portion of their financing is of short-term maturity. Whereas the theoretical models expect financial intermediaries to participate in a full range of maturity structures to obtain the benefits of portfolio diversification, Islamic banks shy away from instruments requiring a medium- or long-term commitment. A review of data on asset maturities collected from six Islamic banks as of 2003 shows that 54 percent of their assets had a maturity of less than one year and 39 percent had a maturity of less than six months. Islamic banks tend not to invest in longer-maturity assets due to their lack of liquidity. Since they rely on short-term maturity, Islamic banks are very restricted in their ability to offer long-term investment opportunities.

Low Participation in Profit- and Loss-Sharing Arrangements

Whereas the theoretical model advocates the promotion of profit- and loss-sharing arrangements, banks' participation in these instruments is low. Banks are reluctant to indulge in profit- and loss-sharing instruments for several reasons, such as the inherit riskiness and additional costs of monitoring such investments, low appetite for risk on the part of both banks and their depositors, and lack of transparency in markets within which Islamic banks are operating. This lack of willingness to take on risk could reflect the lack of transparency in the banking system, which dampens the confidence of depositors. A low level of transparency in the system leads to a low level of trust between investors-depositors and the banks. The result is that depositors tend to be risk averse, and so banks become risk averse; although they may have good investment opportunities on the basis of profit and loss sharing, they may not be able to find depositors willing to take this risk.

Islamic banks often complain that the institutional infrastructure to support profit and loss sharing does not exist. There are no supporting institutions to maintain good-quality information on the credit standing of borrowers and entrepreneurs. There are very few credible trade associations to conduct common monitoring and to share information about debtors. In the presence of informational asymmetry in the system, banks tend to shy away from equity- and partnership-based instruments. Consequently, bank portfolios often are not diversified either geographically or by product. They are exposed to specific sectors or geographic regions, which is not healthy and raises the level of banking environment risk.

Lack of Clarity between Shareholders and Investors-Depositors

In theory, the contractual agreement between the bank and the investors-depositors should be based on a "pass-through" mechanism in which all profits and losses are passed to the depositors-investors. Thus the problem of asset-liability mismatch should not exist. It has been argued that this type of financial intermediation contributes to the stability of the financial system.

However, the practice is very different from the theory. There is no clear differentiation between the shares of investors-depositors and those of equity holders. The means of determining each stakeholder's share is not transparent, as policies and procedures for computing and declaring profits and losses are poorly defined. In some cases, the practice is not truly a pass-through arrangement, and profits are distributed to investment account holders despite losses on the assets, so that the profits are paid out of equity. This phenomenon is termed "displaced commercial risk."

All of these deviations between theory and practice mean that the system is not functioning at its full potential and has adapted itself to a limited functionality. In fact, due to these deviations, the banking system is exposed to risks that it is not supposed to be. These deviations and other bank practices have created heightened risk or at least the perception of it at the institutional and systematic level.

LIQUIDITY RISK

Liquidity is necessary for banks to compensate for expected and unexpected balance sheet fluctuations and to provide funds for growth (Iqbal and Mirakhor 2007). It represents a bank's ability to accommodate the redemption of deposits and other liabilities and to cover the demand for funding in the loan and investment portfolio. A bank is said to have adequate liquidity potential when it can obtain needed funds (by increasing liabilities, securitizing, or selling assets) promptly and at a reasonable cost. The price of liquidity is a function of market conditions and the market's perception of the inherent riskiness of the borrowing institution.

The amount of liquid or readily marketable assets that a bank should hold depends on the stability of its deposit structure and the potential for rapid expansion of the asset portfolio. Generally, if deposits are composed primarily of small, stable accounts, a bank will need relatively low liquidity. A much higher liquidity position normally is required when a substantial portion of the loan portfolio consists of large long-term loans, when a bank has a somewhat high concentration of deposits, or when recent trends show reductions in large corporate or household deposit accounts. Situations also can arise in which a bank should increase its liquidity position; for example, when large commitments have been made on the assets side and the bank expects the client to start using them.

The liquidity management policies of a bank normally comprise a decision-making structure, an approach to funding and liquidity operations, a set of limits to liquidity risk exposure, and a set of procedures for planning liquidity under alternative scenarios, including crisis situations. The decision-making structure reflects the importance that management places on liquidity: banks that stress the importance of liquidity normally institutionalize the structure of liquidity risk management in the asset-liability committee and assign ultimate responsibility for setting policy and reviewing liquidity decisions to the bank's highest level of management. The bank's strategy for funding and liquidity operations should be approved by the board and should include specific policies for particular aspects of risk management, such as the target liabilities structure, the use of certain financial instruments, or the pricing of deposits.

Liquidity needs usually are determined by the construction of a maturity ladder that comprises expected cash inflows and outflows over a series of specified time bands. The difference between the inflows and outflows in each period (that is, the excess or deficit of funds) provides a starting point from which to measure a bank's future liquidity excess or shortfall at any given time (table 9.2 and figure 9.1).

TABLE 9.2   Maturity Profile of Assets and Liabilities

Customers' Deposits	2001	2002	2003	2004	2005	2006
(a) By Type:						
Current accounts	2,134,736	2,622,921	3,291,478	4,762,526	7,015,356	9,264,286
Savings accounts	2,020,814	2,510,461	3,185,930	5,778,598	5,654,891	5,733,414
Investment deposits	8,858,505	11,660,201	13,133,625	16,100,128	20,403,363	32,065,814
Margins	107,616	103,128	146,206	173,662	182,885	579,724
Profit equalization provision (Note 37)	70,938	90,098	126,014	126,102	135,455	89,244
	13,192,609	16,986,809	19,883,253	24,941,016	33,391,950	47,732,482
(b) By maturity:						
Demand deposits	4,263,166	5,239,612	6,749,628	3,840,888	12,988,587	14,887,667
Deposits due within 3 months	2,834,854	3,885,662	4,926,099	6,826,450	5,250,220	18,668,425
Deposits due within 6 months	2,468,876	3,254,781	3,606,573	4,199,553	1,164,639	5,058,889
Deposits due within 1 year	3,625,713	4,606,754	4,600,953	5,074,125	13,988,504	9,117,501
	13,194,610	16,988,811	19,385,256	24,943,020	33,393,955	47,734,488
(c) By geographical areas:						
Within country	12,977,281	16,746,302	19,883,253	24,941,016	31,615,164	39,722,859
Outside country	215,328	240,507	-	-	1,776,786	8,009,623
	13,192,609	16,986,809	19,883,253	24,941,016	33,391,950	47,732,482

(continued)

TABLE 9.2 *continued*

Customers' Deposits	2001	2002	2003	2004	2005	2006
(d) By currency						
Local	12,649,387	16,625,476	19,538,058	24,539,418	30,306,345	36,444,847
Other currencies	543,222	361,333	345,195	401,598	3,085,605	11,287,635
Local and U.S. dollars						
	13,192,609	**16,986,809**	**19,883,253**	**24,941,016**	**33,391,950**	**47,732,482**
Maturity profile						
Assets						
Less than 3 months	8,440,268	9,306,606	10,272,647	11,497,545	15,203,780	31,725,644
3 months to 1 year	1,748,961	1,779,905	2,946,684	6,068,174	5,896,048	10,908,547
Over 1 year	5,144,749	8,511,279	9,558,988	13,047,642	21,898,451	21,799,745
Total assets	**15,333,978**	**19,597,790**	**22,778,319**	**30,613,361**	**42,998,279**	**64,433,936**
Liabilities						
Less than 3 months	7,861,928	9,924,646	12,533,008	18,103,033	21,738,876	38,536,352
3 months to 1 year	6,308,929	8,059,233	8,520,962	9,498,927	17,543,080	17,638,551
Over 1 year	1,163,121	1,613,911	1,724,349	3,011,401	3,716,323	8,259,033
Total liabilities	**15,333,978**	**19,597,790**	**22,778,319**	**30,613,361**	**42,998,279**	**64,433,936**
Liquidity Gaps						
Less than 3 months	578,340	−618,040	−2,260,361	−6,605,488	−6,535,096	−6,810,708
3 months to 1 year	−4,559,968	−6,279,328	−5,574,278	−3,430,753	−11,647,032	−6,730,004
Over 1 year	3,981,628	6,897,368	7,834,639	10,036,241	18,182,128	13,540,712

FIGURE 9.1 Liquidity Mismatches (Derived from Maturity Profile of Assets and Liabilities)

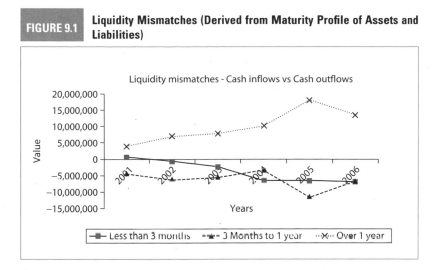

FIGURE 9.2 Cash Flows (Derived from Cash Flow Statements)

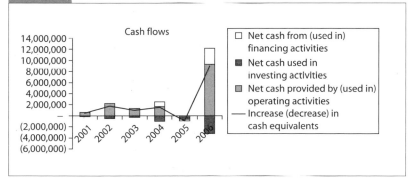

Once its liquidity needs have been determined, the bank must decide how to fulfill them (see figure 9.2). Liquidity management is related to a net funding requirement; in principle, a bank may increase its liquidity through asset management, liability management, or (and most frequently) a combination of both. In practice, a bank may meet its liquidity needs by disposing of highly liquid assets or assets that are nearly liquid, such as assets in the trading portfolio, or by selling less liquid assets, such as excess property or other investments. On the liabilities side, this can be achieved by increasing short-term borrowings or short-term deposit liabilities, by increasing the maturity of liabilities, and ultimately by increasing capital. See box 9.1 for the IFSB guidance on liquidity risk.

| BOX 9.1 | IFSB Principles of Liquidity Risk |

Principle 5.1. [Islamic financial institutions] shall have in place a liquidity management framework (including reporting) taking into account separately and on an overall basis their *liquidity exposures in respect of each category* of current accounts, unrestricted investment accounts, and restricted investment accounts.

Principle 5.2. [Islamic financial institutions] shall undertake liquidity risk commensurate with their ability to have sufficient *recourse to Shariah-compliant funds* to mitigate such risk.

Liquidity risk results when the bank's ability to match the maturity of assets and liabilities is impaired. Such risk results from the mismatch between maturities on the two sides of the balance sheet, creating either a surplus of cash that must be invested or a shortage of cash that must be funded. Lack of liquidity adversely affects the bank's ability to manage portfolios in a diversified fashion and to enter or exit the market when needed.

Liquidity risk as it applies to Islamic banks can be of two types: lack of liquidity in the market and lack of access to funding. In the first type, illiquid assets make it difficult for the financial institution to meet its liabilities and financial obligations. In the second, the institution is unable to borrow or raise funds at a reasonable cost, when needed. Liquidity risk is one of the most critical risks facing Islamic banks for the following reasons:

- Limited availability of a *Shariah*-compatible money market and intrabank market is the leading cause of liquidity risk. Prohibition by *Shariah* law from borrowing on the basis of interest in case of need and the absence of an active interbank money market have restricted Islamic banks' options to manage their liquidity positions efficiently.
- Shallow secondary markets are another source of liquidity risk. The financial instruments that can be traded in the secondary market are limited, and the *Shariah* imposes certain limitations on the trading of financial claims, unless such claims are linked to a real asset. Therefore, there is a need to develop asset-backed tradable securities, known as *sukuk*. Even where instruments are available, the number of market participants is limited.
- Typical avenues of liquidity management available to conventional banks—the interbank market, secondary market for debt instruments, and discount windows from the lender of last resort (central bank)— are all considered as based on *riba* (interest) and, therefore, are not

acceptable. Conventional banks have access to borrowing with overnight to extended short-term maturity through well-developed and efficient interbank markets. This access is vital for meeting the institution's need for short-term cash flow.

■ Certain characteristics of some Islamic instruments give rise to liquidity risks for Islamic banks. For example, liquidity becomes a problem given the cancellation risks in *murabahah* or the inability to trade *murabahah* or *bay' al-salaam* contracts, which can be traded only at par.

■ Islamic banks hold a considerable proportion of funds as demand deposits in current accounts, and these can be withdrawn at any time. Banks guarantee repayment of the principal deposited, and account holders do not have rights to a share in the profits. Some Islamic banks invest only a small fraction of the current account holders' funds and, in the absence of liquid short-term instruments, maintain a high level of idle cash.

These factors have raised Islamic banks' exposure to liquidity risk and limited their ability to invest in long-term and illiquid, but more profitable, assets. Several developments have taken place with a view to meeting this challenge. First, the introduction of *sukuk* (Islamic bonds) is a good development that can provide the foundation for the development of secondary markets. The Central Bank of Sudan has introduced *Shariah*-compatible securities to provide liquidity in the market. Second, progress has been made in establishing an institutional framework to address this problem. In this respect, establishment of International Islamic Financial Markets and the Liquidity Management Center are vital steps toward managing liquidity more effectively.

Malaysia also has taken steps to promote Islamic banks and reduce liquidity risk. The central bank, Bank Negara Malaysia, introduced the Islamic Interbank Money Market (IIMM) in early 1994. The activities of the IIMM include the purchase and sale of Islamic financial instruments among market participants (including the central bank), interbank investment activities through the *mudarabah* interbank investment scheme, and a check clearing and settlement system. The Islamic financial instruments that are currently being traded in the market on the basis of *bay' al-dayn* (sale of debt) are the green bankers acceptances, Islamic bills, Islamic mortgage bonds, and Islamic private debt securities. In addition, financial institutions can sell government investment issues to the central bank, as and when required, to meet their liquidity needs. In turn, financial institutions can buy *Shariah*-compliant investment issues from the central bank.

Whereas the contract of *bay' al-dayn* is commonly accepted and practiced in the Malaysian financial markets, it is not accepted by a majority of *Shariah* scholars outside Malaysia, who maintain that debt can be traded only at par. If trade is not at par, they feel that the practice opens the door to *riba*. *Shariah* scholars in other jurisdictions need to become proactive in finding solutions for reducing liquidity risk.

MARKET RISK

Market risk is the risk that a bank may experience loss due to unfavorable movements in market prices. Realizing its significance, in December 2005 the Islamic Financial Services Board (IFSB) issued a comprehensive document on standards for risk management (see box 9.2). Exposure to market risk may arise as a result of the bank taking deliberately speculative positions (proprietary trading) or may ensue from the bank's market-making (dealer) activities.

Market risk results from changes in the prices of equity instruments, commodities, fixed-income securities, and currencies. Its major components are therefore equity position risk, commodities risk, rate-of-return risk, and currency risk. Each component of risk includes a general aspect of market risk and a specific aspect of risk that originates in the portfolio structure of a bank. In addition to standard instruments, market risk also applies to various derivatives instruments, such as options, equity derivatives, and currency and interest rate derivatives.

The price volatility of most assets held in investment and trading portfolios is often significant. Volatility prevails even in mature markets, although it is much higher in emerging or illiquid markets. The presence of large institutional investors, such as pension funds, insurance companies, or investment funds, also has had an impact on the structure of markets and on market risk. Institutional investors adjust their large-scale investment and trading portfolios through large-scale trades, and in markets with rising prices, large-scale purchases tend to push prices up. Conversely, markets with downward trends become more volatile when large blocks of

---

BOX 9.2 **IFSB Principle of Market Risk**

Principle 4.1. [Islamic financial institutions] shall have in place an appropriate *framework for market risk management* (including reporting) in respect of all assets held, including those that do not have a ready market or are exposed to high price volatility.

securities are sold. Ultimately, this widens the amplitude of price variances and increases market risk.

As banks diversify their business away from the traditional intermediation function and toward market-making and proprietary trading activities, whereby they set aside "risk capital" for deliberate risk-taking activities, their exposure to market risk deepens. The proprietary trading portfolio, therefore, must be distinguished from the investment portfolio. Proprietary trading is aimed at exploiting market opportunities with leveraged funding (for example, through the use of repurchase agreements), whereas the investment portfolio is held and traded as a buffer because its liquidity is relatively stable. Still, both proprietary trading and investment portfolios are subject to market risk.

To summarize, market risk for a financial institution arises in the form of unfavorable price movements, such as yields (rate-of-return risk), benchmark rates (rate-of-return risk), foreign exchange rates (FX risk), and equity and commodity prices (price risk), which have a potential impact on the financial value of an asset over the life of the contract. Islamic banks are further exposed to market risk due to the volatility in the value of tradable, marketable, or leasable assets. The risks relate to the current and future volatility of the market value of specific assets.

Markup Risk

Islamic banks are exposed to markup risk, as the markup rate used in *murabahah* and other trade-financing instruments is fixed for the duration of the contract, while the benchmark rate may change. This means that the prevailing markup rate may rise beyond the rate the bank has locked into a contract, making the bank unable to benefit from higher rates. In the absence of an Islamic index of rate of return, Islamic banks often use the London Interbank Offered Rate (LIBOR) as the benchmark, which aligns their market risk closely with the movement in LIBOR rates.

Price Risk

In case of *bay' al-salaam* (forward sale), Islamic banks are exposed to commodity price volatility during the period between delivery of the commodity and its sale at the prevailing market price. This risk is similar to the market risk of a forward contract if it is not hedged properly. In order to hedge its position, the bank may enter into a parallel (off-setting) *bay' al-salaam* contract. In such cases, the bank is exposed to price risk if there is default on the first contract and is obligated to deliver on the second contract.

Leased Asset Value Risk

In case of an operating *ijarah*, the bank is exposed to market risk due to a fall in the residual value of the leased asset at the expiry of the lease term or, in case of early termination due to default, over the life of the contract.

Currency Risk

Currency risk arises from a mismatch between the value of assets and that of capital and liabilities denominated in foreign currency (or vice versa) or from a mismatch between foreign receivables and foreign payables that are expressed in a domestic currency. Currency risk is of a "speculative" nature and can therefore result in a gain or a loss, depending on the direction of exchange rate shifts and whether a bank is net long or net short in the foreign currency. For example, in the case of a net long position, domestic currency depreciation will result in a net gain for a bank and currency appreciation will produce a loss. Under a net short position, exchange rate movements will have the opposite effect.

Foreign exchange rate movement is another transaction risk arising from the deferred trading nature of some contracts offered by Islamic banks, as the value of the currency in which receivables are due may depreciate or the currency in which payables are due may appreciate. In the absence of any tradable derivatives with which to hedge currency risk, Islamic financial institutions are further exposed to this risk. This is another reason why financial institutions shy away from either exposing themselves to or helping their clients to hedge currency risks.

Securities Price Risk

With a growing market for Islamic bonds (*sukuks*), Islamic banks invest a portion of their assets in marketable securities. However, the prices of such securities are exposed to current yields in the market. Similar to a fixed-income security, the prices go down as yields go up and vice versa. Islamic banks holding such securities are exposed to volatility in yield, unless they hold the security until maturity. Furthermore, the secondary market for such securities may not be very liquid, exposing Islamic banks to distorted prices.

Rate-of-Return Risk

The rate-of-return risk stems from uncertainty in the returns earned by Islamic banks on their assets (see box 9.3 for IFSB guidance on rate-of-return risk). This uncertainty can cause a divergence from the expectations that investment account holders have on the liabilities side. The larger the divergence, the bigger is the rate-of-return risk. Another way of looking at this is to consider the risk generally associated with overall balance sheet exposures, in which mismatches arise between the assets of the bank and the balances of the depositors. For example, an Islamic bank may expect to earn 5 percent on its assets, which is passed on to the investors-depositors. Meanwhile, if current market rates rise up to 6 percent, which is higher than what the bank may earn on its investment, the investors-depositors may also expect to earn 6 percent on their deposits.

The rate-of-return risk is different from the interest rate risk in two ways. First, since conventional banks operate on interest-based, fixed-income securities on the assets side, there is less uncertainty in the rate of return earned on investments held until maturity. Since Islamic banks have a mix of markup-based and equity-based investments, this uncertainty is higher. Second, the return on deposits in conventional banks is predetermined; in contrast, the return on deposits in Islamic banks is anticipated, but not agreed beforehand. In addition, the return on some investments—that is, those based on equity partnerships—are not known accurately until the end of the investment period. Islamic banks have to wait for the results of their investment to determine the level of return that investors-depositors will earn. If, during this period, the prevailing yields or expected rates of return change, the investors may expect to receive similar yields from the bank.

| BOX 9.3 | IFSB Principles of Rate-of-Return Risk |

Principle 6.1. [Islamic financial institutions] shall establish a comprehensive risk management and reporting process to assess the potential impacts of market factors affecting *rates of return* on assets in comparison with the expected rates of return for investment account holders.

Principle 6.2. [Islamic financial institutions] shall have in place an appropriate framework for managing *displaced commercial risk,* where applicable.

Equity Investment Risk

On the assets side, Islamic financial institutions are exposed to equity investment risk in profit- and loss-sharing investments (see box 9.4 for the IFSB guidelines on equity investment risk). These include partnership-based *mudarabah* and *musharakah* investments. Typical examples of equity investments are holdings of shares in the stock market, private equity investments, equity participation in specific projects, and syndication investment.

This risk is somewhat unique to Islamic financial institutions, considering that conventional commercial banks do not invest in equity-based assets. Equity investments can lead to volatility in the financial institution's earnings due to the liquidity, credit, and market risks associated with equity holdings. Although there is credit risk in equity-based assets, there is also considerable financial risk: capital may be lost due to business losses.

Equity investment risk has some distinct features:

- The nature of equity investment requires enhanced monitoring to reduce informational asymmetries. These measures include proper financial disclosure, closer involvement with the project, transparency in reporting, and supervision during all phases of the project, from appraisal to completion. Therefore, Islamic banks need to play an active role in monitoring.
- Both *mudarabah* and *musharakah* are profit- and loss-sharing contracts and are subject to loss of capital despite proper monitoring. The degree of risk is relatively higher than in other investments, and

---

BOX 9.4   **IFSB Principles of Equity Investment Risk**

Principle 3.1. [Islamic financial institutions] shall have in place appropriate strategies, risk management, and reporting processes in respect of the *risk characteristics of equity investments,* including *mudarabah* and *musharakah* investments.

Principle 3.2. [Islamic financial institutions] shall ensure that their *valuation methodologies* are appropriate and consistent and shall assess the potential impacts of their methods on the calculation and allocation of profit. The methods shall be mutually agreed between the institution and the *mudarib* or *musharakah* partners.

Principle 3.3. [Islamic financial institutions] shall define and establish the *exit strategies* in respect of their equity investment activities, including extension and redemption conditions for *mudarabah* and *musharakah* investments, subject to the approval of the institution's *Shariah* board.

Islamic banks should take extreme care in evaluating and selecting the projects, in order to minimize potential losses.

■ Equity investments other than stock market investments do not have organized secondary markets, which raises the costs of an early exit. Illiquidity of such investments can cause financial losses to the bank.

■ Equity investments may not generate steady income, and capital gain might be the only source of return. The unscheduled nature of cash flows makes it difficult to forecast and manage them.

Mudarabah and *musharakah* facilities are equity-type facilities that typically constitute a very small share of total assets, reflecting the significant investment risks they carry. In a sample of Islamic banks examined, the share of *mudarabah* and *musharakah* facilities and traded equities varied from 0 to 24 percent, with a median share of about 3 percent (Grais and Piligrani 2006). A measure of the potential loss in equity exposures that are not traded can be derived from the standard recommended in Basel II (para. 350). Given net equity exposures, the loss can be estimated using the probability of default corresponding to a debt exposure to the counterparties whose equity is being held and applying a fairly high loss given default, such as 90 percent. A measure of both expected and unexpected loss could then be computed from these parameters. In addition, the mudarabah facility may have to be assigned an additional unexpected loss due to operational risk factors, with the extent of operational risk adjustment depending on the quality of internal control systems available to monitor *mudarabah* facilities on the assets side. High-quality monitoring is very important in Islamic banks, since the provider of finance cannot interfere in management of the project funded on a *mudarabah* basis. In the case of *musharakah,* the need for operational risk adjustment may be less, insofar as the bank exercises some control over management. If the banks' equity interest in a counterparty is based on regular cash flow rather than capital gains and is long term in nature and linked to a customer relationship, a different supervisory treatment and a lower loss given default could be used. If, however, equity interest is relatively short term and relies on capital gains (for example, traded equity), a value-at-risk approach, subject to a minimum risk weight of 300 percent, could be used to measure capital at risk (as proposed in Basel II).

In profit- and loss-sharing activities, use of *mudarabah* on the assets side of the balance sheet gives rise to moral hazard problems. While the Islamic bank bears all the losses in case of a negative outcome, it cannot oblige users of the funds (*mudarib*) to take the appropriate action or exert the required level of effort needed to generate the expected level of returns. Such situations can be exploited by the users of funds (Lewis and Algaoud 2002). Also, the bank does not have the right to monitor or to participate in management of the project and hence may lose its principal investment in addition to its potential share of profit if the entrepreneur's books show a loss (Errico and Farahbaksh 1998).

Mudarabah can also expose an Islamic bank to principal-agent problems when the bank enters into the contract as *rab al-mal* (principal) and the user of funds is also the agent. The user of funds may have incentives to expand the expenditures on the projects and to increase the consumption of nonpecuniary benefits at the expense of pecuniary returns, since the increased consumption is borne partly by the bank, while the benefits are consumed entirely by the entrepreneur. A similar problem arises on the liabilities side, when investment account holders place their money with the Islamic bank on a *mudarabah* basis.[2]

The moral hazard problem would be reduced in *musharakah*, where the capital of the partner is also at stake. Furthermore, an equity partnership would minimize the problem of informational asymmetry, as the Islamic bank would have the right to participate in management of the project in which it is investing.[3] However, the *musharakah* asset class has an associated cost in the form of adverse selection and therefore requires extensive screening, information gathering, and monitoring. Each *musharakah* contract requires careful analysis and negotiation of profit- and loss-sharing arrangements, leading to higher costs of intermediation.[4] As a result of the problems associated with both types of contracts, Islamic banks tend to allocate limited funds to these asset classes. This implies an increased reliance on asset-backed securities, which limits the choice of investment and ultimately may hamper the bank's ability to manage risks and diversify its portfolio.

Hedging Risk

Hedging risk is the risk of failure to mitigate and manage different types of risks. This increases the bank's overall risk exposure. In addition to the absence of derivative products with which to hedge risks, illiquid, nonexistent, and shallow secondary markets are other sources of the increasing hedging risk of Islamic banks.

Benchmark Risk

Benchmark risk is the possible loss due to a change in the margin between domestic rates of return and the benchmark rates of return, which may not be linked closely to domestic returns. Many Islamic banks use external benchmarks such as the LIBOR to price the markup in *murabahah* contracts, in part reflecting the lack of reliable domestic benchmark rates of return. If domestic monetary conditions change, requiring adjustments in the returns on deposits and loans, but the margin between external benchmark and domestic rates of return shifts, there could be an impact on asset returns. This is a form of "basis risk" that should be taken into account when computing the rate-of-return risk in the banking book (and also market risks). Existence of this basis risk highlights the importance of developing a domestic rate-of-return benchmark so that both deposits and assets can be aligned to similar benchmarks.

Business Risk

Business risk is associated with a bank's business environment, including macroeconomic and policy concerns, legal and regulatory factors, and the overall financial sector infrastructure such as payment systems and auditors. Business risk also includes the risk of becoming insolvent due to insufficient capital to continue operations. While Islamic financial institutions are very much exposed to the regular business environment, solvency, and financial sector infrastructure risks, they are particularly exposed to rate-of-return risk.

MARKET RISK MEASUREMENT

Given the increasing involvement of banks in investment and trading activities and the high volatility of the market environment, the timely and accurate measurement of market risk is a necessity. This includes measurement of the exposures on a bank's investment and trading portfolios and on- and off-balance-sheet positions. A simplistic approach to market risk assessment treats every market to which the bank is exposed as a separate entity and does not take into account the relationships that may exist among various markets (see table 9.3 and figure 9.3).

Each risk is therefore measured on an individual basis. A more comprehensive approach assumes risk assessment from a consolidated perspective, which takes into consideration the relationships among markets and the fact that a movement in one market may affect several others. For example, a fluctuation in the exchange rate may also affect the price of bonds issued in a particular currency.

TABLE 9.3 Sample Approach to Market Risk Disclosure: Value-at Risk by Category and for Entire Institution

Type of risk or asset classes	Values during period			
	High	Median	Low	End of period
Sukuk (Islamic bonds)				
Equity				
Currency				
Commodity				
Diversification effect				
Aggregate VAR or other measure of risk				

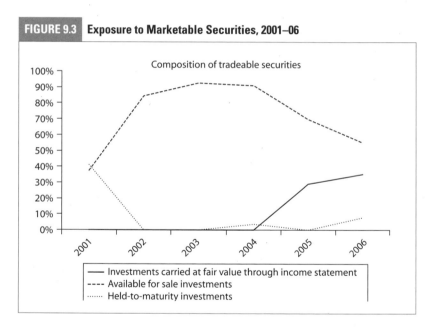

FIGURE 9.3 Exposure to Marketable Securities, 2001–06

Composition of tradeable securities

— Investments carried at fair value through income statement
--- Available for sale investments
······ Held-to-maturity investments

Value at Risk (VAR)

VAR is a modeling technique that typically measures a bank's aggregate market risk exposure and, given a probability level, estimates the amount a bank would lose if it were to hold specific assets for a certain period of time. Inputs to a VAR-based model include data on the bank's positions and on prices, volatility, and risk factors. The risks covered by the model should include all markup risk, currency, equity, and commodity positions inherent in the bank's portfolio, for both on- and off-balance-sheet positions. VAR-based models typically combine the potential change in the value of each position that would result from specific movements in underlying risk factors with the probability of such movements occurring. The changes in value are aggregated at the level of trading book segments or across all trading activities and markets. The VAR may be calculated using one of a number of methodologies. The measurement parameters include a holding period, a historical time horizon at which risk factor prices are observed, and a confidence interval that allows for the prudent judgment of the level of protection. The observation period is chosen by the bank to capture market conditions that are relevant to its risk management strategy. The following is taken into account:

- Value at risk, broken down by type of risk or asset class and in the aggregate, estimated for one-day and two-week holding periods and reported in terms of high, median, and low values over the reporting interval and at period end.
- Information about risk and return in the aggregate, including a comparison of risk estimates with actual outcomes, such as a histogram of daily profit or loss divided by daily value at risk or some other representation of the relationship between daily profit or loss and daily value at risk.
- Qualitative discussion and the comparison of profit or loss and VAR, including a description of differences between the basis of the profit or loss and the basis of VAR estimates.
- Quantitative measure of firm-wide exposure to market risk, broken down by type of risk, that in the bank's judgment best expresses exposure to risk, reported in terms of high, medium, and low values over the reporting period and at period end.

The capacity to assess and measure risk systematically and to manage the net open position effectively is crucial. Methods range from calculation of the net open position (or market factor sensitivity) to value at risk and other more sophisticated estimates of risk. Table 9.4 provides an example of a simplistic but practical method of aggregating assets, as reflected on the balance sheet, to arrive at a net open position. Once forward and unsettled transactions have been taken into account, a projected position is determined at book value, translated into market value, and then disclosed in terms of a common denominator representing the equivalent position in the cash markets. This methodology belongs to the static type of market risk measurement known as standard or table-based tools. Based on the net open position, it is possible to estimate the potential earnings or capital at risk by multiplying the net open position

TABLE 9.4   Simplistic Calculation of Net Effective Open Positions (Assuming Uniform Instruments in Every Market)

Position	Commodities	Fixed-income	Equities	Currencies
Net book value of assets per balance sheet				
Forward transactions				
Position at book value				
Position at market value before transactions in derivatives				
Position in derivatives (delta-equivalent position in options)				
Net effective open position after transactions in derivatives				
Possible movements in market prices (price volatility)				
Impact on earnings and capital				

(market risk factor sensitivity) by price volatility. This estimate provides a simple, one-factor value at risk; it does not, however, take into consideration the correlation between positions.

Risk is based on probabilistic events, and no single measurement tool can capture the multifaceted nature of market risk. Even the simplest aspects of market risk management can present a problem in real-life situations, particularly when a bank does not have adequate portfolio systems. At an absolute minimum, marking to market is a fundamental measure that should be taken to protect a bank's capital. Both the investment portfolio and the trading book should be marked to market on a daily basis to maintain the real value of positions.

The techniques for measuring market risk in Islamic banks, however, are likely limited to traded equities, commodities, foreign exchange positions, and, increasingly, various forms of *sukuks*. A large share of assets also consists of cash and other liquid assets, with such short-term assets typically exceeding short-term liabilities by a large margin. Against this background, exposure to various forms of market risk can be measured by the traditional indicators of exposure:

- Net open position in foreign exchange;
- Net position in traded equities;
- Net position in commodities;

- Rate-of-return gap, measured by currency of denomination;
- Various duration measures of assets and liabilities in the trading book.

Most Islamic banks compute and disclose measures of the *liquidity gap*—that is, the gap between assets and liabilities at various maturity buckets—and hence the rate-of-return or repricing gap should be fairly easy to compute. More accurate measures of *duration gap* may also be available in some banks. (For a discussion of gap and duration measures and their availability in banking statistics, see IMF 2004; for a discussion of gap and duration measures in the context of Islamic banking, see Baldwin 2002.) Duration measures are considered core indicators of financial soundness, but they are not readily available in many banking systems. The impact on earnings of a change in exchange rate, equity price, commodity price, or rates of return can be obtained directly by multiplying the appropriate gap or other indicators of exposure by the corresponding change in price. Such a simple approach will not, however, suffice for computing the impact of changes in interest rates on equity-type exposures of fixed maturity (such as *mudarabah* and *musharakah*). The impact of changes in the rates of return on the expected rate of profits (that is, income) needs to be computed first, or the equity exposures should be adjusted by a multiplicative factor (that a supervisor can specify) before gaps in each maturity bucket are computed. In the presence of longer-maturity assets and liabilities, change in the present value of assets (in the sense of discounted value of projected future cash flow) due to shifts in rates of return would be a more accurate measure of market risk than the estimated change in earnings in a reference period.

In most Islamic banks, the *rate-of-return risk* is likely to be much more important than market risk. The rate-of-return gap and duration gap applied to the banking book measure the exposure to changes in benchmark rates of return and the impact on bank earnings of present values. For example, a simple stress test of applying a 1 percentage point increase in rates of return on both assets and liabilities maturing, or being reprised, at various maturity buckets yields a measure of potential loss (or gain) due to a uniform shift in the term structure of the rate of return. Alternatively, the impact of shifts in the rate of return can be calculated directly from duration measures as follows: Impact of change in the rate of return = $(DA - DL) \Delta ir$, where DA = duration of assets, DL = duration of liabilities, and Δir = change in the rate of return.

It therefore becomes the responsibility of Islamic banks to manage the expectations of their investors-depositors, which makes the rate-of-return risk an issue of strategic risk. In addition, rate-of-return risk has two subcategories: displaced commercial risk and withdrawal risk.

MARKET RISK MANAGEMENT

By its very nature, market risk requires constant management attention and adequate analysis. Prudent managers should be aware of exactly how a bank's market risk exposure relates to its capital (see figure 9.4). Market risk management policies should specifically state a bank's objectives and the related policy guidelines that have been established to protect capital from the negative impact of unfavorable market price movements. Policy guidelines should normally be formulated within restrictions provided by the applicable legal and prudential framework. While policies related to market risk management may vary among banks, certain types of policies typically are present in all banks.

Marking to Market

This refers to the (re)pricing of a bank's portfolios to reflect changes in asset prices due to market price movements. This policy requires that the asset be (re)priced at the market value of the asset in compliance with International Accounting Standard (IAS) 39. The volume and nature of the activities in which a bank engages generally determine the frequency of pricing. It is considered prudent for a bank to evaluate and (re)price positions related to its investment portfolio on at least a monthly basis. Since assets in a trading portfolio are sold and bought on an ongoing

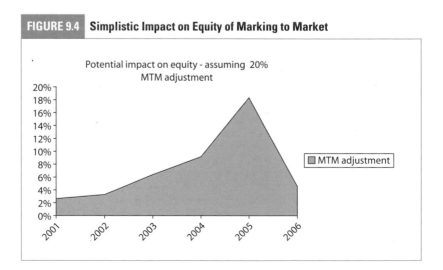

FIGURE 9.4 **Simplistic Impact on Equity of Marking to Market**

Potential impact on equity - assuming 20% MTM adjustment

MTM adjustment

basis, price positions related to a bank's trading portfolio should be evaluated and marked to market at least once a day. The reports prepared in this process should be submitted to and reviewed by the senior bank managers responsible for the bank's investment, asset-liability, and risk management.

Due to the shortage of marketable *Shariah*-compliant securities, the trading portfolio of Islamic banks is either very small or nonexistent. With the emergence of Islamic bonds (*sukuks*), this trend is changing, and more and more Islamic banks are maintaining trading portfolios. A shallow secondary market for Islamic bonds encourages hold-to-maturity behavior. Increased activity in the trading book should be accompanied by the above-mentioned analysis.

Financing assets like *murabahah* and *salaam* are not negotiable or tradable once the initial sale has taken place, which makes marking to market difficult. Since Islamic banks are still exposed to price risk in situations where the client refuses to take delivery of the underlying assets, Islamic banks should mark to market such assets and make doing so part of regular risk monitoring. Other financing assets based on *ijarah* and *istisah* are also not negotiable and not liquid, which makes the task of marking to market more difficult.

It is common practice for Islamic banks to invest their equity capital with the assets of investment account holders. In other words, they co-mingle equity capital with the assets of investment account holders, which makes it difficult to perform any meaningful analysis of equity's exposure to market movements. Given the importance of such analysis, it is strongly recommended that such funds be ring-fenced from the funds of investment account holders and a more formal analysis of different exposures be performed.

The policy regarding marking to market should also address responsibility for pricing and the method used by a bank to determine the new (market) price of an asset. Risk management policy should stipulate that prices be determined and that marking to market be executed by officers who are independent of the dealer or trader and his or her managers. Some jurisdictions have enacted prudential regulations that specifically cover the process of marking to market the value of a bank's assets, sometimes with a high level of detail. In practice, the pricing of positions is less effective if independent, third-party price quotes are not taken into consideration. A bank should routinely acquire from external sources the latest information on the price and performance of assets held in its portfolios.

Position Limits

A market risk management policy should provide for limits on positions (long, short, or net), bearing in mind the liquidity risk that could arise on execution of unrealized transactions such as open contracts or commitments to purchase and sell securities (for example, option contracts or repurchase agreements). Such position limits should be related to the capital available to cover market risk. Banks, especially those with large investment or trading portfolios, would also be expected to set limits on the level of risk taken by individual traders or dealers. These limits are related to several factors, including the specific organization of investment or trading functions and the technical skill level of individual dealers or traders. The sophistication and quality of analytical support that is provided to the dealers or traders also may play a role, as do the specific characteristics of a bank's investment or trading portfolios and the level and quality of its capital. This type of policy should specify the manner and frequency of position valuations and position limit controls.

Stop-Loss Provisions

Market risk management policy should also include stop-loss sale or consultation requirements that relate to a predetermined loss exposure limit (risk budget). The stop-loss exposure limit should be determined with regard to a bank's capital structure and earning trends as well as to its overall risk profile. When losses on a bank's positions reach unacceptable levels, either the positions should be automatically closed or consultations should be initiated with risk management officers or the asset-liability committee in order to establish or reconfirm the stop-loss strategy.

Limits to New Market Presence

Financial innovations involve profits that are much higher than those of standard instruments, because profit is a key factor motivating innovation. In a highly competitive market environment, innovation also pressures competitors to engage in new business in an effort to make profits or not to lose market presence. However, innovation involves a special kind of risk taking, requiring that a bank be willing to invest in or trade a new instrument even though its return and variance may not have been tested in a market setting or even though the appropriate market for the instrument may not yet exist.

A prudent bank should have risk management policies that address its presence in new markets and its trading in new financial instruments. Limits related to a new market presence should be reviewed frequently and adjusted as needed. Because the high spreads initially available in new market segments attract competitors, markets may pick up at a fast pace. Increasing use of a new instrument also helps to increase the breadth and depth of secondary markets and thus their liquidity. Once a market becomes established and sufficiently liquid, a bank should readjust the limits to levels applicable to mature markets.

Due to the fast-changing nature of a bank's trading book and the complexity of risk management, banks engaged in trading must have market risk measurement and management systems that are conceptually sound and implemented with high integrity. The Basel Committee on Banking Supervision's capital adequacy standard for market risk specifies a set of qualitative criteria that must be met for a bank to be eligible for application of the minimum multiplication factor for market risk capital charges.

An independent risk control unit should be responsible for the design and implementation of the bank's market risk management system. The unit should be independent from business trading units and should report directly to senior management of the bank. It should produce daily reports on and analysis of the relationship between the measures of risk exposure and trading limits.

Board and senior management need to be involved actively in the risk control process and regard risk control as an essential aspect of business. Managers who have sufficient seniority and authority should review the daily reports prepared by the independent risk control unit and be willing to enforce reductions in the positions taken by individual traders and in the bank's overall risk exposure.

The market risk measurement system should be closely integrated into the daily risk management process of a bank and be actively used in conjunction with trading and exposure limits. The risk measurement system should be subject to regular back-testing—that is, to ex post comparison of the risk measure generated by the bank's internal model against daily changes in portfolio value and against hypothetical changes based on static positions. The ultimate test is to compare actual profits or losses with budgeted profits.

A routine and rigorous program of stress testing is needed to supplement the risk analysis provided by the model. The results of stress testing should be subject to review by senior management and be reflected in the policies and limits regarding market risk exposure, especially where stress tests reveal particular vulnerability to a given set of circumstances.

Finally, a process is needed to ensure compliance with a documented set of bank policies, controls, and procedures concerning the trading activities and operation of the risk measurement system.

NOTES

1. For detailed discussion on different risks and exposure of Islamic banks, see Iqbal and Mirakhor (2007).
2. This gives rise to fiduciary risk, as discussed previously.
3. Khan (1994) claims that Islamic banks can invest in large enterprises because users of the funds who own large stakes in the business would not put the bank in a disadvantageous position. This might reduce risk overall and improve the profitability of the bank.
4. Sadr and Iqbal (2000) provide empirical evidence that increased monitoring of an Islamic bank resulted in an increase in the share of *musharakah* contracts on the assets side of the balance sheet. Additional monitoring produced higher returns, which recovered the costs of monitoring.

10

Operational and Islamic Banking Risks

Operational risk has received considerable attention in the literature and is now part of the integrated risk management framework of all financial institutions. Islamic banks are also exposed to such risks. In addition, they are exposed to several risks that are very specific to Islamic banks. Such specific risks stem from the nature of their business, business environment, competition, and certain prevailing practices. These risks include displaced commercial risk, withdrawal risk, fiduciary risk, *Shariah risk*, and reputational risk, which are discussed in detail in this chapter.

OPERATIONAL RISK

Operational risk is defined as the risk of loss resulting from the inadequacy or failure of internal processes, as related to people and systems, or from external risks. Operational risk also includes the risk of failure of technology, systems, and analytical models. It is argued that operational risks are likely to be significant for Islamic banks due to their specific contractual features and the general legal environment. Specific aspects of Islamic banking could raise the operational risks of Islamic banks:

- Cancellation risks in the nonbinding *murabahah* (partnership) and *istisnah* (manufacturing) contracts;
- Failure of the internal control system to detect and manage potential problems in the operational processes and back-office functions as well as technical risks of various sorts;

Key Messages

- Islamic banks are perceived to be more exposed to *operational risks* associated with the failure of controls, procedures, information technology systems, and analytical models.
- Distinct features of Islamic financial instruments require enhanced controls and information technology systems. Compliance with *Shariah* also demands better controls and monitoring.
- *Displaced commercial risk* is considered a special risk for Islamic banks, which are exposed to the risk of paying profits out of equity in periods when actual profits are lower than expected.
- *Withdrawal risk* exposes banks to the risk of losing deposits to competition from other Islamic or conventional banks when actual rates of return are lower than expectations or the prevailing rates of return offered by competitors.
- Lack of standardized practices by the *Shariah* boards in different jurisdictions and the challenge of compliance with *Shariah* expose Islamic banks to *Shariah risk*.
- Investors-depositors and the users of funds place a special trust in Islamic banks to be fully compliant with *Shariah*. A breach of trust by a single institution can affect all institutions by exposing them all to *reputational risk*.

- Potential difficulties in enforcing Islamic contracts in a broader legal environment;
- Need to maintain and manage commodity inventories often in illiquid markets;
- Failure to comply with *Shariah* requirements;
- Potential costs and risks of monitoring equity-type contracts and the associated legal risks.

People risk is another type of operational risk arising from incompetence or fraud. An internal control problem cost the Dubai Islamic Bank $50 million in 1998 when a bank official did not conform to the bank's credit terms. This resulted in a one-day run on the bank's deposits to the tune of $138 million, representing 7 percent of the bank's total deposits (Warde 2000).

Technology risk is another type of operational risk. It is associated with the use of software and telecommunications systems that are not tailored specifically to the needs of Islamic banks. The quality of management processes raises specific risks for Islamic banks. As an emerging industry that is required to abide by particular rules, Islamic finance faces the risk of securing management skills fully conversant with the principles of conventional and Islamic finance. Familiarity with either finance rules or *Shariah* rules may not be an issue, but individuals with knowledge of both are hard to find. In addition, compliance with *Shariah* rules requires management information systems that are scarce.

Operational risk is considered high on the list of risk exposures for Islamic banks. A survey conducted by Khan and Ahmed (2001) shows that the managers of Islamic banks perceive operational risk as the most critical risk after markup risk. The survey finds that operational risk is lower in the fixed-income contracts of *murabahah* (cost-plus sales) and *ijarah* (leasing) and higher in the deferred sales contracts of *salaam* (agriculture) and *istisnah* (manufacturing). The relatively higher rankings of the instruments indicate that banks find these contracts complex and difficult to implement.

The three methods of measuring operational risk proposed in Basel II would have to be adapted considerably if they were to apply to Islamic banks. The use of gross income as the basic indicator of operational risk could be misleading in Islamic banks, insofar as the large volume of transactions in commodities and the use of structured finance raise operational exposures that are not captured by gross income. In contrast, the standardized approach that allows for different business lines would be better suited, but it would have to be adapted to the needs of Islamic banks. In particular, agency services under *mudarabah* and commodity inventory management need to be considered explicitly.

RISKS SPECIFIC TO ISLAMIC BANKING

Islamic banks face unique challenges in the following areas: displaced commercial risk, withdrawal risk, governance, fiduciary risk, transparency, *Shariah* risk, and reputational risks. This section deals with each in turn.

Displaced Commercial Risk

The Accounting and Auditing Organization of Islamic Financial Institutions (AAOIFI) has identified displaced commercial risk as the risk when an Islamic bank is under pressure to pay its investors-depositors a rate of return higher than what should be payable under the "actual" terms of the investment contract. This can occur when a bank underperforms during a period and is unable to generate adequate profits for distribution to the account holders.

To mitigate displaced commercial risk, Islamic banks may decide to waive their portion of profits and thus dissuade depositors from withdrawing their funds. Islamic banks often engage in this self-imposed practice. An extreme example is the International Islamic Bank for Investment and Development in Egypt, which distributed all of its profits to investment account holders and nothing to shareholders from the middle to late 1980s (Warde 2000). In 1988 the bank distributed to its depositors an amount exceeding its profits, and the difference appeared in the bank's accounts as "loss carried forward." The practice of forgoing part or all of the shareholders' profits may adversely affect the bank's own capital, which can lead to insolvency risk in extreme cases.

The experience gained from the attempt to mitigate displaced risk has led to the development of two standard practices in the industry. The first practice is for the financial institution to maintain a profit equalization reserve (PER). This reserve is funded by setting aside a portion of gross income before deducting the bank's own share (as agent). The reserve provides a cushion to ensure smooth future returns and to increase the owners' equity for bearing future shocks. Similar to PER, an investment risk reserve (IRR) is maintained out of the income of investors-depositors after allocating the bank's share, in order to dampen the effects of the risk of future investment losses. It has been suggested that the basis for computing the amounts to be appropriated should be predefined and fully disclosed.

In its most general form, risk is uncertainty associated with a future outcome or event. To an investment account holder in an Islamic bank, the risk is the expected variance in the measure of profits that are shared with the depositor. This variance could arise from a variety of both systemic and idiosyncratic (that is, bank-specific) factors. Actual risk in the investment account is dampened in practice by holding PER to reduce or eliminate the variability of return on investment deposits and offer returns that are aligned to market rates of return on conventional deposits or other benchmarks. In addition, banks may use IRR to redistribute over time the income accrued to the investment accounts. Nevertheless, from an investor's point of view, the true risk of *mudarabah* investment in a bank can be measured by a simple measure of profit at risk (PAR). For example, the standard deviation of the monthly profit as a percentage of assets, σp, provides the basis for a simple measure of the risks of holding an investment account.

From a monthly time series of *mudarabah* profits (as a share of assets), its variance (and the standard deviation σp) can be calculated; assuming normality, profit at risk can be calculated as $PAR = Z\alpha \ \sigma p \ \sqrt{T}$, where $Z\alpha =$ is the constant that gives the appropriate one-tailed confidence interval with a probability of $1 - \alpha$ for the standard normal distribution (for example, $Z \ldots 01 = 2.33$ for 0.99 percent confidence interval), and $T =$ holding period or maturity of investment account as a fraction of month (Sundarajan 2004).

Such aggregate PAR for a bank as a whole provides a first-cut estimate of the risks in unrestricted *mudarabah* accounts. Such calculations could also be applied to individual business units within the bank (and to specific portfolios linked to restricted investment deposits). In addition, if specific risk factors that affect the variation in *mudarabah* profits can be identified, σp can be decomposed further in order to estimate the impact of individual risk factors, and this would help to refine the PAR calculation. In practice, however, Islamic banks use profit equalization reserves to smooth the return on investment accounts. As a result, banks themselves absorb the risks in investment accounts insofar as profit equalization reserves are strongly, positively correlated with net return on assets (gross return on assets minus provisions for loan losses). That is, PER is raised or lowered when the return on assets rises or falls, and hence the investment accounts are insulated from both gains and losses. The correlation between PER and return on assets could, therefore, be viewed as a measure of displaced commercial risk.

The practice of maintaining reserves to ensure smooth income over a period of time is becoming common practice, but it has attracted objections as well. While this practice is in alignment with prudent risk management, it raises a governance issue that needs attention. First, limited disclosure of such reserves makes investment account holders uneasy. Second, investment account holders do not have the rights to influence the use of such reserves and to verify the exposure of overall investments. Third, investment account holders with long-term investment objectives may welcome this practice, but investors with a short-term view may feel that they are subsidizing the returns of long-term investors. Finally, some banks require investment account holders to waive their rights to these reserves.

Islamic financial institutions should standardize the practice, and the rights of investment account holders to these reserves should be clearly stated and explained to the depositors. One suggestion is that the profits should be deducted only from long-term depositors, who are more likely to be exposed to such risk, and not from short-term depositors, who are not exposed to it.

Withdrawal Risk

Another type of business risk is "withdrawal risk," which results mainly from the competitive pressures an Islamic bank faces both from other Islamic banks and from conventional banks with Islamic windows. An Islamic bank could be exposed to the risk that depositors will withdraw their funds if they are receiving a lower rate of return than they would receive from another bank. If an Islamic bank is run inefficiently and keeps producing lower returns, depositors eventually will decide to move their money, eroding the franchise value of the bank.

Governance Risk

The importance of governance and the risks associated with poor governance have recently attracted the attention of researchers and policy makers. Governance risk refers to the risk arising from a failure to govern the institution, negligence in conducting business and meeting contractual obligations, and a weak internal and external institutional environment, including legal risk, whereby banks are unable to enforce their contracts.

Fiduciary Risk

Fiduciary risk is the risk that arises from an institution's failure to perform in accordance with explicit and implicit standards applicable to its fiduciary responsibilities. Fiduciary risk leads to the risk of facing legal recourse if the bank breaches its fiduciary responsibility toward depositors and shareholders. As fiduciary agents, Islamic banks are expected to act in the best interests of investors-depositors and shareholders. If and when the objectives of investors and shareholders diverge from the actions of the bank, the bank is exposed to fiduciary risk.

The following are some examples of fiduciary risk:

- In case of partnership-based investment in the form of *mudarabah* and *musharakah* on the assets side, the bank is expected to perform adequate screening and monitoring of projects, and any deliberate or intentional negligence in evaluating and monitoring the project can lead to fiduciary risk. It becomes incumbent on management to perform due diligence before committing the funds of investors-depositors.
- Mismanagement of the funds of current account holders, which are accepted on a trust (*amanah*) basis, can expose the bank to fiduciary risk as well. It is common practice for Islamic banks to use the funds of current account holders without being obliged to share the profits with them. However, in the case of heavy losses on the investments financed by the funds of current account holders, the depositors can lose confidence in the bank and decide to seek legal recourse.
- Mismanagement in governing the business by incurring unnecessary expenses or allocating excessive expenses to investment account holders is a breach of the implicit contract to act in a transparent fashion.

Fiduciary risk can lead to dire consequences. First, it can cause reputational risk, creating panic among depositors, who may rush to withdraw their funds. Second, it may require the bank to pay a penalty or compensation, which can result in a financial loss. Third, it can have a negative impact on the market price of shareholders' equity. Fourth, it can affect the bank's cost and access to liquidity. Finally, it may lead to insolvency if the bank is unable to meet the demands of current investment account holders.

Fiduciary risk emanates directly from the profit- and loss-sharing feature of Islamic finance. AAOIFI (1999) defines fiduciary risk as being legally liable for a breach of the investment contract either for noncompliance with *Shariah* rules or for mismanagement of investors' funds. Such legal liability would expose the bank to both direct and indirect losses.[1] In addition, negligence or misconduct would damage the reputation of the bank. Even a financially sound bank risks losing the confidence—and thus the funds—of its depositors (Ali 2002). Fiduciary risk also exposes equity holders and investment depositors to the risk of economic losses, as they would not receive their share of profits.[2]

In this context, information disclosure facilitates market discipline and enables different stakeholders to protect their own interests by allowing depositors to withdraw their funds, shareholders to sell their shares, and regulators to take the necessary actions in case of mismanagement or misconduct. However, the differences in accounting treatment between Islamic banks have reduced the comparability, consistency, and transparency of financial statements (Archer and Ahmed 2003). This creates uncertainty and limits the potential role of market discipline.

Transparency Risk

Transparency is defined as "the public disclosure of reliable and timely information that enables users of that information to make an accurate assessment of a bank's financial condition and performance, business activities, risk profile, and risk management practices" (Basel Committee on Banking Supervision 1998). Accordingly, lack of transparency creates the risk of incurring losses due to bad decisions based on incomplete or inaccurate information. Lack of transparency arises from two sources: the use of nonstandard conventions for reporting Islamic financial contracts and the lack of uniform standards of reporting among banks. Islamic financial instruments require different conventions of reporting to reflect the bank's true financial picture. Transparency also demands that all banks in the system use a uniform set of standards, which is not the current practice.

The disclosure regime for Islamic banks needs to become more comprehensive and transparent, with a focus on the disclosure of risk profile, risk-return mix, and internal governance. This requires coordinating the rules of supervisory disclosure and accounting standards with the proper differentiation between consumer-friendly disclosure to assist investment account holders and market-oriented disclosure to inform the markets.

Shariah Risk

Shariah risk is related to the structure and functioning of *Shariah* boards at the institutional and systemic level. This risk could be of two types; the first is due to nonstandard practices in respect of different contracts in different jurisdictions, and the second is due to the failure to comply with *Shariah* rules. Differences in the interpretation of *Shariah* rules result in differences in financial reporting, auditing, and accounting treatment. For instance, while some *Shariah* scholars consider the terms of a *murabahah* or *istisnah* contract to be binding on the buyer, others argue that the buyer has the option to decline even after placing an order and paying the commitment fee. While different schools of thought consider different practices to be acceptable, the bank's risk is higher in nonbinding cases and may lead to litigation in the case of unsettled transactions.

The relationship between the bank and the investors-depositors is not only that of an agent and principal; it is also based on an implicit trust between the two that the agent will respect the desires of the principal to comply fully with the *Shariah*. This relationship distinguishes Islamic banking from conventional banking and is the sole justification for the existence of Islamic banks. If the bank is unable to maintain this trust and the bank's actions lead to noncompliance with the *Shariah*, the bank risks breaking the confidence of the investors-depositors. Therefore, the bank should give high priority to ensuring transparency in compliance with the *Shariah* and take actions to avoid lack of compliance.

Some *Shariah* scholars have suggested that, if a bank fails to act in accordance with the *Shariah* rules, the transaction should be considered null and void, and any income derived from it should not be included in the profits to be distributed to the investors-depositors.

REPUTATIONAL RISK

Reputational risk, or "headline risk," is the risk that the irresponsible actions or behavior of management will damage the trust of the bank's clients. Although the fiduciary and *Shariah* risks also stem from negligence and noncompliance, reputational risk is the risk that the irresponsible behavior of a single institution could taint the reputation of other banks in the industry. Negative publicity can have a significant impact on an institution's market share, profitability, and liquidity. The Islamic financial services industry is a relatively young industry, and a single failed institution could give a bad name to other banks that are not engaged in irresponsible behavior. Nevertheless, all Islamic banks in a given market are exposed to such risk. Close collaboration among financial institutions, standardization of contracts and practices, self-examination, and establishment of industry associations are some of the steps needed to mitigate reputational risk.

NOTES

1. The latter effect should impose indirect market discipline on Islamic banks, as is discussed in the next section.
2. For instance, any profits accrued to the bank as a result of investment in non-*Shariah*-acceptable assets would be distributed for charitable purposes.

PART Three

Governance and Regulation

11

Governance Issues in Islamic Banks

For the most part, the corporate governance arrangements of Islamic banks are modeled along the lines of a conventional shareholder corporation (see figure 11.1).[1] This configuration leads to a distribution of rights and responsibilities that essentially leaves control with shareholders. However, Islamic finance raises unique challenges for corporate governance. In particular, two broad sets of issues require specific treatment. The first revolves around the need to reassure stakeholders that the Islamic bank's financial activities comply fully with the precepts of Islamic jurisprudence. Ultimately, the raison d'être of Islamic finance is to meet the desire of stakeholders to conduct their financial business according to *Shariah* principles. Mechanisms are needed to comfort and safeguard them to that effect. This role is played by *Shariah* boards composed of scholars and *Shariah* review units within Islamic banks that ensure compliance with Islamic law.

The second revolves around the stakeholders' need to be comforted in their belief that Islamic banks will promote their financial interests, proving to be efficient, stable, and trustworthy providers of financial services. In practice, depositors and borrowers need to be reassured that Islamic banks deal with liabilities and assets that are competitive and offer an acceptable risk-return tradeoff to their clients.

STAKEHOLDER-BASED GOVERNANCE MODEL

In theory, the Islamic economic system fully supports and endorses a stakeholder view of governance based on Islam's principles of the

---

Key Messages

- The corporate governance of Islamic banks is modeled along the lines of a conventional share-holder corporation, with distinct features such as the existence of *Shariah* boards and the role of investors as depositors.
- *Shariah* endorses a stakeholder-oriented model of corporate governance in light of Islamic tenets of property rights and contracts. Such a stakeholder-oriented model recognizes the rights and responsibilities of different stakeholders and seeks to preserve the rights of all stakeholders.
- The functioning of internal *Shariah* boards raises five issues for corporate governance: independence, confidentiality, competence, consistency, and disclosure.
- Since depositors of Islamic banks are investors, their role as quasi-shareholders has to be recognized. The governance structure should include the protection of rights of different classes of investment account holders.
- On the assets side, Islamic banks may enter into partnerships and take an equity stake. In such cases, Islamic banks themselves become a stakeholder in other institutions and therefore may exert some influence, which may complicate the governance structure.

---

preservation of property rights and the sanctity of contracts. Research has shown that a *Shariah*-based stakeholder-centered model of governance offers a comprehensive framework of governance (for a more detailed analysis, see Iqbal and Mirakhor 2004). As such, the corporate governance model derives from an understanding of three principles of Islam:

- Recognition of the property rights of individuals, legal entities (firms), and the community;
- Significance of contractual obligations, explicit as well as implicit, among economic agents;
- The design of incentive systems to enforce *Shariah* rules and preserve the social order.

The principles of property rights and the treatment of contracts differentiate the functions and obligations of an Islamic financial institution from those of a conventional bank. Islam is a rule-based system geared to protecting the rights of all members of society, both individually and collectivity. The conventional economic system is based on a "shareholder- or owner-centered" governance system. However, there is

FIGURE 11.1 Corporate Governance Structures in Institutions Offering Islamic and Conventional Financial Services

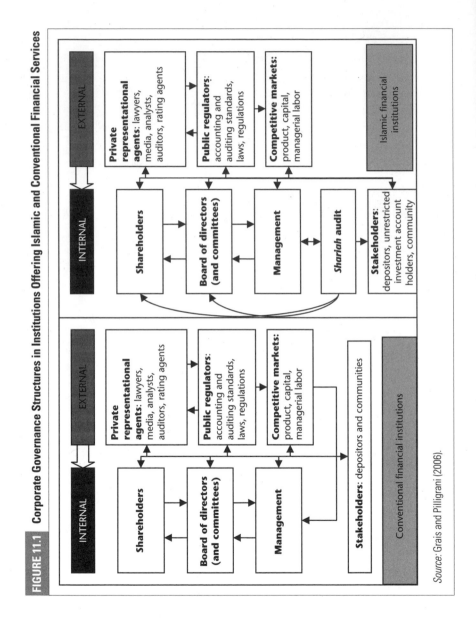

Source: Grais and Pilligrani (2006).

growing acceptance of the idea that stakeholders should be included in the governance structure, but no solid theoretical foundation to date. Questions such as why a stakeholder should be part of the governance system and who should be qualified to be a stakeholder are the subject of debate.

In contrast to the conventional system, the Islamic financial system is based on the active participation of public policy institutions, regulatory and supervisory authorities, and *Shariah* authorities. These institutions collectively monitor the performance of the firm and its faithfulness and commitment to explicit as well as implicit contracts. This structure and process of governance incorporates the legitimate rights and claims of stakeholders whenever a stakeholder's rights are at "risk" due to the activities of the firm. This does not in any way negate or undermine the rights of shareholders to maximize profits, but it does impose on Islamic banks the obligation to protect the rights of stakeholders through explicit or implicit contracts.

ROLE AND RESPONSIBILITIES OF *SHARIAH* BOARDS

A distinctive feature of Islamic banks is the pledge to conduct activities in accordance with the principles of *Shariah*. Islamic banks have created corporate governance structures and processes to reassure stakeholders that all transactions conform to *Shariah* principles and to ensure compliance. *Shariah* supervisory boards, operating either within the Islamic bank itself or through an external institution such as the central bank, ensure conformity with religious principles. Each board has the authority to design, develop, and issue *Shariah*-compliant financial products and legal instruments. *Shariah* boards exist in all Islamic countries with the exception of the Islamic Republic of Iran, where the central bank guarantees and monitors compliance of the whole banking system with *Shariah* (see table 11.1 for an overview).

The internal tasks of *Shariah* supervisory boards vary according to the provisions stipulated in the particular Islamic bank's articles of association or by national regulators. However, a review of 13 Islamic banks for which sufficient information was available revealed that all *Shariah* supervisory boards are entrusted with ex ante monitoring.[2] Next to internal regulations, international and national regulators often implement guidelines for *Shariah* boards. These generally refer to the duty to ensure *Shariah* compliance of transactions and less frequently specify competencies, composition, and decision-making authority. Table 11.2 provides an overview of practice in select countries that have

Table 11.1   Presence of a Centralized *Shariah* Supervisory Board or Islamic Rating Agency in Select Countries

Country	Centralized Shariah board or high Shariah authority or fatwa board	Islamic rating agency
Jordan	No	No
Malaysia	✓	✓
Sudan	✓	No
Bahrain[a]	No	No
Kuwait	✓	No
Pakistan	✓	No
United Arab Emirates	✓	No
Indonesia	✓	No

Source: Grais and Pilligrani (2006).
a. Bahrain is the seat of the International Islamic Financial Market and the International Islamic Rating Agency, which, respectively, set standards for Islamic jurisprudence and rate Islamic instruments on an international scale.

Table 11.2   Regulations Governing *Shariah* Supervisory Boards in Select Countries[a]

Country	Terms of reference	Composition	Decision making	Appointment and dismissal	Fit and proper criteria
Bahrain	✓	✓	Unspecified	✓	✓
Dubai International Financial Center	✓	✓	Unspecified	✓	✓
Indonesia	✓	Unspecified	Unspecified	✓	✓
Jordan	✓	✓	✓	✓	Unspecified
Kuwait	✓	✓	✓	Unspecified	Unspecified
Lebanon	✓	✓	Unspecified	✓	Unspecified
Malaysia	✓	Unspecified	Unspecified	Unspecified	✓
Pakistan	✓	✓	Unspecified	✓	✓
Philippines	✓	✓	Unspecified	Unspecified	✓
Thailand	✓	✓	Unspecified	✓	✓
United Arab Emirates	✓	✓	Unspecified	✓	Unspecified

Source: Grais and Pilligrani (2006).

introduced guidelines or legislative edicts related to the functioning of *Shariah* boards.[3] Whereas all countries in the survey define the terms of reference for *Shariah* boards, rulings on the decision-making process or transparency are not uniform.

In principle, *Shariah* boards are responsible for five main areas: certification of permissible financial instruments through *fatwas* (ex ante *Shariah* audit), verification of transactions' compliance with issued *fatwas* (ex post *Shariah* audit), the calculation and payment of *zakat* (alms giving), disposal of non-*Shariah*-compliant earnings, and advice on the distribution of income or expenses among the bank's shareholders and investment account holders.[4] Each *Shariah* board issues a report to certify the *Shariah* compliance of all financial transactions. This report usually forms an integral part of the institution's annual report.

ISSUES IN *SHARIAH* GOVERNANCE

The functioning of internal *Shariah* boards raises five issues for corporate governance: independence, confidentiality, competence, consistency, and disclosure.

The first issue concerns the *independence* of the *Shariah* supervisory board from the management. Generally, members of *Shariah* boards are appointed by the shareholders of the bank, represented by the board of directors. As such, they are employed by the bank, and their remuneration is proposed by the management and approved by the board. The board members' dual relationship with the Islamic bank as provider of remunerated services and as assessor of the nature of operations can create a conflict of interest. In principle, *Shariah* boards are required to submit an unbiased opinion in all matters pertaining to their assignment. However, their employment status generates an economic stake in the bank, which may compromise their independence. In practice, the conflict-of-interest risk may be mitigated by the ethical standards of the individual members of the *Shariah* board and the high cost that a stained reputation would inflict both on them and on the Islamic bank. Generally, members of *Shariah* boards are highly regarded scholars and guardians of the principles of *Shariah*, making less than truthful assessment and disclosure of *Shariah* compliance unlikely. Similarly, managerial interference in compliance assessments may lead to a loss of confidence on the part of shareholders and other stakeholders, in addition to the imposition of penalties and even dismissal. Thus the cost of false assessments could be heavy. This notwithstanding, a potential conflict of interest is embedded in existing arrangements.

Confidentiality issues may be intertwined with issues of independence. Many *Shariah* scholars sit on various boards. This multiple membership may be a strength, as it may enhance independence vis-à-vis a particular

Islamic bank. However, it entails access to proprietary information of different, possibly competing, Islamic banks. Thus *Shariah* board members may find themselves in the midst of a potential conflict of interest. Malaysia has dealt with this issue by encouraging jurists to sit on the board of only one Islamic bank. While this method would eliminate concerns about confidentiality, the practice poses problems. First, it may exacerbate the lack of competence in areas with a scarcity of *Shariah* experts.[5] Second, it may prevent the formation of an efficient labor market by lessening the economic appeal of the auditing profession. Finally, it may create a symbiotic relationship between the auditor and the Islamic bank that undermines impartiality.

Shariah board members are required to combine a diverse set of *competencies*. They should be knowledgeable in both Islamic law and commercial, banking, and accounting practices. Very few scholars are well versed in all these disciplines. The issue has been addressed by including members from different backgrounds on most *Shariah* boards.[6] The combination of experts rather than expertise poses the challenge of overcoming different perspectives as well as potential failures of communication. Over time, the gap between the supply of and the demand for individuals with both *Shariah* and financial skills is likely to narrow through public policy and formal cross-disciplinary training. Progress in this direction is already noticeable in countries where the Islamic financial industry is well established. However, in countries where Islamic finance is less developed, transitional incentives may be needed.

The fourth issue concerns *consistency of judgment* across Islamic banks over time or across jurisdictions within the same Islamic bank. The activities of *Shariah* boards create jurisprudence by their interpretation of legal sources. As such, it would not be surprising to find conflicting opinions on the admissibility of specific financial instruments or transactions. However, the diversity of opinion is less widespread than expected.[7] Nevertheless, as the industry expands, the number of conflicting rulings on the permissibility of an instrument is likely to grow if no efforts are made to harmonize the standards. This may undermine customer confidence in the industry and have repercussions on the enforceability of contracts.

The last and overarching issue is the *disclosure of all information* relating to *Shariah* advisory. Stable corporate governance systems seek to enhance the soundness of *Shariah* governance. The framework is enhanced by arrangements put in place by regulators and external providers of financial information services. In addition, public rating agencies create a positive climate for *Shariah* compliance. However, private mechanisms for the external governance of *Shariah* compliance are limited. Private rating agencies have not yet developed the necessary skills or found enough incentives to monitor Islamic bank compliance with the *Shariah*.

SHARIAH REVIEW UNITS AND OTHER STRUCTURES

In addition to *Shariah* boards, most Islamic banks, particularly those complying with standards of the Accounting and Auditing Organization for Islamic Financial Institutions (AAOIFI), have established another internal *Shariah* review structure: the *Shariah* review unit.[8] These units are independent of other departments or are an integral part of the institution's audit and control department. They perform an array of tasks similar to that of the audit department: reviewers generally use all powers necessary to ascertain that all financial transactions implemented by management comply with *Shariah* board rulings. In this respect, the role of the internal review unit is limited to complementary ex post monitoring. This makes its task secondary, if more focused and defined, to that of the *Shariah* boards, which are the ultimate arbiters in matters of *Shariah* compliance. In some instances, *Shariah* review units have been given exclusive responsibility for ex post monitoring.[9] These units face many of the same challenges as *Shariah* boards, in particular, regarding independence and competence.

Beyond internal arrangements, the broader *Shariah* governance framework may include features put in place by regulators, such as the provision of financial information to persons outside the institution. Among regulatory arrangements, centralized *Shariah* boards are the most noteworthy in relation to *Shariah* governance. While there are significant differences across countries, centralized *Shariah* boards are usually concerned with ex ante monitoring, mostly understood as standardization of *Shariah* interpretation, and with ex post monitoring of *Shariah* compliance. They also are concerned with issues related to upholding *Shariah* compliance and offer arbitration and recourse to settlement of *Shariah* disputes among members of the same *Shariah* board. See table 11.3 for an overview of centralized boards in select countries (Grais and Pilligrani 2006).

Private mechanisms for external monitoring of *Shariah* compliance are limited. In particular, private rating agencies have not yet developed the necessary skills or have enough incentives to monitor Islamic banks' *Shariah* compliance. "Islamic rating" has so far been the exclusive domain of government-sponsored organizations such as the International Islamic Rating Agency and the Malaysian Rating Corporation. Likewise, other external actors with an interest in Islamic finance, such as financial media

Table 11.3 External *Shariah* Boards in Select Countries

Country	Centralized Shariah board or high Shariah authority or fatwa board
Bahrain	No. But the international Islamic financial market promotes the harmonization and convergence of *Shariah* interpretations in developing Islamic banking products and practices that are universally acceptable.
Indonesia	Yes. The National *Shariah* Board is authorized to issue *fatwas* concerning products, services, and operations of Islamic banks. It also recommends *Shariah* advisers to Islamic banks.
Iran, Islamic Rep. of	No. All are embedded in the by-laws of the central bank.
Jordan	No.
Kuwait	The Fatwa Board in the Ministry of Awqaf and Islamic Affairs is the final authority on *Shariah* disputes. Its advice is binding when it arbitrates on disputes between members of the same *Shariah* board.
Malaysia	Yes. The *Shariah* Council advises the central bank on *Shariah* matters and is the ultimate arbiter in *Shariah* interpretations of disputes. The directives issued by Bank Negara Malaysia in consultation with the *Shariah* Council have binding authority over banks with Islamic windows.
Pakistan	Yes. The *Shariah* Board of the State Bank advises the central bank on matters of *Shariah*. It also produces templates of permissible Islamic financial contracts to ensure compliance with minimum *Shariah* standards.
Sudan	Yes. The *Shariah* High Supervisory Board is responsible for fatwas, contract templates, arbitrage, consultations relating to Islamic legal aspects, training, research, lectures, and seminars.
Saudi Arabia	No.
United Arab Emirates	Yes. The Higher *Shariah* Authority, attached to the Ministry of Justice and Islamic Affairs, is the final arbiter in *Shariah* matters. It is also responsible for *Shariah* supervision.

Source: Grais and Pilligrani (2006).

and external auditors, are generally less concerned with assessments of *Shariah* compliance.[10]

IMPROVEMENT IN *SHARIAH* GOVERNANCE

Shariah governance could be made more efficient and uniform. First, creation of an international standard-setting self-regulatory association would help to harmonize standards and practices. Such an approach could ensure consistency of interpretation and enhance the enforceability of contracts before the civil courts. Review of transactions would be entrusted mainly to internal review units, which, in collaboration with external auditors, would be responsible for issuing an annual opinion on the *Shariah* compliance of transactions. This process would be sustained by reputable agents, like rating agencies, stock markets, financial media, and researchers, that would channel signals to market players. Such a framework would also enhance public understanding of the requirements of *Shariah* and lead stakeholders to play a more effective role in the activities of the institution.

Second, creation of a systemwide board of knowledgeable religious scholars who specialize in Islamic economic and financial principles would be more efficient and lead to optimal governance structures. Countries such as Malaysia and Sudan have adopted this structure, forming a group of highly competent scholars and experts in finance, banking, economics, accounting, and finance to serve on a systemwide or national *Shariah* board.

Such a systemwide *Shariah* board could work closely with regulators and supervisors to devise effective monitoring and supervisory controls that protect the rights of stakeholders according to Islamic principles. The board is responsible for ensuring that compliance with the monitoring system protects the rights of stakeholders with whom the financial institution has explicit or implicit contracts. This structure of governance is more efficient and cost-effective than that of internal *Shariah* boards for the following reasons:

- Each stakeholder is not required to duplicate monitoring;
- Each institution is not required to maintain its own *fatwa*-issuing board;
- The *fatwa*-issuing board consists of knowledgeable experts in finance as well as the *Shariah*;
- There is uniformity of expected behavior, which sets the standards to be followed by individual institutions.

INVESTMENT ACCOUNT HOLDERS AS STAKEHOLDERS

Islamic banks generally have corporate governance structures and systems similar to those of conventional systems for handling agency problems between shareholders and management. In addition, a framework is needed to protect the financial interests of stakeholders, in this case, investment account holders. Generally, Islamic banks offer three broad categories of deposit-investment accounts: current accounts, unrestricted investment accounts, and restricted investment accounts. Each category raises corporate governance issues, but those of unrestricted investment accounts are the most challenging. Current and restricted accounts are considered briefly before turning to unrestricted investment accounts.

Current accounts take one of three general forms: (a) the *amanah* or "trust deposits," where the Islamic bank acts as a trustee and promises to pay back the deposit in full, (b) the *qard hassan*, or goodwill loan, where the bank receives a loan from depositors and owes the principal amount only, and (c) the *wadiah*, or safe deposits and guaranteed banking, with the amount of principal payable on demand. In all cases, the Islamic bank obtains implicit or explicit authorization to use the deposited money for any purpose permitted by the *Shariah* and pays no fixed interest or profit shares to the depositor, with the exception of gifts (*hiba*) distributed at the bank's discretion.[11] Current account holders need protection from the exposure to risky investments or excessive use of their funds to enhance the performance of overall investments or to benefit unrestricted investment accounts.

Investment account holders are like quasi-equity holders, but without any participation in governance of the financial institution. Since they do not participate in governance, they are at the mercy of public policy makers, regulators, and *Shariah* boards. A transparent and efficient governance arrangement is needed to include and protect their rights. The Islamic Financial Services Board, in its Standard on Corporate Governance, issued as an exposure draft, has proposed a governance committee that forms part of the institution and is responsible for safeguarding the interests of investment account holders.

In the case of *restricted investment accounts*, the bank acts as fund manager—agent or nonparticipating *mudarib*—and is not authorized to mix its funds with those of investors without prior permission. The Islamic bank operates these accounts under the principle of *mudarabah*, engaging in tailor-made investments and distributing profits geared to the risk appetite and needs of the client. Restricted account holders are normally savvy high-net-worth investors, whose holdings are large enough to induce them to monitor the agent's behavior directly. They have an interest in full disclosure of all relevant information about returns and risks. In addition, management is responsible for ensuring that their investments are ring-fenced from the rest and that full transparency is present in the identification and distribution of profits and losses.

Unrestricted investment accounts are the third and the most important category of Islamic bank accounts. They constitute the majority of deposits and are a characteristic feature of Islamic finance, posing distinctive challenges for corporate governance. Unrestricted account holders usually enter into a *mudarabah* contract with the Islamic bank,[12] in which the Islamic bank manages their funds and pays a share of returns according to a predetermined profit- and loss-sharing ratio. Unrestricted account holders bear the risk of the performance of the investment pool, except in the case of Islamic bank misconduct, a feature that makes them akin to shareholders. A significant difference is that the agent is appointed by another principal, the shareholder. In short, unrestricted account holders constitute a sui generis category of depositors with neither the capital value nor the returns on their deposits ex ante guaranteed. In principle, this does not constitute a problem, since the allocation of returns is governed by the ratio of the *mudarabah* contract. However, it is common practice to commingle shareholder and investment funds in a common pool, without a mechanism separating the two. Consequently, concern remains over shareholder-controlled management and boards that may favor and protect shareholders' investments at the expense of the holders of unrestricted investment accounts.

With selective application of international norms of corporate governance, regulators should deal with those issues that exclusively jeopardize the interests of Islamic bank stakeholders. The first priority for all depositors is to discontinue the practice of commingling funds because it casts a shadow on Islamic bank compliance with clients' investment mandates. Accordingly, regulatory authorities should stipulate rules and firewalls and establish sanctions for breaches. This is of paramount importance for unrestricted investment accounts. Shortcomings in current practices may require a combination of solutions.

On the one end, rights that normally belong to equity holders may be extended to the holders of unrestricted accounts. Doing so would satisfy the demand of depositors for greater involvement in the strategic management of banks.[13] Otherwise, a step may be taken in the opposite direction by granting unrestricted account holders full debt-holding status and the protection it carries. In most financial systems, regulators act on behalf of debt holders by requiring insurance on all deposits and taking control away from equity holders in case of distress. A *Shariah*-compliant version of deposit insurance could be put in place that would cover current accounts under all circumstances of bank insolvency and unrestricted accounts only in cases of insolvency deriving from fraudulent mismanagement. Alternatively, the sui generis status of unrestricted accounts may be maintained provided that governance structures are created to protect their interests. The key rationale would be to create a permanent institutional channel to facilitate the flow of information from and to unrestricted account holders.

However, the creation of a new agent would bring with it additional agency problems and the risk of multiplying rather than diffusing the asymmetries of information to which unrestricted investment accounts are subject. The creation of a complex body, made up of representatives from several parts of the firm, would certainly reduce the tendency to collusion, as the different members would cross-check each other's behavior. Yet it would not guarantee proper behavior.

Another issue pertains to the reserves that Islamic banks maintain to smooth profits over time. The objective of a profit equalization reserve (PER) is to hedge against future low-income distributions by keeping a portion of current profits to pay out to investment account holders in the future.[14] Whereas this practice is in alignment with prudent risk management, it raises a governance issue that needs attention. First, limited disclosure of such reserves and their use make investment account holders uneasy. Second, investment account holders lack the rights to influence the use of such reserves and to verify the exposure of overall investments. Third, an investment account holder with long-term investment objectives might be comfortable with the practice of retaining profits earned in reserves, but other investors might prefer to have profits paid out as they are earned, even if the payout will vary from period to period and may sometimes be zero. Finally, the latter attitude is all the more likely since Islamic banks require investment account holders to waive their rights to these reserves. For example, the terms and conditions of Islamic Bank of Britain state, "You [the investment account holders] authorize us to deduct from net income your profit stabilization reserve contribution for payment into the profit stabilization reserve account. Upon such deduction you agree that you relinquish any right you may have to the monies in the profit stabilization reserve account."

Islamic financial institutions should standardize their practice in respect of such reserves, and the rights of investment account holders to these reserves should be stated clearly and explained to the depositors. One suggestion is that profits only be deducted from long-term depositors who are more likely to be exposed to displaced commercial risk and not from short-term depositors who are not exposed it.

FINANCIAL INSTITUTIONS AS STAKEHOLDERS

Internal corporate governance arrangements are generally reinforced by external ones that set the framework governing business activity and provide the information necessary for their official and private monitoring. These external arrangements relate to the legal and regulatory prudential framework governing Islamic bank activities and to the infrastructure that permits their monitoring.

Islamic financial institutions carry assets based on partnership contracts, which converts them into stakeholders in the businesses to which they provide financing. This is similar to the "insider" system of governance in the German model of banking, where bankers may also be represented on the board of directors. Little attention is being paid to this aspect, but it does pose challenges for corporate governance.

First, Islamic bank assets are composed of profit- and loss-sharing instruments, akin to those of *mudarabah* and *musharakah*. Due to the high degree of asymmetry of information in equity and profit- and loss-sharing contracts, there is greater need for close monitoring by the Islamic bank. To minimize the costs, institutional arrangements that facilitate monitoring and governance are essential. The absence of such mechanisms is a cause for concern.

Second, as the Islamic financial system places more emphasis on partnership-based instruments, Islamic bank participation in governance matters is critical, enhancing the responsibility and accountability of the management and the decision makers.

Poor corporate governance may impose a heavy cost. The mere extension of international standards and practices to Islamic banks may not be sufficient. Sound corporate governance requires the formulation of principles and enforcement (for more, see Berglöf and Claessens 2004). Many countries where Islamic finance is developing have weak contractual environments.[15] Regulators often lack powers to enforce the rules, private actors are nonexistent, and courts are "underfinanced, unmotivated, unclear as to how the law applies, unfamiliar with economic issues, or even corrupt" (Fremond and Capaul 2002). Furthermore, a "law habit" culture—that is, a propensity to abide by the law—must be rooted in society. While the ability to enforce regulations is inextricably coupled with the overall process of development, legislation enabling transparency, private monitoring initiatives, and investments in the rule of law can pave the way to effective regulatory frameworks.

The Islamic Financial Services Board (IFSB) has recently issued a standard concerning corporate governance of financial institutions offering Islamic products and services. This standard addresses some of the above-mentioned issues and provides a framework for Islamic banks to formulate and implement corporate governance (see box 11.1). The Standard on Corporate Governance defines principles dealing with issues such as general governance principles, rights of investment account holders, *Shariah* governance, and transparency in reporting. For further

BOX 11.1	IFSB Principles of Corporate Governance for Islamic Banks

Principle 1.1. Islamic banks shall establish a comprehensive governance policy framework which sets out the strategic roles and functions of each organ of governance and mechanisms for balancing the Islamic bank's accountabilities to various stakeholders.

Principle 1.2. Islamic banks shall ensure that the reporting of their financial and non-financial information meets the requirements of internationally recognized accounting standards which are in compliance with *Shariah* rules and principles and are applicable to the Islamic financial services industry as recognized by the supervisory authorities of the country.

Principle 2.1. Islamic banks shall acknowledge the right of investment account holders to monitor the performance of their investments and the associated risks and put in place adequate means to ensure that these rights are observed and exercised.

Principle 2.2. Islamic banks shall adopt a sound investment strategy that is appropriately aligned to the risk and return expectations of investment account holders (bearing in mind the distinction between restricted and unrestricted investment accounts), and be transparent in smoothing any returns.

Principle 3.1. Islamic banks shall have in place an appropriate mechanism for obtaining rulings from *Shariah* scholars, applying *fatawa,* and monitoring *Shariah* compliance in all aspects of their products, operations, and activities.

Principle 3.2. Islamic banks shall comply with the *Shariah* rules and principles as expressed in the rulings of the Islamic bank's *Shariah* scholars. The Islamic bank shall make these rulings available to the public.

Principle 4. Islamic banks shall make adequate and timely disclosure to investment account holders and the public of material and relevant information on the investment accounts that they manage.

details, consult IFSB's Standard on Corporate Governance, which was issued in 2007.

NOTES

1. See El-Hawary, Grais, and Iqbal (2005); Grais and Pilligrani (2006); Grais and Iqbal (2006).
2. Annual reports, articles of association, and all information posted on the Web sites of the following Islamic banks were used for this analysis: Bahrain Islamic Bank, Al Rajhi Banking Corporation, Bank Islam Malaysia Berhad, Jordan Islamic Bank, Kuwait Finance House, Bank Muamalat Malaysia, Shamil Bank, Bahrain, Islamic Bank of Britain, Emirates Islamic Bank, Dubai Islamic Bank, Islamic Bank Bangladesh Limited, First Islamic Investment Bank, and Bank Rakyat Malaysia (Grais and Pilligrani 2006).
3. We mention only those countries where authorities have implemented laws or acts or issued circulars and regulations on internal *Shariah* supervisory boards.

4. A *fatwa* is a religious edict or proclamation. It is a legal opinion issued by a qualified Muslim scholar on matters of religious belief and practice. For more, see Briston and El-Ashker (1986) and Abdel Karim (1990).
5. Especially in the area of *fiqh al-muamalat* (Islamic commercial jurisprudence).
6. The practice of AAOIFI (Governance Standard 1) is to include jurists of *fiq al-muamalat*. However, one member may be an expert in Islamic financial institutions and also have knowledge of Islamic commercial jurisprudence.
7. See http://ifptest.law.harvard.edu/ifphtml/index.php?module=Forum Report01&session_id=3886ede153bf015d2c1045ade9f71db5 [April, 4, 2006]. The General Council of Islamic Banks and Financial Institutions sampled about 6,000 *fatwas* and found that 90 percent were consistent across Islamic banks.
8. In AAOIFI member countries and banks, internal *Shariah* review is prescribed by Governance Standard 3. In Pakistan, it is regulated by Annexure-III to IBD Circular no. 02 of 2004.
9. This is the case of large Islamic banks where the *Shariah* boards may not be able to assess large volumes of transactions. Therefore, separate *Shariah* control departments have been established. This seems to be the case in Al Rajhi Banking and Investment Corporation and Dubai Islamic Bank.
10. A notable exception is the multiplication of stock market Islamic indexes, whose major contribution is the identification of *halal* investments. *Halal* conveys goodness and, by extension, has taken the meaning of "permissible."
11. In the case of *amanah* deposits, the authorization must be obtained from the depositor, while in *qard hassan*, this is not needed. For more, see Ahmad (1997).
12. *Wakalah*-based unrestricted investment accounts, where the Islamic bank earns a flat fee, rather than a share of profits, are not considered here.
13. Chapra and Ahmed (2002) find that depositors want to be involved in the strategic management of the bank.
14. Islamic banks also typically maintain an investment risk reserve (IRR) constituted entirely out of appropriations from the investment account holder's share of the profits. This reserve, unlike the PER, may be used to offset losses. Reservations about the use of the PER are also relevant to the IRR.
15. The *2005 Doing Business* report continues to reveal weak enforcement in Middle Eastern countries. Islamic banks operate mostly in jurisdictions where legal protection could be strengthened. The prohibition of *riba* (interest) and *gharar* (gambling) translates into risk-sharing arrangements that may leave stakeholders uncertain about the security of their assets. Furthermore, undivided control with shareholders can create biased decision making, see Tirole (1999).

12

Transparency and Data Quality

In forming a safe environment for stakeholders, corporate governance rules for Islamic banks should focus on creating a culture of transparency. Transparency refers to the principle of creating an environment where information on existing conditions, decisions, and actions is made accessible, visible, and understandable to all market participants. Disclosure refers more specifically to the process and methodology of providing the information and of making policy decisions known through timely dissemination and openness. Accountability refers to the need for market participants, including the relevant authorities, to justify their actions and policies and to accept responsibility for both decisions and results.

TRANSPARENCY AND ACCOUNTABILITY

Transparency is a prerequisite for accountability, especially to borrowers and lenders, issuers and investors, national authorities, and international financial institutions. In part, the case for greater transparency and accountability rests on the need for private sector agents to understand and accept policy decisions that affect their behavior. Greater transparency improves economic decisions taken by other agents in the economy. Transparency also fosters accountability, internal discipline, and better governance, while both transparency and accountability improve the quality of decision making in policy-oriented institutions. Such institutions—as well as other institutions that rely on them to make decisions—should be required to maintain transparency. If actions and decisions are visible and understandable, the costs of

---

Key Messages

- Accounting information has to be useful.
- Relevance, faithful representation, comparability, and understandability are attributes of useful information.
- Financial statements should strive to achieve transparency through the fair presentation of useful information.
- Islamic and international financial reporting standards contain sufficient disclosure requirements to ensure fair presentation.
- Perceived deficiencies in financial reporting standards often relate to inadequate enforcement of and failure to adhere to existing standards.

---

monitoring can be lowered. In addition, the general public is better able to monitor public sector institutions, shareholders and employees have a better view of corporate management, creditors monitor borrowers more adequately, and depositors are able to keep an eye on banks. Poor decisions do not go unnoticed or unquestioned.

Transparency and accountability are mutually reinforcing. Transparency enhances accountability by facilitating monitoring, while accountability enhances transparency by providing an incentive for agents to ensure that their actions are disseminated properly and understood. Greater transparency reduces the tendency of markets to place undue emphasis on positive or negative news and thus reduces volatility in financial markets. Taken together, transparency and accountability also impose discipline that improves the quality of decision making in the public sector. This can result in more efficient policies by improving the private sector's understanding of how policy makers may react to events in the future. Transparency forces institutions to face up to the reality of a situation and makes officials more responsible, especially if they know they will have to justify their views, decisions, and actions. For these reasons, timely policy adjustment is encouraged.

The provision of transparent and useful information on market participants and their transactions is an essential part of an orderly and efficient market; it also is a key prerequisite for imposing market discipline. In order for a risk-based approach to bank management and supervision to be effective, useful information must be provided to each key player. These players include supervisors, current and prospective shareholders and bondholders, depositors and other creditors, correspondent and other banks, counterparties, and the general public. Left alone, markets may not generate sufficient levels of disclosure. While market forces normally balance the marginal benefits and costs of disclosing additional information, the end result may not be what players really need.

Banking legislation traditionally has been used to force disclosure of information. Disclosure has involved the provision of prudential information required by bank supervisors and the compilation of statistics for monetary policy purposes, rather than the provision of information that enables a comprehensive evaluation of financial risks. Nevertheless, even such imperfect information has improved the functioning of markets.

The public disclosure of information is predicated on the existence of quality accounting standards and adequate disclosure methodology. The process normally involves publication of relevant qualitative and quantitative information in annual financial reports, which are often supplemented by biannual or quarterly financial statements and other important information. Because the provision of information can be expensive, disclosure requirements should weigh the usefulness of information for the public against the costs of provision.

It is also important to time the introduction of information well. Disclosure of negative information to a public that is not sufficiently sophisticated to interpret it could damage a bank and possibly the entire banking system. In situations where low-quality information is put forth or users are not deemed capable of properly interpreting what is disclosed, public requirements should be phased in carefully and tightened progressively. In the long run, a full disclosure regime is beneficial, even if some immediate problems are experienced, because the cost to the financial system of not being transparent is ultimately higher than the cost of revealing information.

The financial and capital market liberalization of the 1980s brought increasing volatility to financial markets and, consequently, increased the information needed to ensure financial stability. With the advance of financial and capital market liberalization, pressure has increased to improve the usefulness of available financial sector information through the formulation of minimum disclosure requirements. These requirements address the quality and quantity of information that must be provided to market participants and the general public. Since the provision of information is essential to promote the stability of the banking system, regulatory authorities have placed high priority on improving the quality of information disclosed. Banks are also encouraged to improve their internal information systems in order to develop a reputation for providing quality information.

In the 1990s, the changing structure of financial intermediation further strengthened the case for enhanced disclosure. The substitution of tradable debt securities for bank lending and the increased use of financial instruments to transfer risk reduced the importance of banker-client relationships, while expanding the role of markets and market prices in the allocation of capital and risks in the financial system. This shift also affected disclosure requirements: in order to make informed choices, investors need sound information about the profile and nature of risks involved.

Over the past decade, the issues of transparency and accountability have been increasingly and strongly debated as part of economic policy discussions. Policy makers have long been accustomed to secrecy, which has been viewed as a necessary ingredient for the exercise of power; it has the added benefit of hiding the incompetence of policy makers. However, secrecy also hinders the desired effects of policies. Changes in the changed world economy and financial flows have entailed increasing internationalization and interdependence, placing the issue of openness at the forefront of economic policy making. There is growing recognition on the part of national governments, including central banks, that transparency improves the predictability and therefore the efficiency of policy decisions.

LIMITATIONS OF TRANSPARENCY

Transparency and accountability are not ends in and of themselves; nor are they panaceas to solve all problems. They are designed to improve economic performance and the working of international financial markets by enhancing the quality of decision making and risk management among market participants. In particular, transparency does not change the nature of banking or the risks inherent in financial systems. While it cannot prevent financial crises, it may moderate the responses of market participants to bad news by helping them to anticipate and assess negative information. In this way, transparency helps to mitigate panic and contagion.

A dichotomy exists between transparency and confidentiality. The release of proprietary information may enable competitors to take advantage of a particular situation, a fact that often deters market participants from full disclosure. Similarly, monitoring bodies frequently obtain confidential information from financial institutions, which can have significant market implications. Under such circumstances, financial institutions may be reluctant to provide sensitive information without the guarantee of client confidentiality. However, both unilateral transparency and full disclosure contribute to a regime of transparency.

If such a regime were to become the norm, it would ultimately benefit all market participants, even if in the short term it would create discomfort for individual entities.

TRANSPARENCY IN FINANCIAL STATEMENTS

The objective of financial statements is generally to provide information about an entity's financial position (balance sheet), performance (income statement), changes in financial position (cash flow statement), significant risk exposures, and risk management practices (in the notes) to the entity's stakeholders. The transparency of financial statements is secured by providing full disclosure and fair presentation of the information necessary for a wide range of users to make economic decisions. In the context of public disclosure, financial statements should be easy to interpret. Widely available and affordable financial information supports official and private monitoring of a business's financial performance. It promotes transparency and supports market discipline, two important ingredients of sound corporate governance. Besides being a goal in itself, in that it empowers stakeholders, disclosure could be a means to achieve better governance.

As can be expected, specific disclosure requirements vary among regulators. Nonetheless, there are certain key principles whereby standards should be evaluated (Basel Committee on Banking Supervision 2000). These key principles are summarized in box 12.1.

The adoption of International Financial Reporting Standards (IFRS) has facilitated transparency and the proper interpretation of financial statements. In 1989 the Framework for the Preparation and Presentation of Financial Statements was included in the IFRS in order to accomplish the following:

- Explain concepts underlying the preparation and presentation of financial statements to external users;
- Guide those responsible for developing accounting standards;
- Assist preparers, auditors, and users in interpreting the IFRS and in dealing with issues not yet covered by the standards.

According to international standards, financial statements are normally prepared under the assumption that an entity will continue to operate as a going concern and that events will be recorded on an accrual basis. In other words, the effects of transactions and other events should be recognized when they occur and be reported in the financial statements for the periods to which they relate.

| BOX 12.1 | Criteria for Evaluating Accounting Standards |

Effective accounting standards should satisfy three general criteria (Basel Committee on Banking Supervision 2000): Accounting standards should contribute to—or at least be consistent with (and not hamper)—sound risk management and control practices in banks. They should also provide a prudent and reliable framework for generating high-quality accounting information in banks. Accounting standards should facilitate market discipline by promoting transparent reporting of banks' financial position and performance, risk exposures, and risk management activities. Accounting standards should facilitate and not constrain the effective supervision of banks.

In addition to the general criteria, disclosure should be sufficiently comprehensive to allow assessment of a bank's financial position and performance, risk exposures, and risk management activities. International accounting standards should be suitable for implementation not only in the most advanced financial markets but also in emerging markets.

Certain specific criteria underpin high-quality accounting. Accounting principles should generate relevant and meaningful accounting information. They should generate prudent, realistic, and reliable measurements of financial position and performance and consistent measurements of similar or related items.

In addition, there are certain internationally accepted criteria for accounting standards. Accounting standards should not only have a sound theoretical foundation, but also be workable in practice. Accounting standards should not be overly complex in relation to the issue addressed. They should be sufficiently precise to ensure consistent application, and they should not allow alternative treatments. When alternative treatments are permitted, or judgments are necessary in applying accounting principles, balanced disclosures should be required.

Qualitative characteristics are those attributes that make the information provided in financial statements useful. If comprehensive, useful information does not exist, managers may not be aware of the true financial condition of the bank. Key governance players may be misled, which would prevent the proper operation of market discipline. In contrast, the application of key qualitative characteristics and appropriate accounting standards normally results in financial statements that present a true and fair picture.

Key qualitative characteristics are as follows:

■ *Relevance.* Information must be relevant because it influences the economic decisions of users by helping them to evaluate past, present, and future events or to confirm or correct past assessments. The relevance of information is determined by its nature and material quality. Information overload can force players to sift through a plethora of information for relevant details, making interpretation difficult.

- *Faithful representation:* Information should be free from material errors and bias. The key aspects of faithful representation are reliability, priority of substance over form, neutrality, prudence, and completeness.
- *Comparability.* Information should be presented consistently over time and be congruous with related information and with other entities in order to enable users to make comparisons.
- *Understandability.* Information should be easily comprehensible by users with reasonable knowledge of business, economics, and accounting as well as the willingness to study the information diligently.

The process of producing useful information comprises a number of critical points to ensure the comprehensiveness of the information provided:

- *Timeliness.* A delay in reporting may improve reliability, but compromise relevance.
- *Benefit versus cost.* Benefits derived from information should normally exceed the cost of providing it. Banks in developing countries often lack adequate accounting systems and therefore have difficulty providing relevant information. The level of sophistication of the target audience is also important. Both of these aspects affect the costs and benefits of improved disclosure. However, the mere fact that a bank does not have an accounting system capable of producing useful information is not an acceptable excuse for failing to provide markets with it.
- *Balancing qualitative characteristics.* Providers of information must achieve an appropriate balance of qualitative characteristics to ensure that financial statements are adequate for their particular environment.

In the context of fair presentation, it is better to disclose no information than to disclose information that is misleading. It is therefore not surprising that, when an entity does not comply with specific disclosure requirements, the IFRS framework requires full disclosure of the fact and the reasons for noncompliance. Figure 12.1 summarizes how transparency is secured through the proper application of the concepts contained in the IFRS framework.

DISCLOSURE AND DATA QUALITY

Disclosure requirements related to financial statements have traditionally been a pillar of sound regulation. Disclosure is an effective mechanism for exposing banks to market discipline and presenting quality data, enabling reasonable financial risk analysis. Although a bank is

FIGURE 12.1 Transparency in Financial Statements Achieved through Compliance with the IFRS Framework

Objective of financial statements

To provide a fair presentation of

- Financial position
- Financial performance
- Cash flows

Transparency and fair presentation

- Fair presentation achieved through providing useful information (full disclosure), which secures transparency
- Fair presentation equals transparency

Secondary objective of financial statements

To secure transparency through a fair presentation of useful information (full disclosure) for decision-making purposes

Attributes of useful information

Existing framework

- Relevance
- Faithful representation
- Comparability
- Understandability

Constraints

- Timeliness
- Benefit versus cost
- Balancing the qualitative characteristics

Underlying assumptions

Accrual basis   Going concern

---

normally subject to supervision and provides regulatory authorities with information, this information is often confidential or market sensitive and not always available to all categories of users. Disclosure in financial statements should therefore be sufficiently comprehensive to meet the needs of other users within the constraints of what can reasonably be required. Improved transparency through better disclosure may (but not necessarily) reduce the chances of a systemic banking crisis or the effects of contagion, since creditors and other market participants will be better able to distinguish between the financial circumstances facing different institutions or countries.

Users of financial statements need information to assist them in evaluating a bank's financial position and performance and in making economic decisions. Of key importance are a realistic valuation of assets, including sensitivities to future events and adverse developments, and the proper recognition of income and expenses. Equally important is the evaluation of a bank's entire risk profile, including on- and off-balance-sheet items, capital adequacy, the capacity to withstand short-term problems, and the ability to generate additional capital. Users may also need information to better understand the special characteristics of a bank's operations, in particular solvency and liquidity and the relative degree of risk involved in various dimensions of the banking business.

The issuance of IFRS has followed developments in international financial markets. Over time, the coverage of IFRS has been broadened both to include new topics (for example, disclosure and presentation related to the use of new financial instruments) and to enhance the existing international standards.

Historically, Generally Accepted Accounting Practices (GAAP) did not place heavy burdens on banks to disclose their financial risk management practices. This situation changed in the 1990s with the introduction of International Accounting Standard (IAS) 30 (scrapped with introduction of IFRS 7) and IAS 32 (whose disclosure requirements were transferred to IFRS 7). These standards, which are now largely superseded by IFRS 7, resulted in the requirement on the part of many financial regulators to adopt a "full disclosure" approach.

IAS 30 encouraged management to comment on financial statements describing the way liquidity, solvency, and other risks associated with the operations of a bank were managed and controlled. Although some banking risks may be reflected in financial statements, a commentary can help users to understand their management. IFRS is applicable to all banks, meaning all financial institutions that take deposits and borrow from the general public with the objective of lending and investing and that fall within the scope of banking-related or similar legislation. IAS 32 and IFRS 7 supplement other international accounting standards that also apply to banks. The disclosure requirements, as well as other accounting standards specific to banks, are derived from the IFRS framework. The standard entitled Presentation of Financial Statements gives general guidance on the basic principles, structure, and content of financial statements.

IFRS 7 aims to rectify some of the remaining gaps in financial risk disclosure by adding the following requirements to the existing accounting standards:

■ New disclosure requirements in respect of loans and receivables designated as fair value through profit or loss;

- The amount of change in the financial liability's fair value that is not attributable to changes in market conditions;
- The method used to determine the effects of the changes from a benchmark interest rate;
- Where an impairment of a financial asset is recorded through an allowance account (for example, a provision for doubtful debts as opposed to a direct reduction to the carrying amount of the receivable), a requirement to reconcile changes in carrying amounts in that account during the period for each class of financial asset;
- The amount of ineffectiveness recognized in profit or loss on cash flow hedges and hedges of net investments.
- Gains or losses in fair value hedges arising from remeasuring the hedging instrument and on the hedged item attributable to the hedged risk;
- The net gain or loss on held-to-maturity investments, loans and receivables, and financial liabilities measured at amortized cost.

In addition to the disclosures of IFRS 7, users need information that enhances their understanding of the significance of on- and off-balance-sheet financial instruments to a bank's financial position, performance, and cash flows. This information is necessary to assess the amount, timing, and certainty of future cash flows associated with such instruments. This is addressed under IAS 32, Financial Instruments: Disclosure, which supplements other disclosure requirements and specifically requires that disclosure be made in terms of the risks related to the financial instrument. The specific objectives of the IFRS are to prescribe requirements for the presentation of on-balance-sheet financial instruments and to identify information that should be disclosed about both on-balance-sheet (recognized) and off-balance-sheet (unrecognized) financial instruments.

Although separate IFRS standards were issued (IAS 32, IAS 39, and IFRS 7), they are applied in practice as a unit because they deal with exactly the same accounting phenomenon. IAS 39, which deals with the recognition and measurement of financial instruments, also contains supplementary disclosures to those required by IAS 32. However, it is constantly under review and should be regarded as a work in progress.

IAS 39 establishes principles for recognizing, measuring, and disclosing information about financial instruments in the financial statements. The standard significantly increases the use of fair value accounting for financial instruments, particularly on the assets side of the balance sheet. Despite the introduction of IAS 39, leading accounting standard setters are still deliberating the advantages and disadvantages of introducing fair market value accounting for financial assets and liabilities as well as for the corresponding risks. This process should foster a consistent, market-based approach to measuring the risk related to various financial instruments. However, without prudent and balanced standards for estimating fair value, the use of a fair value model could reduce the reliability of financial statements and increase the volatility of earnings and equity measurements. This is particularly true when active markets do not exist, as is often the case for loans, which frequently account for the lion's share of a bank's assets.

The Basel Committee on Banking Supervision believes that the fair value approach is appropriate in situations where it is workable—for example, when financial instruments are being held for trading purposes. It has expressed concern that some banks may be led to change how they manage their risks as a consequence of applying IAS 39 to their hedging strategies; in doing so, they would be deviating from the Basel-supported principles for best-practice global risk management. Accounting standards should contribute to sound risk management practices and take into account the ways in which trading and banking books are actually managed—not the reverse. However, financial statements should also reflect the reality of transactions in a conceptually consistent manner, and this objective will always produce a certain amount of tension between accountants and practitioners.

Current international accounting standards provide a solid and transparent basis for the development of national disclosure requirements. These standards already require banks to disclose extensive information on all of the categories of risk that have been addressed here, adding transparency to the presentation of financial statements.

DEFICIENCIES IN ACCOUNTING PRACTICES

For several years, but especially in the wake of the East Asian financial crises of the late 1990s, criticism has been voiced regarding deficiencies in bank accounting that have resulted in the incomplete and inadequate presentation of financial information in annual financial reports. Market participants perceive the opacity of financial information not only as official oversight but also as the Achilles' heel of effective corporate governance and market discipline. Market participants need a wide range of economic and financial information for decision-making purposes and therefore react negatively to poor disclosure.

There seems to be a perception among market participants and the general public that the lack of adequate information about a bank's financial position, results, and cash flow are the result of insufficient accounting standards. This misperception seems to stem from general ignorance of the sound accounting standards that already exist.

Contrary to popular belief among non-accountants, the predominant problem is not always a lack of sound and adequate accounting standards, but rather the fact that regulatory and accounting authorities do not enforce the principles underlying existing standards. In fact, the establishment of disclosure requirements is not sufficient in and of itself. Disclosure requirements have to be accompanied by active regulatory enforcement—and perhaps even fraud laws—to ensure that the information disclosed is complete, timely, and not deliberately misleading. Regulatory institutions need to have adequate enforcement capacities.

Both banks and their external auditors may lack proper incentives to disclose more than the regulatory authorities and market discipline demand of them. Market participants, as well as rating agencies, could therefore make a valuable contribution to improving the level of transparency in financial reporting by demanding comprehensive, full disclosure. They could also demonstrate a direct link between investor confidence and transparent disclosure. In addition, disclosure could be improved by peer pressure. A bank's competitors could demonstrate that disclosure is advantageous to an institution because investors and depositors are more likely to provide capital and deposits at lower prices to transparent entities than to nontransparent ones.

A frequent problem with disclosure, especially that which involves a new system, is the hesitancy of a bank's management and supervisors, as well as market participants, to disclose highly negative information. Such information, which has the strongest potential to trigger a market reaction, typically is disclosed at the last possible moment and is often incomplete. Even professional members of the public, such as rating agencies, may be slow to react to and disclose potential problems (see box 12.2 for a survey on public disclosure of banks).

APPLICABILITY OF IFRS TO ISLAMIC BANKS

Islamic banks, however, face a specific problem regarding the applicability of the accounting standards designed for conventional types of business. A number of International Financial Reporting Standards are not applicable to Islamic banks, and issues arise in Islamic finance for which no IFRS exist.

In 1990 the Accounting and Auditing Organization for Islamic Financial Institutions (AAOIFI) was created to address this issue and create an adequate level of transparency in the financial reporting of Islamic banks.

BOX 12.2   Survey on Public Disclosure of Banks

The following is based on a survey of banks conducted by the Basel Committee on Banking Supervision (2002).

Most banks disclosed basic information relating to capital structure and ratios, accounting and presentation policies, credit risk, and market risk. Fewer than half of the banks disclosed information about credit risk modeling, credit derivatives, and securitization. The most notable increases in disclosure involved questions about complex capital instruments, policies and procedures for setting credit risk allowances, securitization, and operational and legal risks, although disclosure regarding securitization was rare.

Most banks released fundamental quantitative data pertinent to their capital structure. While they were less forthcoming about their holdings of innovative and complex capital instruments, the rate of disclosure in this area has generally been improving.

The risk-based capital ratio was almost always disclosed, but fewer than half of the banks provided information on the credit and market risks against which the capital serves as a buffer. Most banks made fairly extensive disclosures about their use of internal models for market risk. The main opportunity for future improvement involves the results of stress testing.

Just over half of the banks described fully their process for assessing credit exposures, and only a few more provided summary information on the use of internal ratings. Fewer than half provided basic information about their credit risk models. These areas of disclosure will become more important under the proposed revision of the Basel Capital Accord, as banks will have to disclose key information regarding the use of internal ratings to qualify for the proposed internal ratings-based approach. In this regard, the large improvement in the disclosure of the internal risk-rating process since the 1999 survey is encouraging. In the area of asset securitization, fewer than half of the banks provided even the most basic information regarding the amount and types of assets securitized and the associated accounting treatment.

Most banks disclosed key quantitative information concerning credit risk, another area with required disclosures. Disclosures of provisioning policies and procedures are improving. About half of the banks discussed the techniques they use to manage impaired assets. However, only a small number of banks disclosed the effect of their use of credit risk mitigants.

Approximately three-fourths of banks discussed their objectives for derivatives and their strategies for hedging risk. The proportion of banks making quantitative disclosures was lower, and trends here are mixed. Approximately two-fifths of banks that use credit derivatives disclosed their strategy and objectives for the use of these instruments, as well as the amount outstanding. However, few provided more detailed information.

While approximately four-fifths of banks provided breakdowns of their trading activities by type of instrument, somewhat fewer provided information about the diversification of their credit risks. Fewer than half supplied a categorical breakdown of problem credits.

There was a dramatic increase in the rate of disclosures of operational and legal risks since the first survey, although the level was still lower than that for more basic market and credit risk information. Basic accounting policies and practices were generally well disclosed.

BOX 12.3	AAOIFI Standards

The following standards are available on the AAOIFI Web site (www.AAOIFI.com):

Financial Accounting Statements

- Objective of Financial Accounting of Islamic Banks and Financial Institutions
- Concepts of Financial Accounting for Islamic Banks and Financial Institutions

Financial Accounting Standards

- General Presentation and Disclosure in the Financial Statements of Islamic Banks and Financial Institutions
- *Murabahah* and *Murabahah* to the Purchase Orderer
- *Mudarabah* Financing
- *Musharakah* Financing
- Disclosure of Bases for Profit Allocation between Owners' Equity and Investment Account Holders and Their Equivalent
- *Salam* and Parallel *Salam*
- *Ijarah* and *Ijarah Muntahia Bittamleek*
- *Istisnah* and Parallel *Istisnah*
- *Zakah*
- Provisions and Reserves
- General Presentation and Disclosure in Financial Statements of Islamic Insurance Companies
- Disclosure of Bases for Determining and Allocating Surplus or Deficit in Islamic Insurance Companies
- Investment Funds
- Provisions and Reserves in Islamic Insurance Companies
- Foreign Currency Transactions and Foreign Operations
- Investments
- Islamic Financial Services offered by Conventional Financial Institutions
- Contributions in Islamic Insurance Companies
- Deferred Payment Sale
- Disclosure on Transfer of Assets
- Segment Reporting

AAOIFI has made a number of important contributions, including the issuance of accounting and auditing standards (see box 12.3).

Between 1998 and 2002, Bahrain, Sudan, and Jordan adopted accounting standards issued by AAOIFI, and Qatar issued accounting standards based on AAOIFI pronouncements. Saudi Arabia requires banks to report according to IFRS and local Saudi standards based on IFRS, but in 2001 banks were asked to review AAOIFI's standards for guidance when accounting for Islamic banking products. While these banks still report using IFRS and Saudi local standards, they now have the additional benefit of AAOIFI's standards for their *Shariah*-based transactions. Indonesia has formed a national body within the Indonesian Accounting Association to prepare and issue Islamic Accounting Standards based on those of AAOIFI, and individual banks in countries such as Kuwait and United Arab Emirates have begun to train staff in the use of AAOIFI's accounting standards.

TRANSPARENCY AND ISLAMIC FINANCIAL INSTITUTIONS

The issues of transparency are especially relevant for Islamic financial institutions due to the private equity nature of certain Islamic instruments and the assumption that these investment account holders have greater incentives than conventional depositors to monitor Islamic bank performance directly. However, an institutional infrastructure is needed to facilitate the production of accurate financial information, the development of agents that can interpret and disseminate it, as well as arrangements to protect its integrity. Islamic banks have made considerable efforts to improve the level of transparency and the quality of information disclosed in the market in recent years. However, several areas still require attention.

In May 2007 the Islamic Financial Services Board issued Exposure Draft no. 4, which deals with "disclosures to promote transparency and market discipline for institutions offering Islamic financial services." The exposure draft clearly states that the need for transparency is, above all, an important *Shariah* consideration as any form of concealment, fraud, or attempt at misrepresentation violates the principles of justice and fairness as mentioned in the *Qur'an*.

The IFSB makes it clear that the intended standard builds on both the guidelines and principles issued by the Basel Committee on Banking Supervision as well as the disclosure standards contained in Pillar 3 of the new Basel Capital Accord (see chapter 13). In addition, it is intended that the requirements of relevant international accounting (financial reporting) standards will be complemented when the exposure draft becomes a standard itself.

Weaknesses in the Current System of Disclosure

Analysts often have difficulty collecting useful information regarding Islamic financial institutions. Contributing to this problem is the lack of uniform reporting standards by the institutions themselves (see table 12.1 for the disclosure practices of Islamic banks). For example, in a survey

TABLE 12.1   Disclosure Practices of Islamic Banks

Disclosure item	*Practice*
Deposit composition: Share of investment deposits to total deposits	Generally disclosed, ranging from 0 to 95 percent, with some banks (36 percent) reporting no investment deposits
Return on restricted investment deposits	Very few disclose this (only one bank in the sample)
Risk management framework and practices	Disclosures are presented at a very general level; some mention the existence of specific committees, such as an asset-liability management committee
Value-at-risk (VAR)	None discloses this (one bank reports using VAR)
Large exposures	Very few banks disclose this (6 percent)

Source: Sundararajan (2004).

conducted by the authors of nine Islamic banks for which balance sheet data were easily available, one bank did not provide sufficient details as to the division of equity and deposits, while the remaining eight did. However, when it came to deposits, only five provided a detailed division of the type of deposits they offer, while the remaining three lumped together different types of deposits. For these three types of deposits, two made no specific reference to special investment accounts, while the other one made no distinction between demand and savings deposits.

Several early studies on the regulation and supervision of Islamic banks note that an appropriate regulatory framework needs to place greater emphasis on accounting standards and information disclosure. Errico and Farabakash (1998) suggest a supervisory framework based on the standards and best practices established by the Basel Committee and an Islamic finance–tailored prudential framework based on the CAMEL (capital adequacy, asset quality, management, earnings, and liquidity) system. Errico and Sundarajan (2002) reinforce this view by recommending the creation of a regulatory framework created along the same lines as a CAMEL framework and the adoption of a Securities and Exchange Commission type of disclosure system. The AAOIFI has promulgated a Statement on the Purpose and Calculations of Capital Adequacy Ratio (CAR) for Islamic Banks, which takes into account differences between deposit accounts in conventional banking and investment accounts in Islamic banking.[1] This statement builds on the capital adequacy principles laid down by the Basel Committee (see also Chapra and Khan 2000; Mulajawan, Dar, and Hall 2002). Archer and

Ahmed (2003) point out features of Islamic finance that require specific accounting, corporate governance, and prudential regulations. They note issues regarding the applicability of the IAS to Islamic banks and further describe efforts undertaken, notably by AAOIFI, to create accounting and auditing regulations, standardize *Shariah* interpretations, and establish capital adequacy ratios for Islamic banks.

Demarcation of Equity and Depositors' Funds

Islamic banks are hybrids of both commercial and investment banks, making them more akin to universal banks. Unlike conventional universal banks, Islamic banks do not erect firewalls to separate legally, financially, and managerially their investment and commercial banking services. As a result, investment account funds are not "ring-fenced" from the funds of others, including equity holders. This commingling of funds is of concern to all stakeholders since it becomes difficult to identify the source of funds invested when the time comes to distribute the profits and losses.

Transparency in *Shariah* Rulings

A transparent financial institution ideally would reveal the duties, decision making, competence, and composition of the *Shariah* board as well as publish all *fatwas* (religious proclamations) issued by the board. This would strengthen stakeholders' confidence in the credibility of *Shariah* board assessments. In addition, public disclosure would provide a venue for educating the public, paving the way for market discipline to play a larger role with respect to *Shariah* compliance. Again, this aspect of transparency is missing from the market. Often the annual reports of a *Shariah* board are not readily available to the public, and other relevant information regarding *fatwas* issued by a *Shariah* board are not available at all. The use of quantitative methods could enhance the level of financial disclosure by producing enhanced measures of risk exposures, especially in the area of credit and equity risk.

NOTE

1. See also Mulajawan, Dar, and Hall (2002) for a discussion of the issue and a suggestion for a modified capital adequacy ratio.

Capital Adequacy and Basel II

Almost every aspect of banking is influenced either directly or indirectly by the availability of capital. This is one of the key factors to be considered when assessing the safety and soundness of a particular bank. An adequate base of capital serves as a safety net for a variety of risks to which an institution is exposed in the course of its business. Capital absorbs possible losses and thus provides a basis for maintaining the confidence of depositors. Capital also is the ultimate determinant of a bank's lending capacity. A bank's balance sheet cannot be expanded beyond the level determined by its capital adequacy ratio (CAR); the availability of capital consequently determines the maximum level of assets.

The cost and amount of capital affect a bank's competitive position. Because shareholders expect a return on their equity, the obligation to earn it affects the pricing of bank products. There is another market perspective as well. In order to create assets, a bank needs to attract deposits (investment accounts and special investment accounts) from the public. Doing so requires public confidence in the bank, which in turn can best be established and maintained by a capital buffer. If a bank faces a shortage of capital, or if the cost of capital is high, the bank stands to lose business to its competitors.

The key purposes of capital are to provide stability and to absorb losses, thereby providing a measure of protection to depositors and other creditors in the event of liquidation. As such, the capital of a bank should have three important characteristics:

- Be permanent;
- Not impose mandatory fixed charges against earnings;

Key Messages

- Capital is required as a buffer against unexpected losses.
- Capital cannot be a substitute for good management.
- A strong base of permanent shareholders' equity and disclosed reserves, supplemented by other forms of qualifying capital (for example, undisclosed reserves, revaluation reserves, general provisions for loan losses, hybrid instruments, and subordinated debt) is needed.
- Capital requirements are different for Islamic banks as recognized by AAOIFI and the IFSB. The IFSB standard on capital requirement provides a framework to determine adequacy of capital for Islamic banks.
- Capital adequacy percentage requirements must be seen as a minimum. In transitional or volatile environments, a risk-weighted capital adequacy requirement of substantially more than 10 percent would be more appropriate.
- Supervisory authority must be willing to set different capital levels for individual banks depending on the specific risk profiles and a bank's capacity to identify, measure, monitor, and control its risks.
- The amount of capital held by a bank must be commensurate with its level of risk. It is management and the board's responsibility to, first, evaluate the bank's risk profile and, second, to equate capital to risk. The board of directors also has a responsibility to project capital requirements to determine whether or not current growth and capital retention are sustainable.

■ Allow for legal subordination to the rights of depositors and other creditors.

The total amount of capital is of fundamental importance. Also important is the nature of bank ownership, specifically the identity of owners who can directly influence the bank's strategic direction and risk management policies. A bank's ownership structure must ensure the integrity of the bank's capital and be able to supply more capital if and when needed. It must not negatively influence the bank's capital position or expose it to additional risk. In addition to owners who are less than fit and proper or who do not discharge their fiduciary responsibilities effectively, the structure of a financial conglomerate may also have a negative impact on the capital of banks in the group.

SIGNIFICANCE OF CAPITAL IN BANKING

Conventional bank capital consists of equity capital, retained reserves, and certain non-deposit liabilities. It is both a means of funding earnings-generating assets and a stability cushion. From the perspective of efficiency and returns, capital is part of a bank's sources of funding that can be applied directly to the purchase of revenue-earning assets as well as be used to raise other funds, with the net benefit accruing to shareholders. From the perspective of stability, bank capital is a cushion for absorbing shocks of business losses and maintaining solvency, with benefits accruing to depositors and other stakeholders. Both financial intermediaries and regulators are sensitive to the dual role of capital. Financial intermediaries tend to be more focused on the earnings-generating role, while regulators tend to be more focused on the stability-cushion role.

A bank's capital structure relates to the ratio of capital to deposits and the ratio of debt capital to equity capital. Its performance, in terms of return on equity capital, is influenced by its ability to calibrate the level of capital required. Efficient risk management can enable the bank to choose a capital structure that allows it to (a) achieve profitability while maintaining stability; (b) reassure markets as to the quality of its business conduct; and (c) have a constructive dialogue with regulators.

Banks have a relatively low ratio of capital to externally provided funding. To encourage prudent management of the risks associated with this unique balance sheet structure, regulatory authorities in most countries have introduced certain capital adequacy requirements. In the late 1980s, the Basel Committee on Banking Supervision took the lead in developing a risk-based capital adequacy standard that would lead to international convergence of supervisory regulations governing the capital adequacy of internationally active banks. The dual objectives for the Basel framework were to strengthen the soundness and stability of the international banking system and, by ensuring a high degree of consistency in the framework's application, to diminish the sources of competitive inequality among international banks.

Thinking along the lines of Basel and recognizing the differences in the nature of intermediation by Islamic banks, the Accounting and Auditing Organization for Islamic Financial Institutions (AAOIFI) drafted a basic standard on capital adequacy of Islamic financial institutions. This standard was further enhanced by the Islamic Financial Services Board (IFSB). In December 2006, a working group of the IFSB issued the first capital adequacy standard for institutions (other than insurance institutions) offering only Islamic financial services. The minimum capital adequacy requirements for both credit and market risks are set out for each of the *Shariah*-compliant financing and investment instruments. Like for conventional financial institutions, in the IFSB standard the minimum capital adequacy requirement for Islamic banks is not lower than 8 percent for total capital.

BASEL I AND BASEL II

The 1980s' initiative resulted in the Basel Capital Accord of 1988 (Basel I). The Basel Accord comprises a definition of regulatory capital, measures of risk exposure, and rules specifying the level of capital to be maintained in relation to these risks. It introduced a de facto capital adequacy standard, based on the risk-weighted composition of a bank's assets and off-balance-sheet exposures that ensures that an adequate amount of capital and reserves is maintained to safeguard solvency. While the original targets were international banks, many national authorities promptly applied the Basel Accord and introduced formal regulatory capital requirements. Since the introduction of the risk-based capital adequacy standard, risk-based capital ratios have increased significantly in all countries that have adopted the standard: the industry average for the G-10 countries increased from 9.3 percent in 1988 to 11.2 percent in 1996. (However, the differences in fiscal treatment and accounting presentations of certain classes of provisions for loan losses and of capital reserves derived from retained earnings may still distort the comparability of the real capital positions of banks from different countries.)

The standard also has played a major role in improving the safety of banking systems in less developed countries and in transitional economies. The capital adequacy standard has been adopted and implemented in more than 100 countries and now forms an integral part of any risk-based bank supervisory approach. Aware that the banking environment in these countries entails higher economic and market risks, many regulators have introduced even higher standards, with 12 to 15 percent often regarded as appropriate for transitional and developing environments.

The world financial system has seen considerable changes since introduction of the Basel I Accord. Financial markets have become more volatile, and a significant degree of financial innovation has taken place. There also have been incidents of economic turbulence leading to widespread financial crisis—for example, in Asia in 1997 and in Eastern Europe in 1998. The risks that internationally active banks must deal with have become more complex. There was an increasing concern that the Basel I Accord did not provide an effective means to ensure that capital requirements match a bank's true risk profile; in other words, it was not sufficiently risk sensitive. The risk measurement and control aspects of the Basel I Accord also needed to be improved. In 1999 the Basel Committee started consultations leading to issuance of a new Capital Accord (Basel II) that is better attuned to the complexities of the modern financial world. While the new framework aims to provide a more comprehensive approach to measuring banking risks, its fundamental objectives remain the same: to promote safety and soundness of the banking system and to enhance the competitive equality of banks.

By 2005, the development of the Basel II Accord had been completed. A significant aspect of the Basel II Accord is the greater use of the banks' internal systems as an input to capital assessment and adequacy calculations and the allowance of more national discretion in determining how specific rules may be applied. This was intended to adapt the standards to different conditions in national financial markets. In addition to minimum capital requirements, Basel II Accord includes two additional pillars: an enhanced supervisory review process and effective use of market discipline. All three pillars are mutually reinforcing and no one pillar should be viewed as more important than another. The countries with well-developed financial systems, which actively participated in its development, are expected to begin adopting Basel II in the course of 2009. Supervisory authorities worldwide are being encouraged to start the procedure, although this may take some time. The Basel II Accord is expected to become a de facto capital adequacy standard in the next year or so. The following discussion is based on and related to Basel II Accord.

PILLAR 1: CAPITAL ADEQUACY REQUIREMENT

The capital adequacy requirement constitutes Pillar 1 under the Basel II Accord. The capital adequacy standard is based on the principle that the level of a bank's capital should be related to the bank's specific risk profile. Measurement of the capital adequacy requirement is determined by three components of risk—credit risk, market risk, and operational risk. For each of these components, a number of models can be used. In principle, these include some form of standardized approach and an approach based on internal systems.

The risk management arrangements of Islamic banks thus bear on their ability to calibrate capital to their business objectives and risk tolerance, to deal with market discipline, and to maintain a dialogue with regulators. Their characteristic of mobilizing funds in the form of risk-sharing investment accounts in place of conventional deposits, together with the materiality of financing transactions, may alter the overall risk of the balance sheet and, consequently, the assessment of their capital

TABLE 13.1   Classification of Capital in the Basel Accords

Classification	Contents
Tier 1 (core capital)	Ordinary paid-up share of capital or common stock, disclosed reserves from post-tax retained earnings, noncumulative perpetual preferred stock (goodwill to be deducted)
Tier 2 (supplementary capital)	Undisclosed reserves, asset revaluation reserves, general provisions or general loan-loss provisions, hybrid (debt-equity) capital instruments, and subordinated term debts[a]
Tier 3	Unsecured debt: subordinated and fully paid up, to have an original maturity of at least two years and not be repayable before the agreed repayment date unless the supervisory authority agrees[b]

a. Eligible Tier 2 capital may not exceed total Tier 1 capital, and long-term subordinated debt may not exceed 50 percent of Tier 1 capital.
b. This will be limited to 250 percent of a bank's Tier 1 capital, which is required to support market risks.

requirements. Indeed, risk-sharing "deposits" would, in principle, reduce the need for a safety cushion with which to weather adverse investment outcomes. Similarly, the materiality of investments is likely to modify the extent of their risk and have a bearing on the assessment of the overall need for capital; asset-based modes of finance may be less risky, and profit-sharing modes more risky, than conventional interest-bearing modes. Nevertheless, Islamic banks operate within a regulatory framework that is likely to impose on them capital requirements with a view to promoting stability and limiting contagion risks (Grais and Anoma 2007).

Defining what constitutes capital is a long-debated issue. However, there is wide acceptance of the capital structure that has been stipulated by the Basel Committee, which segregates capital into three categories, as set out in table 13.1.

To be considered adequately capitalized, international banks in the G-10 countries are required to hold a minimum total capital (Tier 1 and Tier 2) equal to 8 percent of risk-adjusted assets. Tier 1 capital is the same in Islamic banks as in conventional financial institutions. However, in Islamic banks the reserves include the shareholders' portion of the profit equalization reserve (PER), which is included in disclosed reserves.[1] In Tier 2 capital, there are no hybrid capital instruments or subordinated debts, as these would bear interest and contravene *Shariah* principles. However, an issue is the treatment of unrestricted risk-sharing investment accounts, which may be viewed as equity investments on a limited-term basis.

CAPITAL ADEQUACY METHODOLOGY FOR ISLAMIC BANKS

Unlike depositors of conventional banks, the contractual agreement between Islamic banks and investment account holders is based on the concept of sharing profit and loss, which makes investment account holders a unique class of quasi-liability holders: they are neither depositors nor equity holders. Although they are not part of the bank's capital, they are expected to absorb all losses on the investments made through their funds, unless there is evidence of negligence or misconduct on the part of the bank. The nature of intermediation and liabilities has serious implications for the determination of adequate capital for Islamic banks (Grais and Kulathunga 2007):

- Deposits taken on the basis of profit- and loss-sharing agreements should not be subject to any capital requirements other than to cover liability for negligence and misconduct and winding-down expenses.
- Investments funded by current accounts carry commercial banking risks and should be subject to adequate risk weights and capital allocation.
- Restricted investment accounts on the liabilities side form a collection of heterogeneous investment funds resembling a fund of funds; therefore, financial institutions holding such funds should be subject to the same capital requirements as are applicable to fund managers.
- The presence of displaced commercial risk and the practice of income smoothing have indirect implications for the Islamic bank's capital adequacy, which a regulator may take into account when determining the CAR.
- Islamic banks acting as intermediary can face a moral hazard issue. Since, as agent, the bank is not liable for losses but shares the profits with the investment account holder, it may have an incentive to maximize the investments funded by the account holder and to attract more account holders than it has the capacity to handle. This can lead to investment decisions that are riskier than the investment account holder is willing to accept. Such "incentive misalignment" may lead to higher displaced commercial risk, which necessitates higher capital requirements.

Capital requirement standards have been developed for Islamic banks adapting conventional Basel approaches. In December 2006, the Islamic Financial Services Board issued a capital adequacy standard based on the Basel II standardized approach, with a similar approach to risk weights. While the modes of intermediation, financial instruments, and risks may differ between Islamic and conventional financial institutions, the general approach is applicable to both types of financial intermediaries. A better-circumscribed economic capital can allow Islamic banks to manage their resources more efficiently, while providing comfort to their stakeholders. A major difference between Islamic banks and conventional banks relates to investment account deposits. For Islamic banks, the expected losses would be borne by the income, and so the risk capital needed to meet unexpected losses may be less for Islamic banks than for conventional banks.

Theoretically, Islamic banks accept investment deposits that are risk-sharing contracts. The Islamic financial intermediary, as an agent (*mudarib*), would share profits with the depositor, but the depositor would bear losses that are the outcome of market conditions, but not of a *mudarib*'s misconduct. Hence the risk-sharing feature of investment account deposits would reduce the overall risks for Islamic banks in principle. Under the circumstances, and going back to the *murabahah* contract, an Islamic bank would be expected to conduct business in such a way as to deal with expected losses, pricing its products and accumulating provisions accordingly. The Islamic bank would identify economic capital to deal with unexpected losses that are due primarily to misconduct. Unanticipated adverse events that are beyond the reasonable anticipation of the bank would not be cushioned, as profit-sharing investment account "depositors" would share the losses attributable to the assets (or the proportion of assets) financed by their funds.

Determination of Risk Weights

Assigning risk weights to different asset classes reflects the contractual relationship between the bank and the borrower. For conventional banks, most assets are based on debt, whereas for Islamic banks, the assets range from trade financing to equity partnerships; this fact changes the nature of risks. Some instruments carry additional risks that are not present in conventional lending instruments. Therefore, the calculation of risk weights is different for Islamic banks than for conventional banks: (a) assets based on trade are not truly financial assets and carry risks other than credit and market risks; (b) nonfinancial assets such as real estate, commodities, and *ijarah* and *istisnah* contracts have special risk characteristics; (c) Islamic banks carry partnership and profit- and loss-sharing assets that have a higher risk profile; (d) Islamic banks do not have well-defined instruments for mitigating and hedging risk, such as derivatives, which raises the overall riskiness of assets.

In the case of partnership-based contracts such as *mudarabah* and *musharakah*, the bank is exposed to both credit and market risks that need to be analyzed in a similar manner to the methodology of the Basel accords. When such partnership-based assets are acquired in the form of tangible assets—that is, commodities—and are held for trading, the only exposure is to market risk because credit risk is minimized by direct ownership of the assets. However, there is significant risk of capital impairment when direct investment takes place in partnership-based contracts and the investments will be held to maturity. Treatment of this risk within the Basel framework is not straightforward and therefore requires special attention.

This standard comprehensively discusses the nature of risks and the appropriate risk weights to be used for different assets (see box 13.1). The standard deals with the minimum capital adequacy requirements for both credit and market risks for seven *Shariah*-compliant financing and investment instruments: (a) *murabahah*, (b) *salaam*, (c) *istisnah*, (d) *ijarah*, (e) *musharakah* and diminishing *musharakah*, (f) *mudarabah*, and (g) *sukuk*. The discussion of each contract includes risk weights for credit and market risks.

The IFSB standard is defined in two forms: standard and discretionary. In the standard formula, capital is divided by risk-weighted assets excluding the assets financed by investment account holders (see box 13.2). The size of the risk-weighted assets is determined for the credit risk

---

BOX 13.1 **IFSB Principles for Minimum Capital Adequacy Requirements (CAR)**

The minimum capital adequacy requirements for Islamic banks shall be a CAR of not lower than 8 percent of total capital. Tier 2 capital is limited to 100 percent of Tier 1 capital.

In calculating the CAR, the regulatory capital as the numerator shall be calculated in relation to the total risk-weighted assets as the denominator. The total of risk-weighted assets is determined by multiplying the capital requirements for market risk and operational risk by 12.5 (which is the reciprocal of the minimum CAR of 8 percent) and adding the resulting figures to the sum of risk-weighted assets computed for credit risk.

The *Shariah* rules and principles whereby investment account holders provide funds to the Islamic bank on the basis of profit-sharing and loss-bearing *mudarabah* contracts instead of debt-based deposits mean that investment account holders would share in the profits of a successful operation but could lose all or part of their investment. The liability of investment account holders is limited to the capital provided, and the potential loss of the Islamic bank is restricted to the value or opportunity cost of its work.

However, if negligence, mismanagement, or fraud can be proven, the Islamic bank is financially liable for the capital of the account holders. Therefore, account holders normally bear the credit and market risks of the investment, while the Islamic bank bears the operational risk.

first and then adjusted to accommodate for the market and operational risks. To determine the adjustment, the capital requirements for market risk and operational risk are multiplied by 12.5, which is the reciprocal ratio (1 / 0.08) of the minimum CAR of 8 percent.

The second formula, referred to as the supervisory discretion formula, is modified to accommodate the existence of reserves maintained by Islamic banks to minimize displaced commercial, withdrawal, and systemic risks (see box 13.3). In markets where Islamic banks maintain PER and investment risk reserves (IRR), the supervisory authorities are given discretion to adjust the denominator of the CAR formula for them. Supervisors may adjust the formula according to their judgment of the systemic risk and prevalent practices.

In the discretionary formula, the supervisory authority has the discretion to include a specified percentage (represented by α in the formula) of assets financed by investment account holders in the denominator of the CAR. The percentage set by the supervisory authority is applied to

---

BOX 13.2 IFSB Standard Formula for CAR

$$\frac{\text{Eligible capital}}{\text{Total risk-weighted assets PLUS Operational risk} \quad \text{MINUS} \quad \text{Total risk-weighted assets funded by profit-sharing investment accounts}}$$

Notes: Risk weighting includes weights for market and credit risk. Profit-sharing investment account balances include PER and IRR.

BOX 13.3 IFSB Supervisory Discretion Formula for CAR

$$\frac{\text{Eligible capital}}{\text{Total risk-weighted assets PLUS Operational risk} \quad \text{MINUS} \quad \begin{array}{l} 1.\ (1 - \alpha)^*\ \text{Total risk-weighted assets funded by profit-sharing investment accounts} \\ 2.\ \alpha^*\ \text{Risk-weighted assets funded by PER and IRR} \end{array}}$$

Notes: Risk weighting includes weights for market and credit risk. Profit-sharing investment account balances include PER and IRR. α refers to the proportion of assets funded by PSIAs, which is to be determined by the supervisory authorities. The value of α normally does not exceed 30 percent.

TABLE 13.2   Capital Adequacy Standards for Credit Risk: Basel II versus IFSB

Criteria	Basel II	IFSB
Risk weight	Calibrated on the basis of external ratings by the Basel committee	Calibrated on the basis of external ratings by the Basel Committee; varies according to contract stage and financing mode
Treatment of equity in the banking book	>= 150 percent for venture capital and private equity investments	Simple risk weight method (risk weight 300 or 400 percent) or supervisory slotting method (risk weight 90–270 percent)
Credit risk mitigation techniques	Includes financial collateral, credit derivatives, guarantees, netting (on and off balance sheet)	Includes profit-sharing investment accounts (PSIA), or cash on deposits with Islamic banks, guarantees, financial collateral, and pledged assets

Source: Jabbari (2006).

assets financed by holders of both unrestricted and restricted investment accounts. Further adjustment is made for PER and IRR in such a manner that a certain fraction of the risk-weighted assets funded by the reserves is deducted from the denominator. The rationale given for this adjustment is that these reserves reduce the displaced commercial risk.

As Basel II takes into account the capital requirements for operational risk, IFSB's draft on exposure also deals with the issue in detail. Due to difficulties in quantifying the exposures from operational risk, determination of how much capital should be allocated for such risks also becomes complex. The IFSB draft recommends basing the proposed measurement of capital to be allocated to operational risk on either the basic indicator approach or the standardized approach.[2] It is further recommended that, due to the structure of the line of business for Islamic banks, at the present stage, Islamic banks may use the basic indicator approach.

Risk Weights and CAR for Credit Risk

Although the general framework for determining capital requirements in the Basel and IFSB methodology is similar, there are differences in application and determination of weights due to differences in intermediation and instruments. Table 13.2 provides an overview of differences in the approaches taken by Basel II and IFSB.

Figure 13.1 provides a fairly good picture of the mechanics of determining risk weights required to assess the adequate level of capital for an

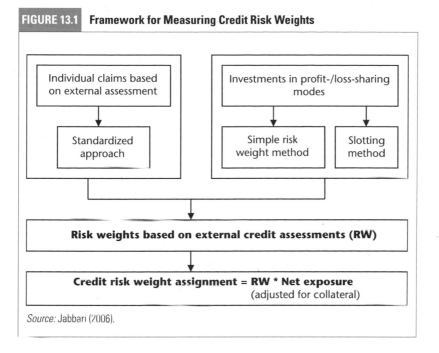

| FIGURE 13.1 | Framework for Measuring Credit Risk Weights |

Source: Jabbari (2006).

Islamic bank. A standardized approach can be taken where an external assessment of credit ratings is available. For investments based on profit sharing or loss bearing, the institution can use either a simple risk-weight method or a slotting method. Risk weights determined through these different approaches are multiplied with the next exposure, excluding any collateral against an asset.

Risk Weights and CAR for Market Risk

Table 13.3 compares the treatment of market risk in the Basel II and IFSB standards. The main differences are that IFSB's standard includes market risk of inventories for the measurement of weights; it allows certain standardized methods of measurement.

IFSB standard lays down an elaborated mechanism for determining market risks weights assignments (see figure 13.2).

Risk Weights and CAR for Operational Risk

The IFSB standard for determining risk weights for operational risk recommends excluding the share of profit-sharing investment account

Table 13.3   Capital Adequacy Standards for Market Risk: Basel II versus IFSB

Criteria	*Basel II*	*IFSB*
Category	Equity, foreign exchange, interest rate risk in the trading book, commodities	Equity, foreign exchange, interest rate risk in the trading book, commodities, *inventories*
Measurement	1996 market risk amendments (standardized and internal model)	1996 market risk amendments (standardized measurement method)

Source: Jabbari (2006).

FIGURE 13.2   Framework for Measuring Market Risk Weights

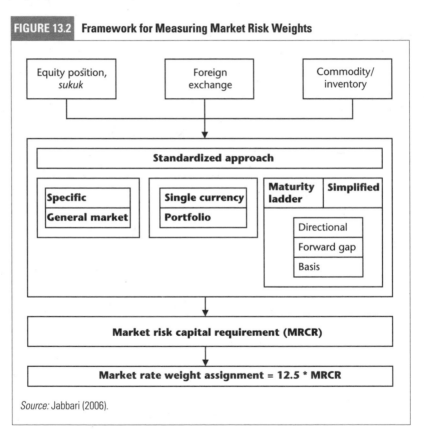

Source: Jabbari (2006).

holders from gross income. This adjustment is necessary because Islamic banks share profits with their depositors-investors (see table 13.4).

CAR Based on IFSB Methodology: An Example

Box 13.4 illustrates a very simple approach to determining the capital adequacy requirement for a hypothetical Islamic bank.

TABLE 13.4   Capital Adequacy Standard for Operational Risk: Basel II versus IFSB

Criteria	Basel II	IFSB
Gross income	Annual average gross income (previous three years)	Annual average gross income (previous three years), excluding profit-sharing investment account (PSIA) holders' share of income

Source: Jabbari (2006).

BOX 13.4   Computation of CAR for an Islamic Bank

Liabilities:

Demand deposits	$200M
Unrestricted investment account deposits	$500M
Restricted investment account deposits	$250M
PER and IRR	$ 50M
Shareholders' capital	$ 20M

Assets:

Trade financing (*murabahah*)	$550M
Salaam / ijarah / istisnah	$250M
Mudarabah and *musharakah* investments	$220M
Total risk-weighted assets	$250M
Risk-adjusted assets financed by investment account holders	$100M
Risk-adjusted assets financed by PER and IRR	$10M
Supervisory authority's discretion (α)	30%
Adjustment for market and operational risk (12.5 × $5M)	$62.5M

CAR according to the standard formula:

$$\frac{\$20}{(\$250M + 62.5M) - (\$100M + \$10M)} = 9.88\%$$

CAR according to the supervisory discretion formula:

$$\frac{\$20}{(\$250M + 62.5M) - (0.7 \times \$100M - 0.3 \times \$10M)} = 8.35\%$$

Source: Iqbal and Mirakhor (2007).

PILLAR 2: SUPERVISORY REVIEW

Supervisory review is the second pillar of Basel II and a critical part of the capital adequacy framework. The supervisory review has two objectives: to assess whether the banks maintain adequate capital necessary for the risks inherent in their business profile and business environment and to encourage banks to have policies and internal processes for assessing and managing capital adequacy that are commensurate with their risk profile, operations, and business strategy. Banks' management is accountable for ensuring that their bank has adequate capital.

The role of supervisors is to review the bank's internal capital adequacy assessments and management processes, to ensure that the bank's capital targets and capital position are consistent with its overall risk profile and strategy, and to enable supervisory intervention if the bank's capital does not provide a sufficient buffer against risk. An important aspect of supervisory reviews is to assess compliance with the minimum standards and disclosure requirements. Supervisors also are expected to have an approach for identifying and intervening in situations where falling capital levels raise questions about the ability of a bank to withstand business shocks.

Supervisors are expected to take appropriate actions if they are not satisfied with the quality of a bank's internal processes and the results of a bank's own risk assessment and capital allocations. They are expected to have at their disposal the necessary enforcement powers and tools. For example, they should be able to require banks to hold capital in excess of the minimum, if so mandated by the risk characteristics of a particular bank or its business environment, and to require prompt remedial action if capital is not maintained or restored.

Four key principles of supervisory review are issued to complement the supervisory guidelines already established (Grais and Kulathunga 2007): (a) Banks must have a process for assessing their overall capital adequacy in relation to their risk profiles and a strategy for maintaining their capital levels. (b) Supervisors should review and evaluate banks' internal capital adequacy assessments and strategies as well as their ability to monitor and ensure compliance with regulatory capital ratios. Supervisors should take appropriate supervisory action if they are not satisfied with the result of this process. (c) Supervisors should expect banks to operate above the minimum regulatory capital ratios and should have the ability to require banks to hold capital in excess of the minimum. (d) Supervisors should seek to intervene at an early stage to prevent capital from falling below the minimum levels required to support the risk characteristics of a particular bank and should require rapid remedial action if capital is not maintained or restored.

The Basel II framework sets special requirements for cooperation between supervisors, especially for the cross-border supervision of complex banking or financial groups. More detailed discussion of the supervisory review process and techniques is provided in chapter 14.

PILLAR 3: MARKET DISCIPLINE

The requirement for market discipline, the third pillar of Basel II, complements the minimum capital requirements and the supervisory review process. Market discipline is based on disclosure requirements. Banks are asked to disclose reliable and timely information that market participants need in order to make well-founded risk assessments, including assessment of the adequacy of capital held as a cushion against losses and of the risk exposures that may give rise to such losses.

The disclosure requirements are based on the concept of materiality—that is, banks must include all information where omission or misstatement could change or influence the decisions of the information users. The only exception is proprietary or confidential information, the sharing of which could undermine a bank's competitive position. Except for large internationally active banks, disclosures are to be made on a semi-annual basis. Banks are expected to have a formal disclosure policy approved by the board of directors, including decisions on what will be disclosed, the frequency of validation reporting, and internal controls over the disclosure process.

The areas that are subject to disclosure are capital structure, capital adequacy, and risk exposure and assessment. The disclosures include qualitative and quantitative aspects. For each area of risk (for example, credit, market, operational, equity), qualitative aspects cover strategies, policies, and processes; the structure and organization of the risk management function; the scope and nature of the risk measurement and reporting systems; the strategies and policies for hedging or mitigating risks; and the processes and systems for monitoring their effectiveness. Quantitative aspects involve disclosures of specific values.

Market discipline contributes to responsible corporate behavior. Market perceptions of—and thus reactions to—a financial intermediary's business conduct and capital strength may be unforgiving. It is thus in the interest of financial intermediaries to define capital resource requirements that take into account the institutional environment in which they operate. The market's perception of market imperfections is likely to influence views on the appropriate level of capital and the capital adequacy of a financial intermediary. For example, the availability of a safety net may lead market participants to require banks to hold less capital in relation to assets. Conversely, anticipation of the high costs of financial distress may induce market participants to require banks to hold more capital in proportion to assets. Similarly, wherever the institutional environment is weak and contract enforcement is uncertain and costly, markets may expect financial intermediaries to adjust the amount of capital they hold.

MANAGING CAPITAL ADEQUACY

A capital adequacy assessment starts with analysis of the components of a bank's capital, as illustrated in figure 13.3. (The figures presented in this section illustrate the analysis of a bank's capital, but do not refer to the same bank.) The core capital components, including common stock and retained earnings, should account for more than half of total capital, as mandated by the 1988 Basel Accord. The identity of shareholders is also important. In extreme circumstances the shareholders may be called on to increase a bank's capital, either by adding new capital or by forgoing dividend payments. However, no amount of capital would be adequate for a bank with malevolent shareholders, incompetent management, or an incompetent board.

The changes in the volume and structure of capital over time are also significant. The bank shown in figure 13.3 experienced some changes in the structure of capital. Any changes in capital structure, especially reductions involving core capital, should be credibly explained. A careful analysis is also needed to explain exactly why and what provoked the loss of capital and to ensure that the bank has learned from the experience and taken adequate measures to prevent a similar situation in the future. The analyst could also compare changes in the volume of capital to the bank's risk profile, which is illustrated in figures 13.3 and 13.4. In general, changes in the volume of capital should be in concert with

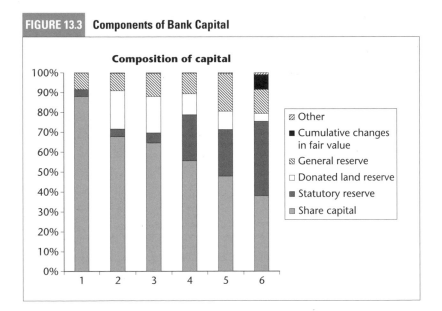

FIGURE 13.3 Components of Bank Capital

expected changes in the risk profile, to provide an adequate cushion for the bank's risk exposures.

In addition to analyzing the structure of a bank's base of capital, the analyst should consider the level and demand for dividends being placed on the bank by shareholders. In periods of economic downturn or situations where the bank's condition is deteriorating, the bank should reduce or eliminate dividend payments to its shareholders.

The next step in the analysis is to assess the bank's risk exposures, on and off the balance sheet. The bank's balance sheet categories are classified according to the risk categories specified in the Basel Accord (and IFSB standards) and are assigned the corresponding risk weight. The analyst should notice the structure of risk-weighted assets and if and how this has changed over time. For example, whether the average risk weights associated with the bank's assets have increased or decreased. The issues to be addressed are whether or not this is a result of the bank's business strategy, whether or not the risk weights reflect actual risk, whether or not the bank is able to understand and adequately manage the higher level of risk, and what appears to be the trend for the future.

Figure 13.4 summarizes the risk profile of a bank, illustrating changes over time in average risk weighting, including on- and off-balance-sheet items; it also projects future trends. It appears that the weighted average of the bank's total risk profile has been reduced in the observation period. The analyst should understand why and what is the trend. For

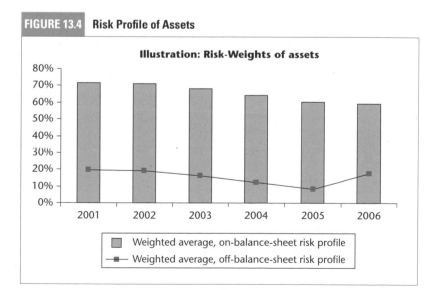

FIGURE 13.4 Risk Profile of Assets

example, the total average could have been reduced because the bank increased its off-balance-sheet business. The weighted average of on-balance-sheet items could have been reduced because the bank started to engage in regulatory capital arbitrage or because of changes in its demand structure.

The final step is to verify the denominator for the capital adequacy calculation by multiplying the amounts of various asset categories by their corresponding risk weights. Once the denominator is determined, the capital adequacy ratio calculation is straightforward. The analyst should, however, also scrutinize a bank's asset quality, to make sure that the capital ratio is realistic. This would normally include checking the bank's policies and practices regarding asset classification and provisions to make sure that it has adequately provided for the impaired value of any of its assets (see chapter 7). It may also include checking the applicable rules concerning general loss reserves.

Table 13.5 illustrates select capital ratios of a bank and their trends over time. A decline in the percentage of core capital in relation to total qualifying capital would indicate that Tier 2 capital or debt instruments are being used to a greater degree in order to meet minimum capital requirements. This situation would, in turn, indicate a relative shift to less permanent forms of capital. The capital ratio indicates whether or not the bank is meeting the minimum capital requirements.

When a bank's capital ratio shows deterioration, this is a cause for concern. The reason could be that the bank has increased the size of its balance sheet, while still meeting minimum capital requirements. Should the growth trend continue, the bank would have to increase capital to be able to maintain the minimum capital ratio. Another reason for a deteriorating capital ratio could be that the bank has changed its risk profile. In such a case, the analyst should investigate whether the bank has adequate policies, procedures, and controls in place to handle the higher risk profile of its operations.

Figure 13.5 illustrates the trend in the capital of a conventional bank over time. The capital is split into Tier 1, Tier 2, and Tier 3 categories, and these are compared to the capital necessary to meet the 8 percent and 15 percent risk-weighted minimum capital requirement. The bank under review has significantly increased its capital as well as its risk-weighted capital ratios. This situation likely indicates that this bank is positioning itself for future growth. While capital adequacy is clearly not an issue, this calls for a review of the bank's internal processes and controls, to ensure that it is adequately prepared to handle the increasing volume of business and, most likely, the increasing degree of risk.

TABLE 13.5   Trend Analysis of Capital Adequacy Ratios

	2001	2002	2003	2004	2005	2006
Actual and projected assets – at past average growth %	15,333,978	19,597,790	22,778,319	30,613,361	42,998,279	64,433,936
Share capital	1,000,000	1,000,000	1,000,000	1,500,000	1,500,000	2,800,000
Retained income & reserves portion of equity	136,560	473,986	548,180	1,195,645	1,627,431	4,561,150
Majority shareholders' equity	1,136,560	1,473,985	1,548,180	2,695,645	3,127,431	7,361,150
Assumed capital requirement @ 15 %	2,300,097	2,939,669	3,416,748	4,592,004	6,449,742	9,665,090
Assumed capital requirement @ 10 %	1,533,398	1,953,779	2,277,832	3,061,336	4,299,828	6,443,394
Shortfall – actual capital to assumed 15 % requirement	(1,163,537)	(1,465,683)	(1,868,568)	(1,896,359)	(3,322,311)	(2,303,940)
Asset growth: 2001–2006	0%	28%	49%	100%	180%	320%
Retained income & reserves portion of equity: growth	0%	247%	301%	776%	1092%	3240%
Equity: Total Asset Ratio	7%	8%	7%	9%	7%	11%

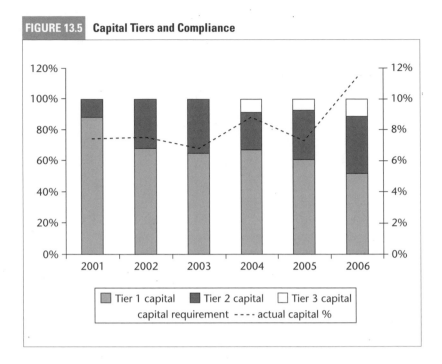

FIGURE 13.5 Capital Tiers and Compliance

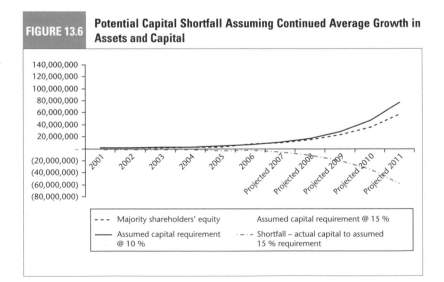

FIGURE 13.6 Potential Capital Shortfall Assuming Continued Average Growth in Assets and Capital

The next question is whether or not a bank can continue to meet its minimum capital requirements in the future. Analysis of this question should include stress tests for situations that might arise in which risk or the bank's capacity to control risk could get out of hand. Figure 13.6 illustrates capital adequacy projections under normal circumstances, made as part of the process of risk management and capital planning. The graph shows the end result of possible situations that a bank may encounter in the future and highlights any projected excess or deficiencies in capital adequacy.

The projection in figure 13.6 is based on a simplistic assumption that both risk-weighted assets and net qualifying capital will grow at the average asset growth percentage of the past five years and that the bank's risk profile will remain the same. This expected business growth clearly would result in a capital shortfall. A bank may take a number of actions to address an expected shortfall in capital adequacy, including the following:

■ Increase Tier 1 capital by asking shareholders to add capital, by retaining earnings, or by issuing new shares in the market;
■ Increase Tier 2 capital—if there is space for this in the bank's capital structure—by issuing the appropriate instruments;
■ Change the business policy to focus on a business with lower capital requirements;
■ Reduce the size of its balance sheet or of its growth.

NOTES

1. The account holder's share of the PER and the whole of the IRR (none of which is attributable to shareholders) are excluded from capital. They are taken into account in measuring the amount of risk-weighted assets attributable to investment account holders. For a discussion of some issues raised by the use of the PER and IRR, see Archer and Karim (2006).
2. Under the basic indicator approach, a fixed percentage, namely 15 percent, of the annual average gross income, averaged over the previous three years, is set aside. Under the standardized approach, this percentage varies according to the line of business, from 12 to 18 percent. It is 18 percent for corporate finance, trading and sales, and payment and settlement; 15 percent for commercial banking and agency services; and 12 percent for retail banking, asset management, and retail brokerage.

14

The Relationship between Risk Analysis and Bank Supervision

anking supervision, based on the ongoing analytical review of banks, serves the public good as one of the key factors in maintaining stability and confidence in the financial system. This chapter discusses the relationship between banking risk analysis and the supervisory process. The methodology for a supervisory review of banks should be similar to that used by private sector analysts, external auditors, or a bank's own risk managers, except that the focus of the analysis differs somewhat.

Bank supervision is an integral part of a much broader and continuous process. It normally includes off-site surveillance and on-site examinations, as summarized in figure 14.1. This process includes the establishment of a legal framework for the banking sector, the designation of regulatory and supervisory authorities, the definition of licensing conditions and criteria, and the enactment of regulations limiting the level of risk that banks are allowed to take. Other necessary steps include establishment of a framework for prudential reporting and off-site surveillance and execution of these activities, followed by on-site supervision. The results of on-site examinations provide inputs for the institutional development of banks and for the improvement of the regulatory and supervisory environment.

In addition to effective supervision, other factors necessary for the stability of banking systems, financial systems, and markets include sound and sustainable macroeconomic policies, a well-developed financial sector infrastructure, effective market discipline, and an adequate banking sector safety net.

Key Messages

- Bank supervisors and financial analysts should view the risk management process in a similar manner.
- The analyst or supervisor should determine what happened, why it happened, the impact of events, and a credible action plan or future strategy to rectify unacceptable trends.
- The supervisory process of off- and on-site supervision is similar to the financial analysis of information, which has to be tested through verification of preliminary conclusions. On-site examination is essential, but could be performed by supervisors, analysts, or external auditors.
- Regulators and supervisors should ensure that all financial institutions are supervised using a consistent philosophy, to ensure a level playing field for financial intermediaries.
- Properly used, banking analysis can enhance the institutional development of the banks concerned.

THE RISK ANALYSIS PROCESS

As discussed in chapter 3, the analytical review of banks follows a number of stages whereby the results of one stage serve as inputs to the next. The ultimate objective of this process is to produce a set of recommendations that, if properly implemented, result in a safe, sound, and properly functioning financial intermediary. Table 14.1 summarizes the stages of the analytical review process.

An analytical review normally comprises a review of financial conditions and specific issues related to risk exposure and risk management. In addition to verifying the conclusions reached during off-site reviews, on-site reviews cover a much larger number of topics and are more concerned with qualitative aspects, including the availability and quality of management information. The questions asked during all phases of the analytic review should focus on what happened, why it happened, the impact of the event or trend, the response and strategy of the bank's management, the recommendations of the analyst, and the vulnerabilities identified. Appendix D summarizes the typical outline for off-site and on-site analytical reviews or diagnostic reports of a bank.

Analytical tools include ratio tables and graphs based on processed input data. These ratios relate to balance sheet structure, profitability, capital adequacy, credit and market risk, liquidity, and currency risk. Taken together, they constitute a complete set of ratios that are normally subject to off-site surveillance. The tables enable analysts to judge the effectiveness of the risk management process and to measure performance. Combined with qualitative information obtained from the questionnaire,

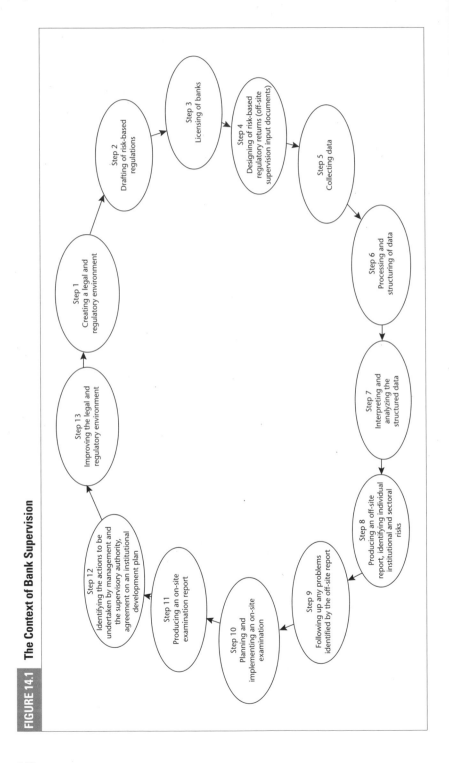

FIGURE 14.1   The Context of Bank Supervision

TABLE 14.1   Stages of the Analytical Review Process

Analytical phase	Source and tools available	Output
Structuring and collection of input data	Questionnaire, financial statements, other financial data	Completed input data, questionnaires, and financial data tables
Processing of data	Completed input data (questionnaires and financial data tables)	Processed output data
Analysis and interpretation of processed or structured output data	Input data and processed output data	Analytical results
Development of an off-site analysis report of the bank's risks	Analytical results and previous on-site examination reports	Off-site examination report or terms of reference for on-site examination
Follow-up through on-site examination, audit, or analytical review	Off-site examination report and terms of reference for on-site examination	On-site examination report and institutional development plan or a memorandum of understanding
Institutional strengthening	On-site examination report and memorandum of understanding for institutional development	Well-functioning financial intermediary
Repeat the process, building on the previous reports and regulatory deficiencies identified	Repeat the process	Repeat the process

these statistical tables make up the raw material on which the analysis contained in off-site reports is based. Graphs provide a visual representation of results and a snapshot of the current situation in a bank. They may also be used during off-site surveillance as a starting point for on-site examination.

During the course of their operations, banks are subject to a wide array of risks. In general, banking risks fall into the following four categories:

- *Financial risks,* as discussed in chapters 5 to 9;
- *Operational risks* related to a bank's overall business strategy and the functioning of its internal systems, including computer systems and technology, compliance with policies and procedures, and the possibility of mismanagement and fraud;
- *Business risks*—often referred to as country risks—associated with a bank's business environment, including macroeconomic, policy, legal, and regulatory factors; financial sector infrastructure and the payment system; and overall systemic risk related to operations;

■ *Event risks,* including all types of exogenous risks that, if they were to materialize, could jeopardize a bank's operations or undermine its financial condition and capital adequacy. Such risks include political events (for example, the fall of a government), contagion due to the failure of a major bank or a market crash, banking crises, natural disasters, and civil wars. Event risks are, in most cases, unexpected until immediately before the event occurs. Banks therefore may not be able to prepare adequately for them other than by maintaining a cushion of capital. The dividing line between the end of an event risk and the beginning of systemic risk is often blurred.

Risk that is inherent in banking should be recognized, monitored, and controlled. Some financial risks are controlled when regulators establish prudential guidelines for a particular type of exposure. The effectiveness of a bank's management of financial risk, monitoring of risk exposure, and compliance with prudential guidelines of bank supervision forms the backbone of the supervisory process, both off- and on-site. Regulations, however, can be costly for a bank. The manner in which regulators apply their functions determines the impact that regulations have on the market as well as their cost. Costs include the provision of information to regulators, maintenance of an institution's internal systems that measure risk and ensure compliance with regulations, and certain business decisions that reduce a bank's profitability. In addition to the direct cost of regulation, hidden costs also exist, such as a bank's compromised ability to innovate or adjust quickly to changing market conditions, which might prevent it from capitalizing on its comparative advantages or competitive position.

With regard to operational risks (with the exception of business strategy risk), regulators typically establish guidelines that banks are expected to follow. Adherence to the guidelines is subject to supervision, typically as part of an on-site examination. A bank's business strategy is also given attention. Initially, as part of the licensing process, the authorities review and implicitly endorse a bank's business strategy. The strategy and its risk implications are always discussed during the process of an on-site examination and possibly also in the context of off-site surveillance. In many countries, senior management is obliged to meet quarterly with supervisory authorities to discuss the bank's business strategy; this is often the case for large banks that have the potential to disrupt market stability.

The category of risks related to a business environment may or may not fall within the scope of supervisory authorities. Regulatory authorities (including the central bank) are closely related to many key aspects of a bank's business environment, however. Entry and licensing regulations effectively determine a banking system's structure and the level and nature of competition. The criteria for issuing licenses must therefore be consistent with those applied in ongoing supervision. If the supervisory authority is different from the licensing authority, the former should have a legal right to have its views considered by the latter.

Monetary authorities also play a critical role in determining the business environment. The choice, design, and use of monetary policy measures and instruments are inextricably related to banking system conditions, the nature of bank competition, and the capacity of the banking system to innovate. In the choice and use of policy instruments, pragmatic considerations (which imply a connection to supervisory authorities) are of prime importance. It is essential to look not only at specific policies or measures, but also at the context in which they are applied. Similar policies may be transmitted, but work in different ways, depending on the structure, financial conditions, and dynamics of the banking system and markets. Supervisory authorities are not involved with other aspects of the business environment that have implications for risk, such as macroeconomic policies, which often determine supply and demand in markets and are a major component of country risk. In addition, authorities usually are not concerned with the tax environment (which directly affects a bank's bottom line), the legal framework, or the financial sector infrastructure (including the payment system and registries), but they may be very influential in proposing changes and improvements in these areas.

Supervisory authorities are also critical with respect to event risks. While these risks may not be foreseen and often cannot be prevented, the authorities play an important role in evaluating their impact on the status and condition of the banking system and of the markets. They also ensure that proper arrangements are put in place to minimize the impact and extent of disruption, to mobilize other authorities to deal effectively with the consequences of certain events, and, ultimately, to oversee the orderly exit of failed institutions.

THE SUPERVISORY PROCESS

All banking systems have at least one regulatory and supervisory authority. However, the locus, structure, regulatory and enforcement powers, and specific responsibilities of each authority are different. This variation is usually a consequence of traditions and of the legal and economic environment of a particular country. Decisions regarding the regulatory and supervisory authorities are sometimes politically motivated. In most countries, the regulatory and supervisory authority for the banking sector is assigned to the central bank, but the current trend is to consolidate all financial supervision in a separate entity, outside the central bank. The responsibilities of bank supervision usually include the following:

- Issuance and withdrawal of banking licenses on an exclusive basis;
- Issuance and enforcement of prudential regulations and standards;
- The authority to prescribe and obtain periodic reports (that is, establish prudential reporting as a precondition for off-site surveillance) and to perform on-site inspections;
- Assessment of fines and penalties and the initiation of emergency actions, including cease and desist orders, management removal and suspension orders, and the imposition of conservatorships;
- Closure and liquidation of banks.

In order to be effective, supervisory authorities must have appropriate enforcement power and an adequate degree of autonomy. These abilities are necessary to resist undue pressures from the government, banks and their shareholders, depositors and creditors, borrowers, and other people who use financial services. Supervisory authorities should command the respect of the banks they oversee.

The Basel Committee on Banking Supervision has identified certain preconditions and set certain standards for effective banking supervision. These standards require the supervisory authority to have a clear, achievable, and consistent framework of responsibilities and objectives as well as the ability to achieve them. If more than one supervisory authority exists, all must operate within a consistent and coordinated framework in order to avoid regulatory or supervisory arbitrage. Where distinctions between banking business and other deposit-taking entities are not clear, the latter could be allowed to operate as quasi-banks, with less regulation. Supervisory authorities should have adequate resources, including the staffing, funding, and technology needed to meet established objectives, provided on terms that do not undermine the autonomy, integrity, and independence of the supervisory agencies. Supervisors must be protected from personal and institutional liability for actions taken in good faith while performing their duties. Supervisory agencies should be obliged to cooperate and share relevant information, both domestically and abroad. This cooperation should be supported by arrangements for protecting the confidentiality of information.

Supervisory authorities, however, cannot guarantee that banks will not fail. The potential for bank failure is an integral part of risk taking. Supervisors have a role to play, but there is a difference between their role in the day-to-day supervision of solvent institutions and their handling of problem institutions in order to prevent contagion and systemic crisis. When approaching systemic issues, the key concern of supervisory authorities is to address threats to confidence in the financial system and contagion to otherwise sound banks. The supervisor's responsibility is to make adequate arrangements that could facilitate the exit of problem banks with minimum disruption to the system; at the same time, the methods applied should minimize distortions to market signals and discipline. Individual bank failure, in contrast, is an issue for shareholders and management. In some cases, a bank failure may become a political issue, especially in the case of a large bank, and involve decisions regarding whether, to what extent, and in what form public funds should be committed to turning the situation around.

An effective supervisory system encompasses some form of off-site surveillance and on-site examination. Off-site surveillance is, in essence, an early-warning device that is based on the analysis of financial data supplied by banks. On-site examination builds on and supplements off-site surveillance and enables supervisory authorities to examine details and to judge a bank's future viability. The extent of on-site work and the method by which it is carried out depend on a variety of factors. In addition to differences in supervisory approaches or techniques, the key determinant of the objectives and scope of supervision is whether they aim only to safeguard the stability of the banking system or if they are also expected to protect the interests of depositors. Some countries have a mixed system of on-site examination based on collaboration between supervisors and external auditors.

Off-Site Surveillance

The central objective of off-site surveillance is to monitor the condition of individual banks, peer groups, and the banking system. Based on this assessment, the performance of a bank is then compared with that of its peer group and the banking sector overall, in order to detect significant deviations from the peer group or from sectoral norms and benchmarks. This process provides an early indication of an individual bank's problems, as well as systemic problems, and assists in prioritizing the use of scarce supervisory resources in areas or activities at greatest risk. Off-site monitoring systems rely on financial reporting in a prescribed format that is supplied by banks according to previously determined reporting schedules. Reporting formats and details vary among countries, although most supervisory authorities systematically collect and analyze data concerning liquidity, capital adequacy, credit risk, asset quality, concentration of exposures, large exposures, market rates, currency, market risks, earnings and profitability, and balance sheet structure. Supporting schedules may also be requested in order to provide greater detail of a bank's exposure to different types of risk and its capacity to bear that risk. Schedules depend on the type and subject of related reports. For example, supervisory authorities may require liquidity to be reported on a weekly or even a daily basis, large exposures on a monthly basis, financial statements quarterly, and asset classification and provisions semiannually.

The sophistication and exact purpose of analytical reviews also vary from country to country. Most supervisory authorities use some form of ratio analysis. The current financial ratios of each bank are analyzed and compared to historical trends and to the performance of its peers in order to assess its financial condition and compliance with prudential regulations. This process may also identify existing or forthcoming problems. Individual bank reports are aggregated to attain group (or peer) statistics for banks of a particular size, business profile, or geographic area and can then be used as a diagnostic tool or in research and monetary policy analysis.

Off-site surveillance is less costly in terms of supervisory resources. Banks provide the information needed for supervisors to form a view of a bank's exposure to the various categories of financial risk. Supervisory authorities then manipulate and interpret the data. Although off-site surveillance allows supervisors to monitor developments concerning a bank's financial condition and risk exposures, it also has limitations:

- The usefulness of reports depends on the quality of a bank's internal information systems and on the accuracy of reporting.
- Reports have a standard format that may not adequately capture new types of risks or the particular activities of individual banks.
- Reports cannot convey all factors affecting risk management, such as the quality of a bank's management personnel, policies, procedures, and internal systems.

On-Site Examinations

On-site examinations enable supervisors to validate the information provided by a bank during the prudential reporting process, to establish the diagnosis and exact cause of a bank's problems with an adequate level of detail, and to assess a bank's future viability or possible problem areas. More specifically, on-site examinations should help supervisors to assess the accuracy of a bank's reports, overall operations and condition, the quality and competence of management, and the adequacy of risk management systems and internal control procedures. Other aspects that should be evaluated include the quality of the loan portfolio, adequacy of loan provisions and reserves, accounting and management information systems, the issues identified in off-site or previous on-site supervisory processes, adherence to laws and regulations, and the terms stipulated in the banking license. On-site examination is very demanding in terms of supervisory resources and usually can address only some of a bank's activities.

On-site examinations can take different forms depending on a bank's size and structure, available resources, and the sophistication, knowledge, and experience of supervisors. Supervisory authorities should establish clear internal guidelines on the objectives, frequency, and scope of on-site examinations. Policies and procedures should ensure that examinations are systematic and conducted in a thorough and consistent manner. In less developed supervisory systems, the examination process often provides only a snapshot of a bank's condition, without assessing potential risks and the availability and quality of systems used by management to identify and manage them. On-site supervision begins with business transactions and proceeds from the bottom up. Results from the successive stages of supervision are compiled and eventually consolidated to arrive at final conclusions regarding a bank's overall financial condition and performance. This approach is characteristic of countries in which management information is unreliable and bank policies and procedures are poorly articulated.

In well-developed banking systems, supervisors typically use a top-down approach that focuses on assessing how banks identify, measure, manage, and control risk. Supervisors are expected to diagnose the causes of a bank's problems and to ensure that they are addressed by preventive actions that can reduce the likelihood of recurrence. The starting point of an on-site examination is an assessment of objectives and policies related to risk management, the directions provided by the board and senior managers, and the coverage, quality, and effectiveness of systems used to monitor, quantify, and control risks. The completeness and effectiveness of a bank's written policies and procedures are then considered, as well as planning and budgeting, internal controls and audit procedures, and management information systems. Examination at the level of business transactions is required only if weaknesses exist in the systems for identifying, measuring, and controlling risks. In many countries, external auditors examine systems and processes at this level.

Early-Warning Systems

In the 1990s supervisory authorities started to refine their early-warning systems—aimed at assessing supervisory risk and identifying potential problems in the financial system and individual banks. The systems generally combine qualitative and quantitative elements. Just as approaches to banking regulation and supervision differ from country to country, the design of early-warning systems also varies. However, there are four generic types: supervisory bank rating systems, financial ratio and peer group analysis systems, comprehensive bank risk assessment systems, and statistical models.

In *supervisory bank rating systems* (of which the most well known is CAMEL—capital adequacy, asset quality, management, earnings, and liquidity), a composite rate is assigned to a bank typically as a result of an on-site examination. *Financial ratio and peer group analysis systems (normatives)* are based on a set of financial variables (typically including capital adequacy, asset quality, profitability, and liquidity) that generate a warning if certain ratios exceed a predetermined critical level, lie within a predetermined interval, or are outliers with regard to past performance of the bank. *Comprehensive bank risk assessment systems* include a comprehensive assessment of the risk profile of a bank, disaggregating a bank (or a banking group) into significant business units and assessing each separate business unit for all business risks. Scores are assigned for specified criteria, and assessment results are aggregated to arrive at the final score for the whole bank or banking group.

Finally, *statistical models* attempt to detect those risks most likely to lead to adverse future conditions in a bank. In contrast with the other three systems, the ultimate focus of statistical models is to predict the probability of future developments rather than produce a summary rating of the current condition of a bank. Statistical models are based on various indicators of future performance. For example, some models estimate a probability of a rating downgrade for an individual bank (for example, probability that the most recent CAMEL rating will be downgraded based on financial data supplied in prudential reporting). Failure-of-survival prediction models are constructed on a sample of failed or distressed banks and aim to identify banks whose ratios, indicators, or change in ratios or indicators are correlated with those of failed or distressed banks. Expected loss models are used in countries where the statistical basis of failed or distressed banks is not large enough to be able to link changes in specific financial variables to probabilities of failure. These models are based on failure probabilities derived from banks' exposure to credit risk and other data, such as the capacity of existing shareholders to supply additional capital. Some regulators have constructed statistical models based on other variables. For example, high growth in assets that is not matched adequately with strengthening of a bank's management and institutional capacity has, in many cases, been the culprit for bank failure. Therefore, a model tracing a high rate of asset growth combined with measures of institutional capacity could be used as an early-warning system.

In many cases, supervisory authorities use more then one early-warning system. The major issues with early-warning systems are the proper choice of variables on which the prediction is based, the availability of reliable input data, and limitations related to quantification of qualitative factors that are critically related to banks' performance (for example, management quality, institutional culture, integrity of internal controls).

CONSOLIDATED SUPERVISION

The institutional classification under which a financial intermediary operates has traditionally been assigned based on predominant financial instruments or services offered by the intermediary. The institutional classification designates regulatory and supervisory authorities for particular institutions and the corresponding regulatory treatment, for example, regarding minimum capital levels, capital adequacy, and other prudential requirements (for example, for liquidity and cash reserves). Increasing financial market integration blurs the difference between various types of financial institutions and creates opportunities for regulatory or supervisory arbitrage, which ultimately increases systemic risk. While perfect neutrality may not be possible or even necessary, authorities should strive to level the playing field with respect to specific markets and to reduce the scope for regulatory arbitrage. In other words, when different financial institutions compete in the same market for identical purposes, their respective regulations must ensure competitive equality.

Regulatory environments that potentially allow for regulatory (or supervisory) arbitrage display at least one of the following features:

- Inconsistent or conflicting regulatory philosophies for different types of financial institutions;
- Deficiencies or inconsistencies in defining risks and prudential requirements for different types of financial institutions;

- Differences in the cost of regulating different financial institutions;
- Lack of coordination between regulatory and supervisory authorities in the financial sector.

Cross-Border Operations

The international expansion of banks increases the efficiency of both global and national markets, but it may create difficulties during the supervisory process. For example, cross-border transactions may conceal a bank's problems from its home-country supervisors. Certain practices by subsidiaries in less regulated environments may be hidden from home-country supervisors but ultimately create losses that can impair the bank's capital. Internationalization may be used as a vehicle to escape regulation and supervision—for example, by transferring problem assets to less stringent regulatory environments or to areas with less effective supervision. Internationally active banks therefore present a challenge to supervisory authorities.

Cooperative efforts are needed to ensure that all aspects of international banking are subject to effective supervision and that remedial actions are well coordinated. Responding to the failure of a number of large, internationally active banks, the Basel Committee on Banking Supervision has issued minimum standards for their supervision. The Basel Concordat is based on the following principles:

- A capable home-country authority should supervise internationally active banks and banking groups on a consolidated basis.
- The creation of a cross-border banking establishment should receive the prior consent of both home- and host-country supervisory authorities. Such bilateral supervisory arrangements should be specified in a memorandum of understanding signed by both authorities.
- Home-country supervisory authorities should possess the right to collect information concerning the cross-border establishment of the banks and banking groups that they supervise. The collection by and exchange of information between authorities should be guided by principles of reciprocity and confidentiality. Confidential information should be safeguarded against disclosure to unauthorized parties.
- If host-country supervisors determine that the home-country supervisory arrangements do not meet minimum standards, they should prohibit cross-border operations or impose restrictive measures that satisfy their standards.

■ Home-country supervisory authorities should inform host-country authorities of changes in supervisory measures that have a significant bearing on the relevant bank's foreign operations.

One of the primary reasons why consolidated supervision is critical is the risk of a damaging loss of confidence and of contagion that extends beyond legal liability. Since supervisory arrangements and techniques differ due to legal, institutional, historical, and other factors, no single set of criteria establishes conclusively whether consolidated supervision is effective or not. In principle, consolidated supervision should assess all risks run by a banking group wherever they occur, including branches and subsidiaries, non-bank financial companies, and financial affiliates. More specifically, consolidated supervision should support the principle that no banking operation, wherever located, should escape supervision. It also should prevent the double leveraging of capital and ensure that all risks incurred by a banking group (no matter where it is booked) are evaluated and controlled on a global basis.

Consolidated supervision should extend beyond the mere consolidation of accounts. Supervisory authorities should consider the exact nature of the risks involved and design an appropriate approach to them. Consolidated accounting may even be inappropriate when the nature of risk varies—for example, when market risk differs from market to market. The offsetting of market risks during the process of accounting consolidation may result in an inaccurate risk exposure position. Liquidity risk should be considered primarily on a market-by-market or a currency-by-currency basis.

Supervision of Conglomerates

Supervisory arrangements involving conglomerates are even more complex. An international financial group active in banking, securities, fund management, and insurance may be subject to a number of regulatory regimes and supervised by authorities in a number of countries. Problems related to a conglomerate's information, coordination, and compliance with prudential regulations—which are complex enough in a single-country environment—are compounded at the international level, particularly when operations involve emerging-market economies.

Financial conglomerates may have different shapes and structural features, reflecting various laws and traditions. Key aspects to be considered in the supervision of conglomerates are the overall approach to supervision, the transparency of group structures, the assessment of capital adequacy, and the prevention of double gearing. In addition, contagion and the effect of intragroup exposures and the consolidated treatment of large exposures play a role because of differences in exposure rules in banking, securities, and insurance.

The problem of consolidated supervision has been addressed internationally by a tripartite group consisting of representatives of the Basel Committee on Banking Supervision and interest groups involved in both the securities and insurance sectors. Their joint statement on the supervision of conglomerates specifies the following:

- All banks, securities firms, and other financial institutions should be subject to effective supervision, including that related to capital.
- Geographically or functionally diversified financial groups require consolidated supervision and special supervisory arrangements. Cooperation and information flow among supervisory authorities should be adequate and free from both national and international impediments.
- The transparency and integrity of markets and supervision rely on adequate reporting and disclosure of information.

The joint statement also recommends accounting-based consolidation as an appropriate technique for assessing capital adequacy in homogeneous conglomerates. This process allows for the straight-forward comparison, using a single set of valuation principles, of total consolidated assets and liabilities as well as the application, at the parent level, of capital adequacy rules to consolidated figures. With regard to heterogeneous conglomerates, the group recommended a combination of three techniques: the building-block prudential approach (whereby consolidation is performed following solo supervision by the supervisory authority), risk-based aggregation, and risk-based deduction.

The best approach to supervision and the assessment of capital adequacy is still broadly debated in international circles, while the supervisory community continuously learns from its experiences.

SUPERVISORY COOPERATION WITH INTERNAL AND EXTERNAL AUDITORS

The Institute of Internal Auditors has defined internal auditing as "an independent, objective activity that . . . helps an organization to accomplish its objectives by bringing a systematic, disciplined approach to evaluate and improve the effectiveness of risk management, control, and governance processes." The internal audit function of a bank should cover all of a bank's activities in all its associated entities. It should be permanent, impartial, and technically competent, operating independently and reporting to a bank's board or to the chief executive officer.

Supervisory authorities normally issue regulatory requirements for banks' internal control systems, aiming to establish some basic principles for the system and the quality of controls applied by banks. Although the extent of regulations varies, internal audit-control regulations normally cover policies and procedures for management of credit risk and other core banking risks, such as liquidity management, foreign exchange and interest rate risks, and risk management of derivatives and computer and telecommunication systems. On-site supervision normally includes an evaluation of the bank's internal controls and the quality of the internal audit function. If satisfied with the quality of internal audit, supervisors can use the reports of internal auditors to identify problems pertaining to control or management in the bank.

External auditors and bank supervisors cover similar ground but focus on different aspects in their work. Auditors are concerned primarily with fair presentation in the annual financial statements and other reports supplied to shareholders and the general public. They are expected to express an opinion on whether financial statements and other prudential returns (when applicable) fairly present the condition and results of a bank's operations. In order to express such an opinion, auditors must also be satisfied with a bank's accounting policies and principles and the consistency of their application, and they must be sure that the bank's key functional systems are coherent, timely, and complete.

Because supervisory resources are scarce and in order to avoid duplication of examination efforts, supervisory authorities have come to rely increasingly on external auditors to assist in on-site supervision. Relying on the assessments and judgment of external auditors implies that supervisors have an interest in ensuring high bank auditing standards and that auditors meet certain quality criteria. In many countries, banking regulations require that the banks' external audits be carried out by auditors who have adequate professional expertise available in their firms and meet certain quality standards.

Auditors are often expected to report to the supervisory authorities any failures by banks to fulfill the requirements related to their banking license and other material breaches of laws and regulations, especially where the interests of depositors are jeopardized. In some countries the external auditors are asked to perform additional tasks of interest to the supervisors, such as to assess the adequacy of organizational and internal

TABLE 14.2   Adapting the External Audit to Specific Circumstances and Needs

Type of analysis or audit	Output	International Standard of Auditing	Comments
Limited assurance review engagement	On-site examination review report	ISA 910	Suggested when the objective is a "validated" understanding of the corporate governance and risk management process
Report of factual findings in connection with an extended (loan) portfolio review	Audit opinion of the loan portfolio or other major asset category	ISA 920	Recommended procedure for any major balance sheet category such as the loan or trading portfolio
Audit of the remainder of the financial data	An opinion on the details of financial statements required in an audit; can be expanded using ISA 920	ISA 700	Optional, to be determined on a case-by-case basis; recommended for change of ownership or restructuring that involves public funds

control systems as well as the consistency of methods and databases used to prepare prudential reports, financial statements, and internal reports.

A supervisor's request to an external auditor to assist in specific supervision-related tasks should be made in the context of a well-defined framework. This process demands adherence to, at a minimum, international accounting and auditing standards. Table 14.2 illustrates the options available in this area.

An important prerequisite for cooperation between the supervisory authorities and external auditors is a continuing dialogue between the supervisory authorities and the national professional accounting and auditing bodies. Such discussions should routinely cover all areas of mutual concern, including generally accepted accounting practices and auditing standards applicable to banks, as well as specific accounting problems, such as appropriate accounting techniques to be introduced in the context of specific financial innovations.

PART Four

Future Challenges

15

Future Challenges

slamic banking has survived well despite the obstacles and skepticism of the critics, although it continues to face many challenges.[1] Its future growth and development will depend largely on the nature of innovations introduced in the market. The immediate need is to develop instruments that enhance liquidity; to develop secondary, money, and interbank markets; and to perform asset-liability and risk management.

AREAS FOR IMPROVEMENT

Although Islamic banks have grown in numbers, the average size of their assets is still small compared to that of conventional banks. As of 2001, no Islamic bank was among the top 100 banks in the world. More than 60 percent of Islamic banks were below the $500 million in assets considered to be the minimum for an efficient conventional bank, and aggregate assets of all Islamic banks were less than those of any single bank among the top 60 banks in the world. Finally, the size of assets of the largest Islamic bank amounted to a meager 1 percent of the assets of the largest bank in the world.

Large institutions have significant potential for efficiency gains due to economies of scale and scope, organizational efficiency, and lower cost of funding. Due to their small size, Islamic banks are unable to reap these benefits.

Key Messages

- Several areas pose challenges for sustaining the growth of Islamic banks.
- The introduction of new products and financial engineering represents a critical challenge requiring immediate attention. New products can be defined either through "reverse engineering" or by "innovation."
- Liquidity-enhancing financial instruments and the development of capital markets are essential for further growth.
- Islamic banks can benefit from economies of scale as well as enhancement of scope. Both approaches offer diversification benefits.
- The measurement and management of risk need to be supplemented with analytical models.
- The risk management framework can be enhanced by improving the transparency in current financial disclosure.

Illiquidity

Islamic banks are operating with a limited set of short-term traditional instruments, and there is a shortage of products for medium- to long-term maturities. One reason for these shortcomings is the lack of markets in which to sell, trade, and negotiate financial assets of the bank. There are no venues for securitizing dormant assets and taking them off the balance sheet. In other words, the secondary markets lack depth and breadth. An effective portfolio management strategy cannot be implemented in the absence of liquid markets, as opportunities for diversification become limited. Since the needs of the market regarding liquidity, risk, and portfolio management are not being met, the system is not functioning at its full potential. There is growing realization that the long-term, sustainable growth of Islamic financial markets will depend largely on the development of well-functioning secondary markets and the introduction of liquidity-enhancing and risk-sharing products.

Limited Scope

In the absence of debt markets, underdevelopment of equities markets, and lack of derivatives markets, financial intermediaries play a critical role in the provision of Islamic financial services. Financial intermediaries not only are the main source of capital and risk mitigation but also are expected to undertake activities with wider scope. The changing global financial landscape will require Islamic banks to go beyond their traditional role as commercial banks and develop areas such as securities, risk management, and insurance that are either lacking or functioning on a limited scale.

The distinction between traditional commercial banking and investment banking is getting blurred, and there is a global trend to mix financial services with non-banking services. Although this trend is prevalent in major industrial economies, it has not been embraced by many of the emerging markets where Islamic finance is practiced. For example, a recent study that ranks several countries in the Middle East according to their level of financial development finds that countries throughout the region have a weak institutional environment and a poorly developed non-bank financial sector (Creane and others 2003).

Concentrated Banking

Islamic banks tend to have a concentrated base of deposits or assets. They often concentrate on a few select sectors and avoid direct competition. For example, one Islamic bank may specialize in financing the agricultural sector, while another might do the same in the construction sector, and neither attempts to diversify to other sectors. This practice makes Islamic banks vulnerable to cyclical shocks in a particular sector. Dependence on a small number of sectors—lack of diversification— increases their exposure to new entrants, especially foreign conventional banks that are better equipped to meet these challenges.

This concentration in the base of deposits or assets reflects a lack of diversification, which increases their exposure to risk. Islamic banks' assets are concentrated in a handful of products. In terms of sector allocation, average financing activities of Islamic banks have been oriented primarily to trade (32 percent), followed by industry (17 percent), real estate (16 percent), services (12 percent), agriculture (6 percent), and others (17 percent; see Kahf 1999). Islamic banks are not fully exploiting the benefits that come from both geographic and product diversification. At present, they rely heavily on maintaining good relationships with depositors. However, these relationships can be tested during times of distress or changing market conditions, when depositors tend to change loyalties and shift to large financial institutions they perceive to be safer.

This risk of losing depositors raises a more serious exposure known as "displacement risk." Displacement risk refers to a situation where, in order to remain competitive, an Islamic bank pays its investment depositors a rate of return higher than what should be payable under the "actual" terms of the investment contract; it does this by forgoing part or all of its equity holders' profits, which may adversely affect its own capital.

Islamic banks engage in such practices to induce investment account holders not to withdraw their funds. By diversifying their base of depositors, Islamic banks could reduce their exposure to displacement or withdrawal risks. With the changing face of banking and the introduction of Internet-based banking, achieving a high degree of geographic diversity on the liabilities side is conceivable and should be encouraged.

Weak Risk Management and Governance Framework

Several studies have identified weaknesses and vulnerabilities among Islamic banks in the areas of risk management and governance. Operational risk, which arises due to the failure of systems, processes, and procedures, is one area of concern. Weak internal control processes may present operational risks and expose an Islamic bank to potential losses. Governance issues are equally important for Islamic banks, investors, regulators, and other stakeholders. The role of *Shariah* boards brings unique challenges to the governance of Islamic financial institutions. Similarly, human resource issues, such as the quality of management, technical expertise, and professionalism, are also subject to debate.

STEPS FORWARD: SOME RECOMMENDATIONS

Improvement can be made in several areas to promote and enhance the functioning of Islamic banks and other institutions providing Islamic financial services. However, certain areas deserve immediate attention, and these are discussed further in this section.

Financial Engineering

Financial engineering and financial innovations are driving the global financial system toward greater economic efficiency by expanding the opportunities for sharing risk, lowering transaction costs, and reducing asymmetric information and agency costs. Financial engineering involves the design, development, and implementation of innovative financial instruments and processes as well as the formulation of creative solutions. Financial engineering may lead to a new consumer-type financial instrument, or a new security, or a new process or creative solution to corporate finance problems, such as the need to lower funding costs, manage risk better, or increase the return on investments.

For Islamic financial institutions, a financial engineering challenge is to introduce new *Shariah*-compatible products that enhance liquidity, risk management, and portfolio diversification. Generally, attempts to apply financial engineering techniques to Islamic banking will require committing a great deal of resources to understanding the risk-return characteristics of each building block of the system and offering new products with different risk-return profiles that meet the demand of investors, financial intermediaries, and entrepreneurs for liquidity and safety. Securitization is a prime candidate for financial engineering. New financial innovations are also needed to satisfy the demand for instruments at both ends of the maturity structure: extremely short-term deposits and long-term investments. Money markets that are *Shariah*-compatible do not exist at present, and there is no equivalent of an Islamic interbank market where banks could place, say, overnight funds or could borrow to satisfy a need for temporary liquidity. Although securitization of a pool of lease portfolios could help to develop the interbank market, the volume of transactions offered by securitization may not be sufficient to meet the demand (Iqbal 1999).

With increased globalization, integration and linkages have become critical to the success of any capital market. Such integration becomes seamless and transparent when financial markets offer a wide array of instruments with varying structures of maturity and opportunities for portfolio diversification and risk management. Financial engineering in Islamic finance will have to focus on the development of products that foster market integration and attract investors and entrepreneurs to the risk-return characteristics of the product rather than to the fact of the product being Islamic or non-Islamic.

As impressive as the record of growth of individual Islamic banks may be, so far they have served mostly as intermediaries between Muslim financial resources and major commercial banks in the West. It has been a one-way relationship. No major Islamic bank has been able to develop ways and means of intermediating between the supply of Western financial resources and the demand for them in Muslim countries. There is an urgent need to develop marketable *Shariah*-based instruments by which asset portfolios generated in Muslim countries can be marketed in the West.

Related to the challenge of financial engineering is another operational challenge for Islamic banks: the need to standardize the process for introducing new products in the market. Currently, each Islamic bank has its own religious board that examines and evaluates each new product without coordinating the effort with other banks. Each religious board adheres to a particular school of thought. This process should be streamlined and standardized to minimize time, effort, and confusion.[2]

Development of new products and financial engineering are resource-intensive activities. All major conventional banks have dedicated departments that conduct background market research, product development, and analytical modeling. These activities demand financial and human resources, which are costly. Conventional financial institutions can justify these costs, because they are able to recover them, in most cases, from the volume of business generated as a result of the innovative product. Costs associated with the development of new products are rising due to the increasing complexity of the business environment as a result of regulatory or accounting and reporting standards.

Islamic financial institutions are, in general, of small size and cannot afford to invest substantial funds in research and development. They are unable to reap the benefits of economies of scale. Considering the importance of financial engineering, Islamic financial institutions should seriously consider making joint efforts to develop the basic infrastructure for introducing new products. Conducting basic research and development collectively may save some of the costs required to build this infrastructure individually. A good example of such collective effort would be to sponsor research in the development of analytical models, computer systems, and tools to analyze the risk and return on different instruments.

Financial engineering is an area where Islamic financial institutions could benefit from more experienced Western institutions, which are more sophisticated in engineering and marketing the right product to the right client. Conventional investment banks, which have invested heavily in the infrastructure for developing new products, can work for or with Islamic financial institutions to develop *Shariah*-compliant products. Once a financial engineering shop is set up, it can develop different products with different risk and return profiles. In this respect, Islamic financial institutions would do well to develop synergies and collaborate with conventional institutions. Islamic financial institutions could outsource the development part to conventional institutions and keep the marketing part to themselves, a division of labor that could benefit both institutions.

Risk Management and Diversification

Financial markets are becoming more integrated and interdependent, thus increasing the probability of expeditious contagion effects and leaving little room for swift measures against unexpected risk. Insufficient understanding of the new environment can create a sense of greater risk even if the objective level of risk in the system remains unchanged or is even lower. The current wave of capital market liberalization and globalization is prompting the need for enhanced risk management measures, especially for the developing economies and emerging markets. Whereas risk management is practiced widely in conventional financial markets, it is underdeveloped in Islamic financial markets.

Due to limited resources, Islamic banks are often unable to afford high-cost management information systems or the technology to assess and monitor risk in a timely fashion. With weak management and lack of proper risk-monitoring systems, the risk exposure of Islamic banks is high.

Providing a more diverse mix of financial services or spreading risks over a larger geographic area imply at least the potential for improved diversification, so the same protection against financial distress can be attained with fewer resources.[3] For Islamic financial institutions, geographic expansion of the depositor base could achieve diversification on the liabilities side. Diversification on the assets side could reduce the variance of the returns that accrue to claimholders of the financial intermediary. Also, geographic and sectoral diversification on the assets side could break up the financial institution's concentration in a region or a sector and thus reduce its exposure by creating less perfectly correlated risks. Geographic spread of products can further help the financial intermediary to improve its credit risk by selecting borrowers with the best credit and avoiding those with the weakest. With diversification, Islamic banks would be able to extend the maturity frontier.

Islamic financial intermediaries need to adopt appropriate risk management not only for their own portfolio but also for that of their clients. Diversification and risk management are closely associated with the degree of market incompleteness. In highly incomplete markets, financial intermediaries are in a better position to provide diversification and risk management for the client because the responsibility for risk diversification shifts from the investors to the financial intermediary, which is considered to be better at providing intertemporal risk management. Islamic financial institutions need to take immediate steps to devise an infrastructure for implementing proper measures, controls, and management of risk and to create innovative instruments to share, transfer, and mitigate financial risk so that entrepreneurs can concentrate on what they do best: managing exposure to business risk in which they have a comparative advantage.

Exposure can also be reduced by working closely with clients to reduce their exposure, which will ultimately reduce the intermediary's exposure. In other words, if the debtor of the bank has lower financial risk, this will result in better quality credit for the bank. Furthermore, monitoring becomes vital in cases where Islamic banks invest in equity-based instruments because an institution with limited resources may not be equipped to conduct thorough monitoring. An institution with adequate resources may develop processes, systems, and training to undertake effective monitoring. There is clearly a need for Islamic financial institutions that can offer guarantees, enhance liquidity, underwrite insurance against risks, and develop hedging tools for a fee.

Finally, Islamic financial institutions need to realize the importance not only of financial risk and its management but also of operational risk, which is risk due to the failure of controls and processes. Currently, there is a serious lack of a risk culture and of enterprise-level sponsorship of active risk management. Formulating a strategy for risk management in Islamic financial markets will require (a) holding comprehensive and detailed discussion of the scope and role of derivatives within the framework of the *Shariah*; (b) expanding the role of financial intermediaries with special emphasis on facilitating risk sharing; (c) applying *takaful* (*Shariah*-compliant mutual insurance) to insure financial risk; and, finally, (d) applying financial engineering to develop synthetic derivatives and off-balance-sheet instruments.

Challenges for Risk Management

Implementation of a risk management framework requires close collaboration among the management of Islamic financial institutions, regulators, and supervisors. Implementation of risk management at the institutional level is the responsibility of management, which should identify clear objectives and strategies for the institution and establish internal systems for identifying, measuring, monitoring, and managing various risk exposures. Although the general principles of risk management are the same for conventional and Islamic financial institutions, there are specific challenges in the management of risk in Islamic financial institutions:

- *The need to establish supporting institutions.* Such institutions include a lender of last resort, a deposit insurance system, a liquidity management system, secondary markets, a legal infrastructure favorable to Islamic instruments, and an efficient system for resolving disputes.
- *The need to achieve uniformity in and harmonization of Shariah standards across markets and borders.* The current practice of maintaining separate *Shariah* boards for each institution is inefficient and should be replaced by a centralized *Shariah* board for a jurisdiction.

■ *The cost of developing risk management systems.* Many Islamic financial institutions are too small to afford the costs. Efforts should be made to collaborate with other institutions to develop systems that are customized to the needs of Islamic financial institutions and that address the need for instrument-specific modeling.

■ *The challenges of integrating Islamic financial institutions with global financial markets.* Efforts should be made to enhance transparency in financial reporting and develop accounting and reporting standards across markets.

■ *The scarcity of highly skilled human resources.* Efforts should be made to develop customized research and training programs on risk management. Such training programs should certify participants after successful completion of the program.

Non-Bank Financial Services

For further growth, the role of intermediation should be extended beyond its traditional setup. In particular, there is a need to broaden the scope and range of financial services offered, similar to the concept of a "financial products supermarket." Such a supermarket would act like an "all-in-one-bank" covering all sorts of financial services. In this role, the Islamic bank would serve as a one-stop shop catering to different types of customers, ranging from private individuals, institutions, high-net-worth individuals, and corporations and offering products that serve their investment, borrowing, risk management, and wealth management needs. For example, such an institution would serve retail customers, manage investment portfolios, and provide various services for corporate customers. At the same time, like a broker, the financial products supermarket would be a retail firm that manages assets and offers payment and settlement services.

As financial systems become more sophisticated, institutional investors have grown significantly in size and importance. For instance, contractual savings with defined benefits, like insurance and pension funds, are managing a large volume of assets. In a financial system where securities markets are underdeveloped, which is the case of Islamic financial markets, financial intermediaries will have to provide a broader set of services, including non-bank financial services. Most Islamic banks are not adequately equipped to provide typical investment banking services, such as underwriting, guarantees, market research, and fee-based advisory services. The refinement and development of fee-based services would enhance the functionality of Islamic financial services. Fee-based contracts like *joalah*, *wakalah*, and *kifalah* require further development if they are to be recognized and operationalized to exploit the full capabilities of Islamic banks.

Performance Benchmarks

The practice of measuring performance of an asset by comparing its return and risk relative to a well-defined benchmark is well established in a market-centered financial system. Markets are good at offering an efficient, measurable, and consistent benchmark for different asset classes and securities. The absence of benchmarks makes it difficult to evaluate the performance of Islamic financial institutions. The dearth of transparent benchmarks that can be used to compare risk-adjusted returns complicates the task of evaluating the efficiency of financial institutions. Such benchmarks are valuable tools for measuring the relative performance of different asset classes and, ultimately, the performance of the financial intermediary. The current practice of using interest based benchmarks such as the London Interbank Offered Rate (LIBOR) has been accepted on an ad hoc basis in the absence of better benchmarks, but several researchers have raised the need to develop benchmarks based on the rate of return, reflecting Islamic modes of financing.

Payment System

The absence of risk-free or high-grade investment securities and the dominance of trade-financed asset-backed securities are of concern to regulators, as they threaten the payment system and increase its vulnerability to risk and illiquidity. In this context, it has been suggested that the concept of narrow banking be applied to Islamic banks. Fischer originally presented the concept of narrow banking, which is banking that specializes in deposit-taking and payment activities but does not provide lending services. Stability and safety are achieved if deposits are invested only in short-term treasuries or their close equivalents. In the context of the Islamic financial system, Islamic banks do not have access to relatively risk-free securities like treasuries. One alternative, suggested by El-Hawary, Grais, and Iqbal (2004), is to segment the balance sheet of Islamic banks so that demand and short-term deposits are invested only in high-grade, liquid asset-backed securities, reducing the risk to the payment system. This concept needs to be refined further by developing a secondary market to enhance the liquidity and standardizing contracts to reduce the riskiness of asset-backed securities.

Institutionalization of Instruments

If the Islamic financial services industry is to grow, various institutions are desperately needed. Institutions to support equity-style financing and investment are the most critical. Due to the nature of trade- and asset-related financing instruments, Islamic banks tend to act as more than mere financiers. Institutions are needed to support such instruments. For example, specialized institutions are needed to administer, maintain, and facilitate lease-related operations and to work closely with the banks to provide funding. Standardizing the operations and instruments will pave the way for pooling heterogeneous assets for securitization purposes—a much-needed functionality for enhancing liquidity in the market.

Universal Banking

The nature of financial intermediation and the style of financial products and services offered make Islamic banks a hybrid between commercial and investment banking, similar to a universal bank. Universal banking benefits from economies of scope due to its close relationship, established client base, and access to private information gained through the relationship. Combining different product lines (such as banking and insurance products) or commercial and investment banking lines may increase the relationship value of banking at a much lower average cost of marketing. Islamic financial institutions could realize the benefits of universal banking by strengthening this aspect.

For example, by expanding the scope of services, Islamic banks could spread the fixed cost, in terms of both physical and human capital, of managing a client relationship over a wider set of products, leading to more efficient use of resources. Through expansion, Islamic banks could use their branch networks and other channels to distribute additional products at low marginal cost. As universal banks, Islamic banks would be able to capitalize on their good reputation established in one product or service to market other products and services with relatively little effort. Finally, expanding the scope of Islamic banks would benefit consumers, who would save on searching and monitoring costs by purchasing a bundle of financial services from a single provider instead of acquiring them separately from different providers.

Despite its advantages, universal banking has inefficiencies as well, and these should be avoided. For example, universal banks can stymie innovation by extracting informational rents and protecting established firms with close ties to the bank from competition.

Regulation, Governance, and Transparency

Corporate governance in Islamic finance entails implementation of a rule-based incentive system that preserves social justice and order among all members of society (Iqbal and Mirakhor 2001). Islamic banks emphasize service to multiple stakeholders. Governance processes and structures inside and outside the firm are needed to protect the ethical and pecuniary interests of shareholders and stakeholders.

Having a *Shariah* board for every institution is not efficient; only one set of *Shariah*-compliant rules is needed for appropriate corporate governance. A *Shariah* board for the system as a whole, consisting of scholars from different disciplines including *Shariah*, economics, finance, and commercial law, is needed to ensure that rules are defined and enforced so that economic agents comply fully with their contractual obligations to all stakeholders (Iqbal and Mirakhor 2003). Complementing existing arrangements, a harmonized systemwide *Shariah* board could be guided by standardized contracts and practices, set by an international standard-setting self-regulatory association. Such an approach would ensure consistency of interpretation and enhance the enforceability of contracts before civil courts.

To enhance *Shariah* compliance further, relying on a body external to the institution is likely to improve the consistency of interpretation and application of *Shariah*. Chapra and Habib (2002) propose having chartered audit firms acquire the necessary knowledge to undertake a *Shariah* audit. The idea of a market for *Shariah* audit firms presents some advantages if externalization is reconceptualized as a complement—rather than an alternative—to the internal *Shariah* audit. External *Shariah* companies would perform a role that reflects their chartered counterparts in conventional finance, thus introducing an additional layer in the *Shariah* verification process. This option would entail a clear separation of ex ante and ex post audit. However, it is unclear whether switching to a market for *Shariah* auditing firms would guarantee *Shariah* compliance.

Implementation of financial disclosure is another priority. Ideally, jurisdictions where Islamic banks are present should implement accounting and reporting practices in line with standards of the Accounting and Auditing Organization of Islamic Financial Institutions (AAOIFI). This could be accomplished by adopting the official AAOIFI standards, creating AAOIFI-inspired national standards, or integrating select AAOIFI standards with existing accounting and auditing standards. AAOIFI standards present multiple advantages. First, the process of conducting periodic reviews ensures that only the best accounting and auditing practices are used. Second, they allow comparability across Islamic banks in different jurisdictions, although they may limit comparability between Islamic and conventional banks. Third, stakeholders involved in Islamic finance will find it easier to gain familiarity with a single accounting framework instead of multiple national ones. In spite of increased comparability across sectors, the simple extension of International Financial Reporting Standards (IFRS) or national conventional standards is not likely to bring the same clarity, because it may not allow the disclosure of relevant information.

Poor corporate governance imposes heavy costs, but the mere extension of international standards to Islamic banks may not be sufficient. The principles and practices of Islamic financial services require a thorough review from the corporate governance perspective. Sound corporate governance requires the formulation of principles and enforcement (for more, see Berglöf and Claessens 2004). Many countries where Islamic finance is developing have weak contracting environments: regulators often lack the power to enforce rules, private actors are nonexistent, and courts are "underfinanced, unmotivated, unclear as to how the law applies, unfamiliar with economic issues, or even corrupt" (Fremond and Capaul 2002). Furthermore, a "law habit" culture—that is, a propensity to abide by the law—must be rooted in society. While the ability to enforce regulations is inextricably coupled with the overall process of development, legislation enabling transparency, private monitoring initiatives, and investments in the rule of law by willing authorities can pave the way to the emergence of regulatory frameworks.

Development of Capital Markets

Responding to the current wave of oil revenues and growing demand for *Shariah*-compliant products, Islamic capital markets are expanding at a quickening pace, and stakeholders are starting to realize their potential. Development of institutional infrastructure, such as accounting standards and regulatory bodies, is a step in the right direction.[4] However, the market needs host governments to undertake strong leadership and constructive policy actions.

Well-developed Islamic capital markets will not only benefit borrowers and institutional investors, they also can enhance the stability of Islamic banks, providing them with improved portfolio, liquidity, and risk management tools. Ultimately, these developments will help to integrate Islamic financial markets, as well as the institutions that form them, into the broader conventional international financial system.

On the supply side, the volume of Islamic investments, with a preference for *Shariah*-compliant instruments, has grown to form a critical mass that can support a well-functioning and efficient capital market. It is evolving into a truly international market. Not only highly rated borrowers, such as the multilateral development banks (for example, the World Bank), but also developing-country borrowers with lower credit ratings, such as Pakistan, have successfully raised a considerable volume of funds in this market.

On the demand side, countries in the developing world, especially the middle-income countries, will require a significant volume of investments in infrastructure over the next decade. For Indonesia alone, additional infrastructure investments of $5 billion (2 percent of GDP) are required annually, to reach a 6 percent medium-term growth target (World Bank 2004). Because the domestic capital markets of these borrowers are often too shallow to satisfy their large investment needs, they will have to access external sources of financing.

Furthermore, Muslim stakeholders in middle-income countries are increasingly expressing their preference for *Shariah*-compliant financing. In turn, financial intermediaries, including private sector commercial and investment banks, as well as development finance institutions, will have to start paying more attention to the "nonfinancial" needs of their clients.

For the multilateral development banks, the development of Islamic capital markets is a highly relevant topic. First, multilateral development banks are deeply involved in infrastructure finance and are naturally interested in the Islamic capital market as a new and alternative source of financing. Second, by channeling the funds available in Islamic financial markets, which are mostly based in the countries with high savings such as the Gulf Cooperation Council countries and Malaysia, to finance investments in developing countries, multilateral development banks can create a new model for international cooperation while responding to the stakeholders' voices on both sides. Third, multilateral development banks can promote financial stability by encouraging the development of Islamic capital markets and providing the momentum to integrate the Islamic financial markets into the international financial system.

In the near future, structures such as *ijarah* (a lease) and *murabahah* (a cost-plus sales contract used to purchase commodities) that provide investors with a predetermined return as well as full recourse to the obligor probably will have more market potential than other structures. This will be driven primarily by investor preferences, but a large proportion of potential borrowers will prefer to lock in their borrowing costs rather than engage in pure profit-sharing schemes.

While the future appears promising, certain obstacles lie ahead, and market participants and regulators need to take concrete steps to support market takeoff. First and most important, market development requires strong sponsorship and leadership on the part of the host-country government, especially regarding legal and regulatory issues. For example, for an *ijarah* transaction, the owner of operating assets enters into a leasing transaction. While the owner of operating assets is often the government itself or related public sector bodies, the relevant laws and regulations in the host country may not allow these bodies to pledge or lease assets needed to structure an *ijarah* transaction. This is a fundamental point; the host country's policy actions are a key prerequisite for further market development.

In addition, borrowers, investors, and intermediaries need to nurture the market patiently. Islamic transactions are often less cost-efficient than conventional bond issues. Each new issue incurs higher legal and documentary expenses as well as distribution costs because it involves examining structural robustness in addition to evaluating the credit quality of the obligor. Since the terms available in Islamic capital markets are derived mostly from pricing levels in the more liquid conventional bond markets, there is no inherent cost advantage for borrowers tapping Islamic markets. Borrowers, therefore, need to formulate a comprehensive, long-term, and strategic view on how to reduce the overall cost of tapping Islamic markets, rather than focus on a single transaction. Investors can support market development by expressing their preference for *Shariah*-compliant instruments, namely, in their bid prices. Intermediaries can lead the process, perhaps through further standardization of transaction schemes and instruments.[5]

Globalization

Globalization is a multifaceted process that is connecting the nations and peoples of the world. Its main dimensions are cultural, sociopolitical, and economic. Its economic dimensions include growing trade flows, unhindered movements of finance, investment, and production, and standardization of processes, regulations, and institutions, all facilitated by the free flow of information and ideas. Globalization is the result of lower costs of information and transportation and liberalization of trade, finance, investment, capital flows, and factor movements.

As globalization gathers momentum and as more economies liberalize and integrate into the global economy, the new finance will grow and so will risk sharing and asset-based securitization: both are the core of Islamic finance. So far, globalization is considered unfair because the risks and rewards of the process are not shared equitably. But as equity-based and asset-backed financing grows, the fruits of globalization could be distributed more widely and more equitably among participants, at least in terms of the financial linkages. Issues such as protectionism in industrial countries, segmented labor markets, impediments to the transfer of technology, and the like remain and will require full international cooperation if they are to be addressed and mitigated.

As globalization proceeds, its main engines—the new finance and advances in information technology—will shift the methods and instruments of financing trade, investment, and production in favor of spreading and sharing risk rather than shifting risk via fixed-price debt contracts. This will be the result of financial innovations that are dissecting, analyzing, and pricing risk better, so that—combined with efficient availability of information and the adoption of best international standards of transparency, accountability, and good governance in public and private sectors—the raison d'être of fixed-price debt contracts will erode. This will pave the way for risk-sharing financial contracts, such as those promoted by Islamic finance. As risk-sharing financial instruments gain wider acceptance and earn the confidence of investors, a financial system founded on the risk-sharing principles promoted by Islamic finance will become more and more feasible.

Mircofinance

Microfinance institutions have experienced impressive growth in the last two decades, and the award of the Nobel Prize to Dr. Mohammed Yunis of Bangladesh in October 2006 for his pioneering work with Grameen Bank has enhanced the prominence of this sector. The conventional microfinance industry has been growing at 13 percent a year since 1999, and today there are more than 320 sustainable institutions operating under this banner. Microfinance mainly targets the poor or the "non-banked" segment of the society. Whereas microfinance institutions have been successful in conventional markets, there are only a few cases of such institutions operating on Islamic finance principles. In an Islamic system, instruments like *qard hassan* can play a vital role in serving the poor, and the role each instrument can play needs to be reviewed.

This phenomenal success in conventional finance has forced even private investors to regard microfinance as a potential and viable asset class. Unlike conventional microfinance institutions, only very limited information is available on microfinance institutions operating under Islamic finance. A relatively small number of interest-free loans are operating in

Pakistan, and there are some small-scale, micro-rural banks in Indonesia.[6] However, no organized institutions are known to be operating on the basis of *qard hassan* except in the Islamic Republic of Iran, where it has been used effectively to provide finance for the needy and where these institutions are widespread throughout the country (for further details, see Sadr 2007).

Iqbal and Mirakhor (2007b) argue that an Islamic form of microfinance based on *qard hassan* has its own benefits, which are worth investigating:

■ It is flexible with respect to collateral. No physical collateral is normally required, but a co-signature for the loan by capital contributors is, more often than not, a substitute for physical collateral.

■ Documentary procedures are usually very simple.

■ Loans are usually small in size, approval procedures are rapid, and disbursement is quick.

■ No interest charges are involved, although some funds charge as much as 1 percent to cover administrative costs.

■ The fund has easy access to capital contributors, borrowers, and co-signers because of its local base.

■ The fund managers, who are drawn from the capital contributors, are fully accountable.

Microfinance and *qard hassan* microfinance have both similarities and differences. Both target the same groups and have devised effective ways of avoiding informational problems by relying on peer monitoring, in the case of traditional microfinance, and familiarity with the borrower and his or her reputation in the case of *qard hassan* microfinance. Moreover, neither requires collateral as a prerequisite for a loan. There are two crucial differences, however. The first is that traditional microfinance charges interest, an abomination from an Islamic perspective. The second is that *quard hassan* has no collective punishment for the group if one of its members defaults on a loan: a capital contributor has to introduce the borrower and, at times, co-sign for the loan, but if there is a default, the co-signer does not have to withdraw from the fund (Iqbal and Mirakhor 2007b).

Islamic finance that claims to promote social justice and advocates equal opportunity for less fortunate segments of society needs to develop a microfinance industry. A well-developed microfinance industry will promote economic development in underdeveloped Islamic countries. As poor segments of society are economically empowered, they will move from being "non-bankable" to being "bankable," expanding the base of depositors and investors.

NOTES

1. For further discussion of issues see Iqbal and Mirakhor (1999); Iqbal (2005); and Iqbal and Mirakhor (2007).
2. Informal discussions with practitioners revealed that religious boards sometimes are extremely rigid on minor technical matters and make the process of introducing a new product difficult and lengthy, resulting in missed business opportunities.
3. Hughes and others (1999) examine the tradeoffs among expected profit, variability and efficiency of profit, and insolvency risk for large U.S. banking organizations in the early 1990s. They find that when organizations are larger in a way that produces geographic diversification, especially via interstate banking that diversifies macroeconomic risk, efficiency tends to be higher and insolvency risk tends to be lower.
4. These institutions include the IFSB, AAOIFI, Liquidity Management Center, International Islamic Financial Markets, and International Islamic Rating Agency.
5. For example, in the Malaysian market, market participants have developed a few well-standardized structures, such as *bai' bithaman ajil*. The costs of structuring and distributing these standardized Islamic deals in Malaysia are now reduced to a competitive level, making them a viable alternative to conventional debt instruments.
6. See www.akhuwat.org.pk.

REFERENCES

AAOIFI (Accounting and Auditing Organization for Islamic Financial Institutions). 1999. "Statement on the Purpose and Calculation of the Capital Adequacy Ratio for Islamic Banks." AAOIFI, Bahrain, March.

Ahmad, Ausaf. 1997. *Structure of Deposits in Selected Islamic Banks.* IRTI Research Paper 48. Jeddah, Saudi Arabia: Islamic Development Bank.

Al-Deehani, Talla, Rifaat A. A. Karim, and Victor Murinde. 1999. "The Capital Structure of Islamic Banks under the Contractual Obligation of Profit Sharing." *International Journal of Theoretical and Applied Finance* 2 (3, July): 243–83.

Ali, Ahmad. 2002. "The Emerging Islamic Financial Architecture: The Way Ahead." Paper presented at the Fifth Harvard University Forum on Islamic Finance, April 6–7.

Allen, Franklin, and Douglas Gale. 2004. "Financial Intermediaries and Markets." *Econometrica* 72 (4): 1023–61.

Archer, Simon. 2005. "Adapting Basel II: The IFSB Draft Standard; Issues of Risk-Bearing Capital and Risk Management." Paper presented at "The Islamic Financial Services Forum: The European Challenge," Central Bank of Luxembourg, November 8–9.

Archer, Simon, and T. Ahmed. 2003. "Emerging Standards for Islamic Financial Institutions: The Case of the Accounting and Auditing Organization for Islamic Financial Institutions." Unpublished mss. World Bank, Washington, DC.

Archer, Simon, and Rifaat A. A. Karim. 2006. "On Capital Structure, Risk Sharing, and Capital Adequacy in Islamic Banks." *International Journal of Theoretical and Applied Finance* 9 (3, May): 269–80.

Baldwin, K. 2002. "Risk Management in Islamic Banks." In R. Abdel Karim and Simon Archer, eds., *Islamic Finance: Innovation and Growth,* 176–97. Bahrain: Euromoney Books and AAOIFI.

Barth, James R., Gerard Caprio, and Ross Levine. 2006. *Rethinking Bank Regulation: Till Angels Govern.* New York: Cambridge University Press.

Basel Committee on Banking Supervision. 1998. *Enhancing Bank Transparency.* Basel: Bank for International Settlement, September.

———. 2000. *Report to G7 Finance Ministers and Central Bank Governors on International Accounting Standards.* Basel: Bank for International Settlement, April.

————. 2002. "Results of the 2000 Disclosure Survey: Public Disclosures of Banks." Basel: Bank for International Settlement, May.

Berger, Allen, and Christa Bouwman. 2005. "Bank Capital and Liquidity Creation." Paper presented at the European Finance Association Meetings, Moscow, June (http://ssrn.com/abstract=672784).

Berglöf, Erik, and Stijn Claessens. 2004. "Enforcement and Corporate Governance." Working Paper 3409. Washington, DC: World Bank.

Briston, R., and A. El-Ashker. 1986. "Religious Audit: Could It Happen Here?" *Accountancy* 6 (4, October): 120–21.

Burns, Robert L. 2004. "Economic Capital and the Assessment of Capital Adequacy." Supervisory Insights. Federal Deposit Insurance Corporation (www.fdic.gov/regulations/examinations/supervisory/insights/siwin04/economic_capital. html).

Chapra, M. Umer, and Habib Ahmed. 2002. *Corporate Governance in Islamic Financial Institutions*. Occasional Paper 6. Jeddah, Saudi Arabia: Islamic Research and Training Institute, Islamic Development Bank.

Chapra, M. Umer, and Tariqullah Khan. 2000. *Regulation and Supervision of Islamic Banks*. Occasional Paper 3. Jeddah, Saudi Arabia: Islamic Research and Training Institute, Islamic Development Bank.

Creane, Susan, Rishi Goyal, A. Mushfiq Mobarak, and Randa Sab. 2003. *Financial Development in the Middle East and North Africa*. Washington, DC: International Monetary Agency.

Diamond, Douglas, and Raghuram Rajan. 2000. "A Theory of Bank Capital." *Journal of Finance* 55 (6, December): 2431–65.

El-Hawary, Dahlia, Wafik Grais, and Zamir Iqbal. 2004. "Regulating Islamic Financial Institutions: The Nature of the Regulated." Policy Research Working Paper 3227. Washington, DC: World Bank.

Errico, Luca, and Mitra Farahbaksh. 1998. "Islamic Banking: Issues in Prudential Regulations and Supervision." IMF Working Paper WP/98/30. Washington, DC: International Monetary Fund.

Fremond, Olivier, and Mierta Capaul. 2002. "The State of Corporate Governance: Experience from Country Assessments." Policy Research Working Paper 2858. Washington, DC: World Bank.

Gersbach, Hans. 2002. "The Optimal Capital Structure of an Economy." Grabengasse, Germany: Alfred-Weber-Institut, University of Heidelberg.

Grais, Wafik, and Zamir Iqbal. 2006. "Corporate Governance Challenges of Islamic Financial Institutions." Paper presented at the "Seventh Harvard Forum on Islamic Finance." Harvard University, Boston, MA, April 22–23.

Grais, Wafik, and Anoma Kulathunga. 2007. "Capital Structure and Risk in Islamic Financial Services." In Simon Archer and Rifaat A. Karim, eds., *Islamic Finance: The Regulatory Challenges*. John Wiley and Sons (Asia).

Grais, Wafik, and Matteo Pellegrini. 2006a. "Corporate Governance of Business Offering Islamic Financial Services: Issues and Options." World Bank Policy Paper 40543. Washington, DC: World Bank Group.

————. 2006b. "Corporate Governance and *Shariah* Compliance in Institutions Offering Islamic Financial Services." Working Paper. Washington, DC: World Bank.

Hughes, J. P., W. Lang, L. Mester and C. G. Moon. 1998. 'The dollars and sense of bank consolidation' working paper 10, Federal Reserve Bank of Philadelphia.

IMF (International Monetary Fund). 2004. *Compilation Guide for Financial Soundness Indicators.* Washington, DC: IMF.

IFSB (Islamic Financial Services Board). 2005a. *Capital Adequacy Standard for Institutions (Other Than Insurance Institutions) Offering Only Islamic Financial Services.* Exposure Draft 2. Kuala Lumpur, Malaysia: IFSB.

————. 2005b. *Guiding Principles of Risk Management for Institutions (Other Than Insurance Institutions) Offering Only Islamic Financial Services.* Exposure Draft 1. Kuala Lumpur, Malaysia: IFSB.

Iqbal, Zamir. 2005. *"Impact of Consolidation on Islamic Financial Services Industry,"* 2nd International on Challenges Facing the Islamic Financial Services Industry, April 6–7, Tehran, Iran.

Iqbal, Zamir, and Abbas Mirakhor. 1999. "Progress and Challenges of Islamic Banking." *Thunderbird International Business Review* 41 (4–5, July–October): 381–405.

————. 2002. "Development of Islamic Financial Institutions and Challenges Ahead." In Simon Archer and Rifaat Abdel Karim, eds., *Islamic Finance: Growth and Innovation.* London: Euromoney Books.

————. 2004. "A Stakeholders Model of Corporate Governance of Firm in Islamic Economic System." *Islamic Economic Studies* 11 (2, March): 43–63.

————. 2007. *Introduction to Islamic Finance: Theory and Practice.* John Wiley and Sons (Asia).

————. 2007b. *Qard Hasan* Mircofinance, New Horizon, No. 64, Apr–Jun 2007, UK.

Iqbal, Zamir, and Hiroshi Tsubota. 2005. *"Emerging Islamic Markets."* The *Euromoney International Debt Capital Markets Handbook.* London: Euromoney Publishing.

Islamic Development Bank (IDB) and Islamic Financial Services Board (IFSB). 2005. Ten Year Master Plan for Islamic Financial Industry Development: Ten-year Framework and Strategies, Jeddah, Saudi Arabia.

Jabbari, A. Nadia. 2006. Capital Adequacy Standard for institutions offering Islamic financial Services, Islamic Financial Services Board 2nd International Research Conference on Islamic Banking: Risk Management, Regulation & Supervision Kuala Lumpur, February 7–8.

Kahf, Monzer. 1999. "Islamic Banks at the Threshold of the Third Millennium." *Thunderbird International Business Review* 41 (4–5, July–October): 445–60.

Khan, M. Fahim. 1994. "Comparative Economics of Some Islamic Financing Techniques." *Islamic Economic Studies* 2 (1, December): 81–102.

Khan, Mohsin. 1987. "Islamic Interest-Free Banking: A Theoretical Analysis." In Khan and Mirakhor, eds., *Theoretical Studies in Islamic Banking and Finance.* Houston, TX: IRIS Books.

Khan, Tariqullah. 1996. *An analysis of risk sharing in Islamic finance with special reference to Pakistan*, Doctoral Thesis, Department of Economics, Loughborough University, United Kingdom.

Khan, Tariqullah, and Habib Ahmed. 2001. *Risk Management: An Analysis of Issues in Islamic Financial Industry.* Occasional Paper 9. Jeddah, Saudi Arabia: Islamic Development Bank.

Klingebiel and Laeven. 2002. *Managing the Real and Fiscal Effects of Banking Crises.* Washington, DC: World Bank.

Lewis, Mervyn K., and Latifa M. Algaoud. 2001. *Islamic Banking.* Cheltenham, UK: Edward Elgar.

Mehra, Rajnish. 2004. "The Equity Premium: Why Is It a Puzzle?" *Financial Analysts Journal* (January–February): 54–69.

Minsky, Hyman. 1982. *Inflation, Recession, and Economic Policy.* London: Wheatsheaf Books.

Mirakhor, Abbas. 1989. "General Characteristics of an Islamic Economic System." In Baqir Al-Hasani and Abbas Mirakhor, eds., *Essays on Iqtisad: The Islamic Approach to Economic Problems*, 45–80. Silver Spring, MD: Nur Corporation.

Modigliani, Franco, and Merton Miller. 1958. "The Cost of Capital: Corporation Finance and the Theory of Investment." *American Economic Review* 48 (3, June): 261–97.

Mulajawan, Dadang, Humayon A. Dar, and Maximilian J. B. Hall. 2002. "A Capital Adequacy Framework for Islamic Banks: The Need to Reconcile Depositors' Risk Aversion with Managers' Risk Taking." Economics Research Paper ERP 02-13. Loughborough University.

Prescott, E. C., and Rajnish Mehra. 1985. "Equity Premium: A Puzzle." *Journal of Monetary Economics (Netherlands)* 15 (2): 145–61.

Sadr, S. Kazem. 2007. "Qard-ul-Hassan Financing and Institutions." Paper prepared for the first international conference on Inclusive Islamic Financial Sector Development, "Enhancing Islamic Financial Services to Micro and Medium-Sized Enterprises," Islamic Research and Training Institute, Jeddah, and Centre for Islamic Banking, Finance, and Management, Universiti Brunei Darussalam, Brunei, April 17–18.

Sadr, Kazem, and Zamir Iqbal. 2002. "Choice between Debt and Equity Contracts and Asymmetrical Information: Some Empirical Evidence." In Munawar Iqbal and David T. Llewellyn, eds., *Islamic Banking and Finance.* London: Edward Elgar.

Sundararajan, V. 2004. "Risk Measurement, Risk Management, and Disclosure in Islamic Finance." Seminar on Comparative Supervision of Islamic and Conventional Finance, Beirut, Lebanon, December 7–8.

Sundararajan, V., and Luca Errico. 2002. *Islamic Financial Institutions and Products in the Global Financial System: Key Issues in Risk Management and Challenges Ahead.* IMF Working Paper WP/02/192. Washington, DC: International Monetary Fund.

Tirole, Jean. 1999. *Corporate Governance.* CEPR Discussion Paper 2086. London: Centre for Economic Policy Research.

Udovitch, Abraham L. 1981. "Bankers without Banks: Commerce, Banking, and Society in the Islamic World of the Middle Ages." Princeton Near East Paper 30. Princeton, NJ: Princeton University Press.

Van Greuning, Hennie, and Sonja Brajovic Bratanovic. 2002. "Analyzing and Managing Banking Risk." Washington, DC: World Bank.

Van Greuning, Hennie, 2006. "International Financial Reporting Standards: a practical guide." Washington, DC: World Bank.

Van Greuning, Hennie and Zamir Iqbal, "Banking and the Risk Environment." In Simon Archer and Rifaat Ahmed Abdel Karim, eds., *Islamic Finance: The Regulatory Challenge.* John Wiley and Sons (Asia), Singapore.

Warde, Ibrahim. 2000. *Islamic Finance in the Global Economy.* Edinburgh: Edinburgh University Press.

World Bank. 2004. *Indonesia: Averting an Infrastructure Crisis; A Framework for Policy and Action.* Washington, DC: World Bank.

———. 2005. *Doing Business in 2005: Removing Obstacles to Growth.* Washington, DC: World Bank.

APPENDIX A: GLOSSARY

Amanah. Safe keeping.

Bai' bithaman ajil. Sale contract where payment is made in installments after delivery of goods. Sale could be for long-term and there is no obligation to disclose profit margins.

Bay' al-dayn. Sale of debt.

Bay' al-muajjil. Sale with deferred payment.

Bay' al-salaam. Purchase with deferred delivery.

Fatwa. A legal opinion issued by a qualified Muslim scholar on matters of religious beliefs and practice.

Fiqh. An Islamic scholar.

Fiqh al-muamalat. Islamic commercial jurisprudence.

Gharar. Any uncertainty created by the lack of information or control in a contract; ignorance in regard to an essential element in a transaction.

Halal. Goodness; permissible.

Hiba. Gifts.

Ijarah. A leasing contract, technically a contract of sale.

Istisnah. A manufacturing contract that facilitates the manufacture or construction of an asset at the request of the buyer.

Joalah. Agreement with an expert in a given field to undertake a task for a pre-determined fee or commission(as in a consultancy agreement or contract).

Kifalah. Stewardship Guarantee or Surety.

Maysur. Games of chance involving deception. Same as Myisur.

Mudarabah. A contract in which the owner of capital forms a partnership with an entrepreneur or manager who has certain entrepreneurial skills and both agree to share the profits and losses of the venture undertaken. There are two types of funds: multipurpose—having more than one investment purpose or objective (multipurpose)—and specific purpose.

Mudarabat. Plural of *Mudarabah*

Mudarib. A fund manager or agent.

Murabahah. A cost-plus sales contract, which is used to purchase commodities.

Murabahat. Plural of *Murabahah* Short-term commodity finance based on *Murabahah* contracts.

Musharakah. A profit- and loss-sharing contract. An equity partnership.

Musharakat. Plural of *Musharakah.*

Musharik. The partner in a musharakah contract.

Myisur. Same as Saysur (duplicate)

Qard hassan. Goodwill loan, in which the bank receives a loan from depositors and owes the principal amount only.

Qard-ul-Hasan.

Qimar. Gambling.

Qur'an. The basic source of law for Muslims, which includes all of the constitutive rules of law.

Rab al-mal. Supplier of funds, the principal.

Riba. Interest. Literally, it means excess, addition, and surplus, while the associated verb implies "to increase, to multiply, to exceed, to exact more than was due, or to practice usury."

Sadaqah. Voluntary charitable contribution.

Salaam. Agriculture-based sales contract.

Sarraf. Financier in the early days of Islam.

Shariah. The constitutive and regulative rules based on the Qur'an.

Shiraka. Partnership.

Sukuk. Islamic asset-backed certificates.

Sunnah. Explanations rendered by the Prophet Muhammad.

Takaful. Shariah-compliant mutual insurance; literally, a mutual or joint guarantee.

Ummah. Muslim Community.

Waqf. Charitable Trust or endowment.

Wadiah. Safe deposits and guaranteed banking, with the principal amount payable on demand.

Wakalah. Representation. Entrusting a person or legal entity (*Wakil*) to act on one's behalf or as one's representative.

Wakalah Accounts. Unrestricted investment account in which the bank earns a flat fee rather than a share of profits.

Wakalat. Plural of *Wakalah*.

Zakah. An obligatory charitable contribution. One of the five basic pillars of Islam.

APPENDIX B: IFSB STANDARD
ON RISK MANAGEMENT

The following premises relate to the sound processes of credit risk management in Islamic financial services.

Islamic financial institutions can embrace the role of financiers, suppliers, *mudarib*, and *musharakah* partners. They concern themselves with the risk of a counterparty's failure to meet their obligations by receiving deferred payment and making or taking delivery of an asset. A failure could relate to a delay or default in payment or in delivery of the subject matter of salaam or parallel *istisnah*, entailing a potential loss of income and even capital.

Due to the unique characteristics of each type of financing instrument, such as the nonbinding nature of some contracts, the commencement stage involving credit risk varies. Therefore, credit risk shall be assessed separately for each financing instrument to facilitate appropriate internal controls and risk management systems.

Islamic banks shall consider other types of risks that give rise to credit risk. For example, during the life of a contract, the risk inherent in a *murabahah* contract is transformed from market risk to credit risk. In another example, the invested capital in a *mudarabah* or *musharakah* contract is transformed into debt in case of proven negligence or misconduct of the *mudarib* or the *musharakah*'s managing partner.

In case of default, Islamic banks are prohibited from imposing any penalty except in the case of deliberate procrastination. In the latter case, they are prohibited from using the amount of the penalty for their own benefit; they must donate the amount levied to charity.

OPERATIONAL CONSIDERATIONS

Islamic banks shall have in place a framework for managing credit risk that includes identification, measurement, monitoring, reporting, and control of credit risks. Adequate capital should be held against the credit risks assumed. Islamic banks shall also comply with relevant rules, regulations, and prudential conditions applicable to their financing activities.

Islamic banks shall assess credit risk in a holistic manner and ensure that its management forms part of an integrated approach to the management of all financial risks. Given the nature of Islamic financing instruments, the source of credit risk may be the same as that of market or operational risks. For example, in a salaam contract, changes in market risk factors (for example, commodity prices) as well as in the external environment (for example, bad weather) affect the likelihood of default.

Islamic banks shall have in place the following:

- An appropriate credit strategy, including pricing and tolerance for undertaking various credit risks;
- A risk management structure with effective oversight of credit risk management;
- Credit policies and operational procedures including credit criteria and credit review processes, acceptable forms of risk mitigation, and limit setting;
- An appropriate measurement and careful analysis of exposures, including market- and liquidity-sensitive exposures;
- A system (a) to monitor the condition of ongoing individual credits to ensure the financings are made in accordance with the Islamic bank's policies and procedures; (b) to manage problem credit situations according to an established remedial process; and (c) to determine adequate provisions to be made for such losses.

PRINCIPLE 2.1

Islamic banks shall have in place a strategy for financing, using the various Islamic instruments in compliance with *Shariah*, whereby they recognize the potential credit exposures that may arise at different stages of the various financing agreements.

The board of directors shall define and set the institution's overall level of risk appetite, risk diversification, and asset allocation strategies applicable to each Islamic financing instrument, economic activity, geographic spread, season, currency, and tenor. Islamic banks shall be mindful of and take into account the permissible types of financing instruments available in different locations wherever they undertake cross-border transactions. They will take into account seasonal aspects resulting from a shift in or termination of the use of certain financing instruments, thus affecting the overall concentration exposures of their financing portfolio. For example, the Islamic bank may offer *salaam* contracts during a certain season where a product can most likely be delivered and sold at maturity.

Islamic financing strategies shall include a list of all types of applicable and approved transactions and financings. The approved list must include formal exclusions from any engagement by the Islamic bank in prohibited industries, such as pork meat, alcohol, gambling, and tobacco. The approved list will be kept up to date and communicated to the relevant personnel within the institution, and an internal compliance function will be organized and empowered to ensure that such rules are applied.

Islamic banks shall be aware of the commencement of exposure to credit risk inherent in different financing instruments and in various jurisdictions when developing the strategy. The nonbinding promise and legal enforcement vary among Islamic banks or from one jurisdiction to another, which may give rise to operational risks and other risk management problems relating to *Shariah* compliance.

When setting the level of risk appetite relating to counterparties, Islamic banks shall ensure that (a) the expected rate of return on a transaction is commensurate with the risks incurred and that (b) excessive credit risks (at both the individual and portfolio levels) are avoided.

PRINCIPLE 2.2

Islamic banks shall carry out a due diligence review in respect of counterparties prior to choosing an appropriate Islamic financing instrument.

Islamic banks shall establish policies and procedures defining eligible counterparties (retail or consumer; corporate or sovereign), the nature of approved financings and types of appropriate financing instruments. Islamic banks shall obtain sufficient information to permit a comprehensive assessment of the risk profile of the counterparty prior to granting the financing.

Islamic banks shall have a policy for carrying out due diligence in evaluating counterparties, in particular, for transactions involving the following:

- *New ventures with multiple financing modes.* The bank shall carry out due diligence on customers or sovereigns using multiple financing modes to meet specific financial objectives designed to address the *Shariah*, legal, or tax issues of customers.
- *Creditworthiness that may be influenced by external factors.* Where significant investment risks are present in participatory instruments,

especially in the case of *mudarabah* financings, additional counter-party reviews and evaluations will focus on the business purpose, operational capability, enforcement, and economic substance of the proposed project, including the assessment of realistic forecasts of esti-mated future cash flows.[1] Risk-mitigating structures should be put in place as far as possible.

Islamic banks in their policy for approval shall engage appropriate experts, including a *Shariah* adviser or *Shariah* board, to review and ensure that new, ad hoc financing proposals or amendments to existing contracts are *Shariah* compliant at all times. They may also engage an appropriate technical expert (for example, an engineer) to evaluate the feasibility of a proposed project and to assess and approve progress billings to be made under the contract.

In a financing involving several related agreements, the Islamic bank will need to be aware of the binding obligations arising in connection with credit risks associated with the underlying assets for each agreement. The Islamic bank shall ensure that all components of the financial struc-ture are contractually independent (although these may be executed in a parallel manner) in spite of their interrelated nature, in order to avoid noncompliance with *Shariah*.

PRINCIPLE 2.3

Islamic banks will have in place appropriate methodologies for measur-ing and reporting the credit risk exposures arising under each Islamic financing instrument.

The Islamic bank will develop and implement appropriate risk meas-urement and reporting methodologies relevant to each Islamic financing instrument in respect of managing its counterparty risks, which may arise at different stages of the contract. Depending on the instrument used, the Islamic bank may employ an appropriate methodology that takes into account the price volatility of the underlying assets. The methodology selected shall be appropriate to the nature, size, and complexity of the insti-tution's credit-related activities. The Islamic bank shall ensure that adequate systems and resources are available to implement this methodology.

PRINCIPLE 2.4

Islamic banks shall have in place *Shariah*-compliant credit risk–mitigat-ing techniques appropriate for each type of Islamic financing instrument.

The Islamic bank shall clearly define its credit risk–mitigating techniques including, but not limited to, having in place markup rates set according to the risk rating of the counterparties, where expected risks should have been taken into account in the pricing decisions; permissible and enforceable collateral and guarantees; clear documentation as to whether or not purchase orders are cancelable;[2] and clear governing laws for contracts relating to financing transactions.

The Islamic bank shall establish limits on the degree of reliance and the enforceability of collateral and guarantees. It shall protect itself against legal impediments that may restrict the accessibility of collateral needed to enforce its rights in respect of a debt. The Islamic bank shall formally agree with the counterparty at the time of signing the contract on the redemption and use of collateral if the counterparty defaults in payment.

The Islamic bank shall define the action to be taken by it when a customer cancels a nonbinding purchase order. The policies will describe how the bank will (a) monitor and control its exposure to suppliers, especially during delivery when a customer is acting as an agent; and (b) identify whether the risks associated with the assets will be borne by the supplier or the customer (which acts as agent and accepts the assets from the supplier). For example, the Islamic bank may enter into a purchase contract with a supplier on a "sale or return" basis, with an option to return the purchased item within a specified period.

The Islamic bank shall have appropriate credit management systems and administrative procedures in place to undertake early remedial action in the case of financial distress of a counterparty or, in particular, for managing potential and defaulting counterparties.[3] This system will be reviewed on a regular basis. Remedial actions will include both administrative and financial measures.

Administrative measures may, inter alia, include (a) negotiating and following up proactively with the counterparty through frequent contact; (b) setting an allowable time frame for payment or offering debt-rescheduling or restructuring arrangements (without an increase in the amount of the debt); (c) resorting to legal action, including attaching any credit balance belonging to defaulters according to the agreement between them; and (d) making a claim under Islamic insurance.

Financial measures include, among others, (a) imposing penalties to be donated to charity in accordance with the *Shariah* rule, where approved by the Islamic bank's *Shariah* board or committee and (b) establishing the enforceability of collateral or third-party guarantees.

The Islamic bank shall set appropriate measures for early settlements, which are permissible under their *Shariah* rules and principles for each Islamic financing instrument. Some customers may expect a discount, which the Islamic bank can give of its own volition as a commercial decision made on a case-by-case basis. Alternatively, irrespective of industry practice, the Islamic bank can grant a rebate, at its discretion (not to be mentioned in the contract) to customers by reducing the amount of the debt in subsequent transactions.

The Islamic bank shall assess and establish appropriate policies and procedures pertaining to the risks associated with its own exposures in parallel transactions. For instance, the Islamic bank enters into an *istisnah* contract as a seller to provide manufactured goods or a building to a customer. The Islamic bank then enters into another (parallel) *istisnah* contract as a buyer with a supplier (manufacturer or builder), using the specifications drawn up for the original contract. If the supplier fails to deliver the manufactured goods or the building according to the agreed specifications, the Islamic bank will be in default of its obligation. If necessary, as in the case of some Islamic banks, a separate engineering department will be established, or an outside expert will be engaged to evaluate, approve, and monitor the technical aspects. The Islamic bank may also stipulate that the party to the first contract must inspect the manufactured goods or building from time to time during the production or construction process to verify that the specifications are being met.

The Islamic bank shall establish appropriate policies and procedures that require it to honor its commitment to the parallel contract counterparty. In certain countries, where a parallel contract must be transacted with the first salaam contract in order to mitigate the exposure to market risk, there must be no legal linkages between the two contracts.

The Islamic bank shall have in place a system to ascertain and fulfill its obligations in respect of leased assets that are permanently impaired through no default of the lessee. In case of such impairment, the Islamic bank either has to provide the lessee with a replacement asset with a similar specificity or has to refund the additional amounts (capital payments) included in the IMB lease rentals as compared with those in an operating *ijarah*. In *ijarah* and IMB , the Islamic banks (as lessors) retain ownership of the leased asset throughout the contract and are liable for the consequences of any damage to the asset that is not caused by the lessee's misconduct or negligence. The Islamic banks shall establish appropriate risk management policies to mitigate losses arising from such damage during the term of the lease.

The Islamic bank shall ensure that there is sufficient Islamic insurance coverage of the value of the assets, subject to availability. If necessary, the Islamic bank shall engage an insurance adviser at an early stage to review the insurance coverage of the leased assets.

If a loss arises from negligence by the lessee, the Islamic bank is permitted to claim compensation from the lessee. The Islamic bank (as lessor) bears the risks associated with the leased assets and cannot use lessees' guarantees to recover the amount of the losses on the leased assets (unless these are due to misconduct, negligence, or breach of contract on the part of the lessees).

The Islamic bank shall have in place an appropriate policy for determining and allocating provisions to be made for estimated impairment in the value of each asset.

NOTES

1. IFIs will be mindful that the counterparty risk will not commence prior to execution of other contracts or before certain events take place. In the case of certain *murabahah* transactions, the long period preceding the delivery of imported goods from abroad gives rise to other risks that may not all be covered by *takaful* or insurance.
2. In some jurisdictions, a purchase order backed by a promise to purchase would constitute a binding contract according to contract law and would be legally enforceable if adequately evidenced.
3. The *Shariah* differentiates between two kinds of defaulter: (a) the affluent or able (willful defaulter or procrastinator) and (b) the insolvent defaulter who is unable to pay his debts due to reasons permitted by *Shariah*.

APPENDIX C: PROPOSED OUTLINE FOR BANK ANALYTICAL REPORTS

1. Executive Summary and Recommendations

2. Institutional Development Needs

3. Overview of the Financial Sector and Regulation

4. Overview of the Bank and Its Risk Management Culture
   4.1 Historical background and general information
   4.2 Group and organization structure
   4.3 Accounting systems, management information, and internal control
   4.4 Information technology
   4.5 Risk management culture and decision-making process

5. Corporate Governance
   5.1 Shareholders, ownership
   5.2 Board of directors, supervisory board
   5.3 Executive management
   5.4 Internal audit, audit committee of the board
   5.5 External auditors

6. Balance Sheet Structure and the Changes Therein
   6.1 Composition of the balance sheet
       Asset structure: Growth and changes
       Liabilities structure: Growth and changes
   6.2 Overall on- and off-balance-sheet growth
   6.3 Low and nonearning assets

7. Income Statement Structure and the Changes Therein (Profitability/Earnings)
   7.1 Sources of income: Changes in the structure and trends of income
   7.2 Structure of assets compared to structure of income
   7.3 Margins earned on various components of intermediation business
   7.4 Operating income and operating expenses breakdown
   7.5 Return on assets and shareholders' funds

8. Capital Adequacy
   8.1 Capital retention policies
   8.2 Compliance with capital adequacy requirements
   8.3 Potential future capital requirements
   8.4 Structure of shareholders' funds
   8.5 Risk profile of balance sheet assets

9. Credit Risk Management
   9.1 Credit risk management policies, systems, and procedures
   9.2 Profile of borrowers
   9.3 Maturity of loans
   9.4 Loan products
   9.5 Sectoral analysis of loans
   9.6 Large exposures to individuals and connected parties
   9.7 Loan and other asset classification and provisioning
   9.8 Analysis of loans in arrears
   9.9 Connected lending (to related parties)

10. Organization of the Treasury Function
    10.1 Organization of the treasury function—policy and governance framework
    10.2 Asset-liability management
    10.3 Market operations—funding and investment of expected shortfalls and surpluses
         Funding on the local and international markets
         Investment portfolio management and proprietary trading (position taking)
    10.4 Risk analytics
         Risk measurement and management (liquidity, counterparty/credit, market, and currency risk)
         Performance measurement and analysis

Risk reporting
Governance, compliance, and operational risk
Quantitative strategies and risk research (model development, etc.)
10.5 Treasury operations
Cash management
Settlements
Accounting
Information services

11. Investment Portfolio Management
    11.1 Size and structure of investment portfolio compared to short-term liabilities
    11.2 Benchmark for performance measurement
    11.3 Eligible investments
    11.4 Credit and market risk measurement tools used
    11.5 Active management of the investment portfolio
    11.6 Risk management and budgeting
    11.7 Risk reporting

12. Proprietary Trading/Market Risk Management
    12.1 Market/price risk management policies, systems, and procedures
    12.2 Structure of the proprietary trading portfolio
    12.3 Use of derivatives
    12.4 Value-at-risk, position limits and stop loss provisions
    12.5 Market risk attached to off-balance-sheet activities and derivatives

13. Asset-Liability Management (ALM)
    13.1 Market rate risk management policies, systems, and procedures
    13.2 Forecasting of market rates
    13.3 Measures to determine the potential impact of exogenous rate movements on the bank's capital

14. Liquidity Risk Management
    14.1 Liquidity risk management policies, systems, and procedures
    14.2 Compliance with regulatory requirements
    14.3 Access to and sources of deposits: Profile of depositors
    14.4 Maturity structure of deposits
    14.5 Large depositors and volatility of funding

INDEX